Earl Mindell's Nutrition & Health for Dogs

Earl Mindell, R.Ph., Ph.D., and Elizabeth Renaghan

Earl Mindell's Nutrition & Health for Dogs

KEEP YOUR DOG
HEALTHY AND HAPPY
WITH NATURAL
PREVENTATIVE CARE AND REMEDIES

Prima Publishing

This book is not intended to replace medical guidance. Persons should consult their veterinarians before administering any specific treatment or nutritional plan that is discussed in this book to their dog. Responsibility for adverse effects resulting from the use of information in this book rests solely with the reader.

PRIMA PUBLISHING and colophon are registered trademarks of Prima Communications, Inc.

Interior Design by Trina Stahl

Library of Congress Cataloging-in-Publication Data
Mindell, Earl.
    Earl Mindell's nutrition & health for dogs : keep your dog healthy and
happy with natural preventative care and remedies / Earl Mindell and
Elizabeth Renaghan.
        p.   cm.
    Includes bibliographical references and index.
    ISBN 0-7615-1158-X
    1. Dogs—Nutrition.   2. Dogs—Health.   3. Dogs—Food.
I. Renaghan, Elizabeth.   II. Title.
SF427.4.M56 1998
636.7'084—dc21   97-49020
                                                                             CIP

98 99 00 01 02 BB 10 9 8 7 6 5 4 3 2 1
Printed in the United States of America

How to Order
Single copies may be ordered from Prima Publishing, P.O. Box 1260BK, Rocklin, CA 95677; telephone (916) 632-4400. Quantity discounts are also available. On your letterhead, include information concerning the intended use of the books and the number of books you wish to purchase.

Visit us online at http://www.primapublishing.com

Contents

Acknowledgments

FIRST AND FOREMOST, we would like to thank Virginia Hopkins for putting this project together and for her inspiration and editing through the years.

We are deeply grateful to Dr. Beverly Cappel-King, who shared her time and considerable expertise as a holistic veterinarian as well as her miracles in healing dogs with nutrition. Thanks as always to agent Richard Curtis for his guidance. A heartfelt thanks to our friends and family for their support and for believing in this book for so many years, with a special thanks to the four-legged members of our families: Dudley, for his unconditional love and patience; Winkin, who is a shining, energetic example that nutrition is the key to optimum health; and Sunshine, Sky, and Crystal, for leading the way.

Introduction

DURING MORE THAN twenty-five years of writing about health and nutrition, hundreds and maybe even thousands of people have thanked me for giving them the information they need to lead a healthy, energetic life. I have found that once a person learns how the food he or she is eating affects every aspect of life and then experiences the difference when positive lifestyle changes are made, there is no going back. There is nothing like optimal health to convince a person that diet, exercise, clean water, and taking some supplements work wonders.

As I learn more about the nutritional needs of dogs, I find that confusion and misconceptions abound. Few people, including veterinarians, realize that a dog's body functions much the same as a human body and has similar nutritional needs. You could probably go into your refrigerator right now and make a nutritious, balanced meal for your dog.

The commercial dog food industry is a multimillion-dollar business that depends on hiding the truth about what is good nutrition for a dog. For example, the dog food industry has perpetuated the myth that your dog is healthiest and happiest when she gets the same food every day. That is no more true than it would be for you. Your dog thrives on a variety of fresh foods, including fruits and vegetables. If you compare your dog's nutritional needs to the ingredients in the majority of commercial dog foods, you will understand why dogs are dying younger than they should be and are plagued by chronic illnesses.

The foundation for good health for your dog is the same as it is for you: good nutrition, exercise, clean water, and love. For optimal health, you can build on that foundation with specific food and supplements. I will tell you about the specific nutritional needs your dog has that are different from yours and how to keep her immune system strong.

It is also important to support your dog nutritionally against those illnesses that she might be genetically predisposed to. Just as with people (for example, one family may have a high incidence of cancer and another a high incidence of heart disease), different breeds of dogs are genetically predisposed to certain illnesses. In this book, you will learn which illnesses your breed is prone to and how to avoid or delay the onset of the more common illnesses.

The focus of this book is on how your dog's body functions nutritionally, what your dog's nutritional needs are, and easy, flexible, affordable ways to keep your dog in optimal health through all phases of her life.

The nutritional information I will give you is a guideline for formulating a diet and supplement plan for your dog. Each and every dog is different and has different nutritional needs. I will explain to you why each nutrient is needed so you can create a diet for your dog's specific needs. The recommended amounts to feed are also meant to give you a general sense of what is appropriate for that size of dog. What your dog actually eats needs to be balanced for her unique combination of age, level of exercise, and individual metabolism. In the same way, your dog's multivitamin-mineral supplement does not have to exactly fit the recommended dosages (which we are very grateful to Dr. Beverly Cappel-King for providing), as long as it is close and contains the proper balance of vitamins and minerals.

You will find that as you pay closer attention to your dog's health, your bond with your best friend will become stronger and that having a dog in your life will become an even greater privilege and joy than it is now.

PART ONE

Creating Optimum Nutrition for Your Dog

CHAPTER ONE

Feeding Your Dog for Naturally Great Health

YOU ARE WHAT you eat. It is a common saying that few people take seriously, yet good nutrition is the foundation for good health. If your dog does not have a soft, shiny coat, eyes that are bright, clear, and alert, clean teeth, pink gums, and a lean, muscular body, then she is not in good health. The good news is that you can restore and maintain your dog's health through proper nutrition.

Most commercial dog food is low in nutrients and high in additives and preservatives. Dog food companies are not required to make human-grade dog food, meaning it is not fit for human consumption. Yet with a few exceptions your dog's body functions much the same as yours and your dog has similar nutritional requirements for optimal health.

A dog is not conditioned to complain about her aches and pains as we are, and she will instinctively hide physical problems, because in any pack of animals the predators look for the weakest members. That is why it is important to do a quick health check, head to tail, on your dog each week. Start with the head and look for clean teeth, dark pink gums, bright clear eyes, and clean ears. Work your way back, looking for any signs of weight gain or loss, a soft, shiny, mat-free coat and a clean underbelly free of fleas and flea dirt. Last, and the least desirable, check your dog's rear end to be sure it is clean, with no sign of worms.

> "Dog food companies are not required to make human-grade dog food, meaning it is not fit for human consumption. Yet with a few exceptions your dog's body functions much the same as yours and your dog has similar nutritional requirements for optimal health."

If your dog does not pass the health check, a simple change in diet could bring her back to optimal health. In this chapter, you will learn what to look for in a commercial dog food and what to steer clear of. I will take the mystery and labor out of home-cooked meals and help you integrate fresh foods into your dog's diet. In later chapters, I will give you feeding guidelines for special needs in cases such as obesity, illness recovery, and pregnant and nursing dogs.

If you are not feeding your dog an all-natural, human-grade dog food and are going to change to all-natural food or home-cooked meals, it is best to make the change slowly. Time after time I have had people tell me they tried home-cooked meals or all-natural diets, and it made their dogs terribly sick with diarrhea and mucousy stools. What made the dogs sick was the body's attempt to detoxify from the toxin-filled food they had been eating. The dogs' bodies were struggling to come back to a natural state by getting rid of all the chemicals and preservatives that had been accumulating. A gradual change to a natural diet will detoxify your dog gradually, creating less of a shock to her system and fewer side effects such as diarrhea.

Each dog is a unique individual, with specific nutritional needs. For example, although golden retrievers look alike and generally have similar personalities and health problems, each golden retriever has different dietary needs depending on how his or her body processes foods, activity level, age, genetic makeup, environment, and a whole host of other internal and external factors. In this chapter, I will give you nutritional guidelines to use as a starting point in tailoring a diet to specifically meet your dog's needs. As you gradually introduce new foods to your dog, watch her carefully for any negative or positive reactions. Keep an eye out for things like changes in her coat, eye clarity, energy level, and weight.

What to Look for When Choosing a Commercial Dog Food

Although there are over 300 pet food manufacturers in the United States, your choice of truly high-quality foods is extremely limited. Most commercial dog foods are either canned, semimoist, or dry. Semimoist can be eliminated from your list of choices, because it is very high in sugar and other flavor additives, which have no nutritional value and are addictive. Canned and dry dog foods are your remaining choices, with dry foods being the most popular because they are less expensive, less cumbersome, and easier to use. Here are your three most important criteria in choosing a dry dog food.

The first thing to look for is meat that is human-grade or inspected by the United States Department of Agriculture (USDA). USDA-inspected meat is, by definition, fit for human consumption. Optimally, buy a dog food made of organic, human-grade, or USDA meat. Organic meat comes from animals raised without the use of antibiotics or fattening hormones such as estrogen, or steroids. If the meat is not USDA or human-grade, it is usually coming from diseased, drugged, and decaying animals, including dogs and cats.

There are many reports of rendering plants throughout the U.S. that receive dead dogs and cats, process them into meat meal, and sell them to dog food manufacturers. These animals are most likely riddled with diseases such as cancer, heart disease, and liver and kidney disease. Sodium pentobarbital, which is used to euthanize dogs and cats, survives the rendering process and will be in the meat meal that is sold to the dog food manufacturers. A rendering plant in Baltimore processes over 1,800 animals a month, including dogs, and sells its products to Alpo, Ralston Purina, and Heinz pet food companies. This meat can be listed on the dog food label as meat meal or meat and bone meal.

The second criterion in choosing a dog food is to look for natural preservatives. Check the label for the antioxidants vitamin E and vitamin C. Stay away from chemical antioxidants such as ethoxyquin, butylated hydroxyanisole (BHA), and butylated hydroxytoluene (BHT). Ethoxyquin is a chemical that is manufactured by Monsanto for use in making rubber and preserving animal feed. It is labeled as a poison by Monsanto, is listed as a pesticide by the Department of Agriculture, and has been banned from use in human food. The Occupation Safety and Health Administration (OSHA) lists BHA and BHT as chemical hazards in the laboratory. They have been linked to various forms of cancer, most commonly kidney, liver, and bladder cancer.

Natural antioxidants such as vitamins E and C are the best preservatives, because they are natural to your dog's body and she can use what she needs and easily excrete any she does not need.

> "Sodium pentobarbital, which is used to euthanize dogs and cats, survives the rendering process and will be in the meat meal that is sold to the dog food manufacturers."

The third criterion for dry dog food is freshness. Look for a brand with a maximum shelf life of six months. Just as you look for the expiration date when you buy milk, yogurt, or cottage cheese, start looking for the date on the bag of dry food. Look for a bag that is under three months old, and please do not buy a 40-pound bag of food for your Chihuahua. By the time a toy breed eats 40 pounds of dog food, the dog food will be stale and rancid. Rancid fats and oils cause oxidation, a process within your dog's body in which unstable oxygen molecules, known as free radicals, attack healthy cells in an attempt to stabilize themselves. The healthy cell becomes unstable from the attack and becomes a free radical looking for a healthy cell to stabilize it. Free radical damage contributes to cancer, heart disease, eye disease, arthritis, allergies, and kidney disease.

The smell of the rancid oil in dog food is often not detectable, which makes the date on the bag your only indicator of freshness. Some dog food companies put the date the food is made on the bag, and some put the expiration date on the bag. The person you buy the food from should know which system the company uses. Buy enough food for a maximum of a month and keep it in a dark, dry area in a tightly closed container or close the bag tightly.

Canned dog food will not have an expiration date on it, but the other two criteria are the same: human-grade meat and natural preservatives.

Ideally, your dog should be eating fresh, naturally preserved food made with meat that you would put on your dinner table. In the Resources section, I have listed some dog food companies whose products fit these criteria. I have indicated the companies that use organic meat, and I recommend that you feed your dog organic meat if it is available in your area.

HOW TO READ DOG FOOD LABELS

Dog food labels are just as confusing as people food labels, so we will not try to read and understand each ingredient. You can scan the label and look for red flags.

The ingredients in dog food are listed in descending order by weight. The ingredient that weighs the most is first but is not necessarily the primary ingredient. If you add a cup of beef and a cup of oats, the oats will weigh significantly less than the beef.

Meat should be the first ingredient. If the label does not specify the type of meat, such as chicken, lamb, or beef, cross that food off your list. If the meat is simply listed as meat, it could be dog, cat, or a decaying raccoon someone found on the side of the road on the way to work.

Steer clear of by-products. They can be any part of the animal except for the meat, hair, horn, teeth, and hoofs, which means that it could be feathers, feet, and heads. Minced feathers and feet will not directly hurt your dog, but their nutritional value is highly questionable.

Meal and digest are fine. Meat meal is chopped or ground meat, bone, and organs. Poultry meal is chopped or ground meat, bone, and skin. Digest is meat that is predigested through a chemical or enzymatic process. You would not want your only source of meat to be digest, so be sure additional sources, such as meal, are listed. You also want meat that is naturally digested, with enzymes and not chemicals. If the shelf life of the food is six months or less, you can feel confident that the meat is naturally digested and does not contain chemicals.

The next ingredients listed are usually the grains and fats. Look for whole grains, such as ground brown rice. Avoid terms like "hulls," "mill run," and "by-products." These refer to the waste that is left after the grains are processed for human consumption. Ironically, what is considered the waste is the most nutritious part of the grain, but it still does not give you the complete balance of nutrients that whole grains do.

> "Many dog food manufacturers add beet pulp to their dog food in an attempt to satisfy the myth that the harder the dog's stool the better. Your dog's stool should not be rock hard; it should be soft and slightly formed."

Fats should be specifically identified. It should say poultry fat or beef fat, not simply animal fat, and it should be naturally preserved, usually with vitamin E.

The rest of the ingredients can range from a simple list of vitamins and minerals, which you will recognize after reading this book, to various plants, such as vegetables, herbs, and kelp.

Stay away from beet pulp. If you see beet pulp on the label, cross that food off your list. Beet pulp is another common ingredient in dog food that would be thrown in the garbage by the sugar beet processor if the dog food manufacturers did not buy it. Many dog food manufacturers add beet pulp to their dog food in an attempt to satisfy the myth that the harder the dog's stool the better. Your dog's stool should not be rock hard; it should be soft and slightly formed. As beet pulp passes through the intestine and the colon, it absorbs water and swells up to ten times its dry state, which causes it to pass very slowly and produce hard stools.

Diarrhea for more than a day or two is one of the few early indicators that your dog has an intestinal disorder. An artificial stool hardener like beet pulp will put you days behind in identifying and treating an illness. Beet pulp also has a high sugar content. Dogs get just as addicted to sugar as we do, and it also makes them fat, hyperactive, and diabetic.

Gastric torsion is one of the leading causes of death in large and giant barrel-chested dogs, such as the basset hound, Bernese mountain dog, bloodhound (leading cause of death), boxer, briard, bullmastiff, Chinese shar-pei, chow chow, Doberman pinscher, English setter, German shepherd, Gordon setter, greyhound, Irish setter, Labrador retriever, Russian wolfhound, Saint Bernard, Scottish deerhound, standard poodle, and weimaraner. The exact cause of gastric bloat and torsion has not been determined, probably because there is not one exact cause, but many breeders believe that feeding dry food without adding water is one cause. Dry food fed without water absorbs water from the stomach and swells. Adding beet pulp will cause additional swelling and additional risk. There is more on gastric torsion in Chapter 9, Natural Prevention and Treatment of Common Dog Diseases.

You have probably studied the guaranteed analysis on pet food labels, scratched your head, and wondered what it should mean to you. Because there are no regulations of the quality of the ingredients in dog food, unless you know the ingredients are of high quality, it is useless information. The guaranteed analysis lists minimum or maximum percentages of ingredients, such as crude protein, fat, and fiber. The catch is that they do not have to tell you exactly what sources the protein, fat, and fiber come from.

For example, lots of foods contain protein, but your dog's ability to absorb and use the protein varies. Eggs are a great source of protein, because your dog's body will absorb and use all the protein in an egg. An old leather shoe is a poor source of protein, because your dog's body cannot absorb the protein in an old leather shoe, and yet it could be legally listed on the ingredient label as meat by-products and could be included as a source of protein. If the food contains high-quality ingredients, then you can use the guaranteed analysis to narrow down your choices of dog food by finding a brand with optimal amounts of protein, fat, and fiber.

If you are going to feed your dog dry or canned food, be sure all the ingredients have nutritional value for your dog, and also add a variety of fresh, raw foods every day. Contrary to what the dog food manufacturers would like you to believe, a variety of nutrient-rich foods is the best way to give your dog a balanced diet.

Home-Cooked Meals

Many people shy away from home-cooked meals for their dogs. They do not know where to start, they think it will be too time-consuming, or they are worried that their pets will not get proper nutrition. Preparing homemade food does take more time than throwing a cup of dry food in a dish, but not much more, and it really is very simple.

Your dog is an omnivore, meaning she eats both animal and plant foods. In the case of a dog, the need for animal food is predominant. The approximate nutritional proportions for a healthy meal for a dog are 25 percent organ meat (liver, kidney, heart), 25 percent muscle meat, 25 percent grains, and 25 percent vegetables. For example, for a 50-pound dog, one meal might consist of one-half cup liver, one-half cup ground beef, one-half cup minced or grated carrots and broccoli, and one-half cup brown rice and oats, sprinkled with a multivitamin-mineral supplement.

Ground meat is an economical and easy source of muscle meat. Buy the ground meat that is packaged by the store. Meat that is packaged by the store usually was ground in the store. This reduces the risk of contamination that occurs in large meat-processing plants or in transporting the meat.

When it comes to fat content, you can live vicariously through your dog and buy the ground beef, lamb, turkey, or chicken with the highest fat content. Your dog needs some fat in her diet.

If your dog is lazy and inactive, you might want to avoid turkey, and if she is hyperactive, you might want to try adding turkey to her diet. Have you ever wondered why, after a turkey dinner, you never want to do the dishes or play a game of touch football—you just want to take a nap? Turkey contains the amino acid tryptophan, which acts as a mild sedative.

If possible, try to find an affordable source of organic organ meats. The liver and kidney are the organs that filter waste from the body, and toxins can accumulate there. If you have a grocery store nearby that sells organic meat, the butcher may be able to lower the price if you buy in bulk. If you do not have a big freezer, your friends may be interested in organic organ meat for themselves and/or their dog(s). Your local health food store may also know of a source. If you cannot find an organic source, it is best to skip the organ meats.

If you feed your dog raw meat, which is the healthiest way to do it, freeze the meat in meal-size packages and take out enough each morning for the next day and put it in your refrigerator.

For the carbohydrate portion of the meal, buy whole grains such as brown rice, oats, buckwheat, barley, grits, millet, amaranth, whole wheat couscous, or quinoa, a whole grain that is high in protein. Your dog's saliva does not contain the starch-digesting enzymes that we have, so she cannot digest large pieces or quantities of starchy food. Add some extra water and cook the grains a littler longer than you would cook them for yourself. If you see the grains in your dog's stool, that means she is not digesting them and they need to be cooked longer. Cooking breaks down the starches in the grains, making them easier to digest. You can cook enough for a week at one time.

> "Most vegetables are good for your dog. Dark green leafy vegetables and red, orange, and yellow vegetables are the most nutritious."

Most vegetables are good for your dog. Dark green leafy vegetables and red, orange, and yellow vegetables are the most nutritious. Onions should be avoided, because they contain a substance called n-propyl disulfide, which alters and eventually destroys the red blood cells of dogs, causing hemolytic anemia and sometimes death. If your dog has arthritis, try avoiding vegetables from the nightshade family (tomato, potato, peppers, eggplant), as these vegetables can sometimes aggravate arthritis.

Either slightly cook the vegetables or, to preserve the enzymes, chop or grate them finely and serve them raw. I often just give my dog a little bit of what the rest of the family is getting for dinner and leave some in the fridge for the next morning. After all, our dogs are not the only ones who should eat their peas and broccoli!

You do not have to be strict about the food proportions that you give. Older dogs who have never eaten vegetables may not have a taste for them unless the vegetables are well disguised in a little butter or olive oil. Dogs fed vegetables early in life will more easily eat them plain and raw. Each dog's needs are different, and they will vary throughout her life. The quantities given are a guideline. If she tends to leave grains in her dish, cut back a little on the grains. Meat, grains, and vegetables are the basics. Any whole nutritious foods can be added, such as fruits, yogurt, eggs, unsalted nuts, cheese, beans, and cottage cheese.

How much food to feed each day will also vary with each dog. Just as every person's body uses food differently, so does a dog's. You will be giving your dog more food with home-cooked meals than with a dry dog food, because dry dog food does not have water in it, so it is concentrated. As a starting point, use the following guidelines for total amounts to feed each day:

small dogs up to 20 pounds	1 to 2 cups
medium dogs from 20 to 50 pounds	2 to 7 cups
large dogs from 50 to 100 pounds	7 to 10 cups
giant dogs over 100 pounds	10 to 14 cups

Many dog owners find that once their dog gets used to her home-cooked meals she will eat what she needs and leave the rest, becoming trim and fit and full of energy. Unless they have experienced trauma around food, such as not getting enough to eat as a newborn, dogs will eat to meet their energy and nutritional needs. Most dogs are overweight because their food contains addictive sugars or is high in calories with little nutritional value.

Mix together the meat, grains, and vegetables, add supplements, which you will learn about later in this chapter, mix thoroughly, and serve with a smile, knowing you are putting your dog on the road to a long, healthy life.

Fresh Foods

Fresh foods have been forgotten in most canine diets. There are hundreds of human studies that testify to the fact that a diet high in fresh, raw fruits and vegetables is a key to a long, healthy life. Where are the studies on dogs that would prove the same thing? The majority of studies done on dog nutrition are funded by dog food manufacturers who could not call their foods "complete and balanced" if they did a nutritional study that included fresh foods. Fortunately there are a few studies being done that are independent of the dog food manufacturers. One impressive study of 900 cats found that the cats fed a diet including raw meat and raw milk led long and healthy lives, while the cats fed pasteurized milk and cooked meat suffered from many ailments, including kidney, heart, thyroid, and gum disease. Another impressive testimony to the benefits of fresh foods is Taffy, a border collie who holds the *Guinness Book of Records* title for canine longevity in Britain. Taffy ate fresh foods and lived to be twenty-seven years old.

The difference between raw meat and milk and pasteurized milk and cooked meat is that the raw food contains enzymes. An enzyme is a protein molecule produced by living organisms. There are at least 1,300 different enzymes in your dog's body, each with a different function, such as digesting food or processing waste materials in the blood. Enzymes are essential to all life on earth.

According to Humbart Santillo, author of *Food Enzymes: The Missing Link to Radiant Health,* "There is a connection between the strength of our immune system and our enzyme level. The greater the amount of enzyme reserves, the stronger our immune system, the healthier and stronger we will be." Enzymes are only found in raw food because they are destroyed in food that is heated over 105 degrees Fahrenheit. Any food that is heat processed, roasted, baked, or fried does not contain enzymes.

> "The majority of studies done on dog nutrition are funded by dog food manufacturers who could not call their foods 'complete and balanced' if they did a nutritional study that included fresh foods."

Not surprisingly, there is a high incidence of digestive enzyme deficiencies in dogs. Although many enzymes are made by the body, it is also important to get them from raw foods. Most dogs do not get fresh food their entire lives unless they can get away with sneaking in a few mouthfuls of grass when they go outside.

> "Digestive enzymes help break down your dog's food, enabling the nutrients to be absorbed. Normally, living creatures begin life with plenty of digestive enzymes, which may be depleted if they are never given any fresh, raw food."

Digestive enzymes help break down your dog's food, enabling the nutrients to be absorbed. Normally, living creatures begin life with plenty of digestive enzymes, which may be depleted if they are never given any fresh, raw food. The enzymes in raw food do not replenish your dog's reserves as much as they digest a portion of that food so that your dog's body does not use as many.

German shepherds are prone to a digestive enzyme deficiency that causes many intestinal problems, including poor digestion and the inability to absorb the nutrients from foods. Nutrient deficiencies cause a long list of chronic problems, including skin problems, allergies, diarrhea, and vomiting. A diet of fresh, raw foods would be all these German shepherds would need to properly digest and absorb their food. For severe cases, there are digestive enzyme supplements for dogs.

Try to give your dog as much fresh, raw meat, vegetables, and fruits as you can. If you feed your dog raw vegetables from the time she is a puppy, she will usually always like them. If your older dog will not chew on a carrot, then grate, mince, or blend it and add it to her food. If you are in the kitchen preparing fresh whole foods and your dog shows an interest in them, give her some. Sometimes dogs will be more willing to try something new if they think it is people food. And yes, raw beef, poultry, and lamb is very good for your dog. Not only will the enzymes help digest the meat, but they will help clean your dog's teeth.

Water

Oxygen is the only nutrient that is more important in sustaining life than water. Your dog could live for weeks without food but would only last a few days without water. Approximately 60 percent of your dog's total weight is water. That means that if your dog weighs 50 pounds, then 30 pounds of that weight is water! The entire body is highly dependent on water, including the brain, blood, and muscles, which are each over 70 percent water. The most important nutrient you give your dog is water, so it is vital your dog have access to pure, clean water at all times.

Although 70 percent of the earth is covered by water, it is hard to find clean drinking water. In 1991 and 1992 the Natural Resources Defense Council found 250,000 violations of the Safe Drinking Water Act, which affected more than 120 million people. Environmental Protection Agency (EPA) data shows that the tap water of approximately 30 million people in the U.S. fails to meet at least one of its health standards each year, and yet its standards are shamefully inadequate. The EPA health standards include about 100 contaminants that should not be found in tap water, but over 2,000 contaminants have been found in drinking water supplies throughout the U.S. Your tap water could (and probably does) contain contaminants such as bacteria, viruses, parasites, lead, gasoline, radioactive gases, cancer-causing industrial compounds, chlorine, fluoride, aluminum, nitrates, lead, chemical salts, sulphates, fecal material (*E. coli*), and pesticides.

According to the U.S. Centers for Disease Control, 1,000 to 1,200 people die each year from contaminated drinking water and another 400,000 to 27 million people become sick. These numbers probably reflect only a small portion of the actual deaths and illnesses from contaminated water, because there is no official reporting system for water-related health problems. Gathering statistics on water-related health problems is also difficult because many doctors do not consider water when diagnosing an illness, and the toxins in water cause gradual deterioration of the body over many years. Human health care professionals who consider the role of polluted water in illness are rare, and it is unheard of among health care professionals who take care of our dogs. When was the last time you called your vet because your dog had diarrhea or vomiting and she asked about your dog's drinking water?

The average dog weighs about 60 pounds, while the average person weighs more than twice that. The smaller the dog, the higher the metabolic rate and the more susceptible to pollutants, because the body processes everything more quickly, including toxins. What might take months to make a human sick might take only days to make a small dog sick. The same drinking water that is making 27 million people sick each year is undoubtedly making a significantly higher number of dogs seriously ill and shortening the life span of many toy breeds.

"The same drinking water that is making 27 million people sick each year is undoubtedly making a significantly higher number of dogs seriously ill and shortening the life span of many toy breeds."

GET THE LEAD OUT

Among the hundreds of contaminants in our drinking water, lead is probably the most common and the most dangerous contaminant. Over 98 percent of homes in the U.S. have pipes that contain lead or lead solder, leaving over 30 million people drinking water with high levels of lead. High concentrations of lead can permanently damage the brain, kidneys, and central nervous system and cause hyperactivity, reproductive problems, slowed growth, headaches, heart disease, retardation, digestive problems, anemia, muscle and joint pain, and even death. In 1986, Congress amended the 1974 Safe Drinking Water Act and banned all future use of lead pipe and lead solder in public drinking water systems. This does not include your faucets, which to this day may contain up to 8 percent lead. A study of water that sat in twenty-five new faucets for a few hours contained from 30 to 1,300 parts per billion of lead, which is 2 to 100 times the daily amount that can cause serious symptoms in people. Again, whatever the danger to people, the danger to your dog is magnified.

If you must use tap water, both for yourself and your dog, run the water for a minute first to clear out any accumulated toxins. If you believe your dog has been exposed to lead, give her an extra mineral supplement for a few days. Magnesium and zinc are instrumental in helping rid your dog's body of lead.

There are hundreds of contaminants that enter the water through the air, ground, and pipes that are eliminated from municipal water supplies by adding chlorine, which is yet another contaminant. Some communities are also poisoning their water supply with fluoride.

THE GREAT FLUORIDE SCANDAL

The decision to add fluoride to our drinking water can only be attributed to one of the most successful and deceptive marketing campaigns in modern history. Before fluoride was added to our drinking water, it was considered an extremely toxic environmental pollutant that destroyed crops and animals. The handbook *Clinical Toxicology of Commercial Products* considers fluoride to be more poisonous than lead. Because it was considered an environmental pollutant, industries whose waste products contained large amounts of fluoride (mostly aluminum and fertilizer manufacturers) were incurring huge expenses to dispose of their waste. The need to inexpensively dispose of fluoride waste products was brought to the government's attention by the "right" people, which prompted the mysterious transformation of fluoride from an environmental pollutant to a supposedly harmless substance that would be trickled into the nation's water supply to prevent tooth decay.

The studies used to support the proposal to put fluoride in our drinking water to prevent tooth decay are in direct opposition to studies done independently of the companies that needed to get rid of their fluoride. It reminds me of the two men who went for job interviews at a company's research facility. The first man went to his interview and was given a research project and asked how he would conduct the study. The man went through a lengthy discussion on how he would conduct his study and left feeling very confident he would get the job.

The second man went in for his interview and was given the same research project and was asked how he would conduct the study. The second man got the job by simply asking one question: What results do you want?

Studies that were done by people who did not have a financial interest in fluoride found it to be linked to weak bones, skin problems, stomach pain, headaches, cancer, immune disorders, arthritis, and discolored teeth. Fluoride has not been linked to a reduction in tooth decay or stronger bones in adults in any independent study. One of the many independent studies on fluoridated water involved over 39,000 children ages five to seven throughout the United States. The children using fluoridated water did not show a reduction in tooth decay when compared to those children using nonfluoridated water.

The U.S. is one of the few countries left in the world that puts fluoride in its water. The same decline in tooth decay that we have seen in the U.S. has also been seen in countries that do not use fluoride in their water. In fact, the decline in tooth decay is attributable to better dental hygiene and better nutrition, not fluoride.

Another fluoride myth is that it will build strong bones and repair weak, brittle bones. Using fluoride will make bones look more dense on X rays for a few years, but in truth the bone is weak and brittle, and after four to six years the fracture rate of people taking it increases dramatically. It is fascinating how the studies promoting the use of fluoride-like drugs, such as Fosamax for osteoporosis, all end at four to six years!

Avoiding fluoride is not easy, so if you live in a community that does not add fluoride to its water supply, consider yourself lucky. Boiling water concentrates fluoride, and the only filtration system that removes fluoride is a reverse osmosis system. If fluoride is in your tap water, use bottled water that

> "The U.S. is one of the few countries left in the world that puts fluoride in its water. The same decline in tooth decay that we have seen in the U.S. has also been seen in countries that do not use fluoride in their water. In fact, the decline in tooth decay is attributable to better dental hygiene and better nutrition, not fluoride."

guarantees it does not contain fluoride, distilled water, or water from a reverse osmosis system.

OUR BIGGEST WATER-BORNE CARCINOGEN

Chlorine is added to municipal water systems to destroy microorganisms that carry disease. Unfortunately, this disinfectant can also make you and your dog sick. Chlorine in water creates cancer-causing by-products called trihalomethanes, which are formed during the chlorination process. The Natural Resources Defense Council estimates that trihalomethanes cause more than 10,000 cases of rectal and bladder cancer in humans a year. According to the National Cancer Institute, drinking chlorinated water doubles your risk for bladder cancer. Fortunately, most water filters remove chlorine.

If you use well water, you have probably been congratulating yourself on having clean, untreated water, but the only contaminants you are avoiding are chlorine and fluoride. The same nearby farms, military bases, landfills, underground gasoline storage tanks, golf courses, fields, orchards, and pesticide-spraying neighbors that pollute municipal water supplies are also poisoning your well water.

In your dog, short-term bouts of diarrhea or vomiting and hyperactivity or more serious long-term effects, such as cancer, liver and kidney disease, and arthritis, could all be caused by polluted drinking water.

There are a few easy solutions to clearing up the contaminants in your tap water. First, you can have your water tested to find out what contaminants you need to eliminate. To have your water tested, call the Environmental Protection Agency's safe drinking water hotline, at (800) 426-4791. If you live in Alaska or Washington, D.C., call (202) 382-5533. The EPA will give you a list of certified testing labs in your area.

Once you find out which contaminants you need to eliminate, look in the yellow pages of your phone book under "water" and "water purification systems." Depending on the level of contaminants and your budget, you can buy a filter for your faucet, a water distiller, or a reverse osmosis system. For information on where to buy filters, see the Resources section in the back of this book.

New technology for water filtration is coming out every year, so do your research before buying. If you do not want to bother with having your water tested or changing filters, you can have bottled water delivered to your house, or if you have the time and the inclination, there may be a place near you where you can bring your own container and get bottled water for around twenty-five cents a gallon. Whatever your source, be sure to get a written evaluation of what is in the water.

If you and your dog travel a lot or go camping, you can buy purification filters at most sport stores or department stores. Read the label carefully. Some types of portable filters only purify water from freshwater rivers, lakes, or streams and not tap water. Look for one that filters chlorine and parasites such as *Giardia*.

THE WATER BOWL

Your dog's water bowl can also be a source of contaminants. Use a glass, stainless steel, or American-made ceramic bowl. Many foreign-made ceramics contain high levels of lead, which will leach into the water. Plastic and aluminum will also leach and contaminate the water you worked so hard to keep clean and fresh.

Place the water away from possible contamination by pesticides, cleaning sprays, or other animals. Wild animals such as rodents carry many diseases that could be lethal to your dog. Rodent urine has recently been found to carry a deadly strain of leptospirosis that is different from the vaccine your dog gets.

Clean your dog's water bowl at least once a day, and if you are not home during the day, be sure the supply is large enough to last through the day.

CHAPTER TWO

Treats

MANY PEOPLE SERVE their dogs only the highest-quality foods at mealtime and then fall short when it comes to treats. Even a few low-quality treats a day can compromise your dog's health. The same cautions I gave you in choosing a dog food hold true for treats, and the best treats are fresh raw foods. I once knew a golden retriever named Tyler who thought the best treat in the world was an ice cube. His owner was on a tight budget, so she used ice cubes for rewards.

Some of the dog food manufacturers listed in the Resources section make high-quality treats, or you can use carrot sticks, dried meat, or home-cooked cookies. If you like to cook, you can try making home-made treats and store them in the freezer. For a refreshing treat on a hot day, give one to your dog right from the freezer.

The following are two of Dr. Beverly Cappel-King's favorite recipes for dog treats.

Dr. Bev's Delectable Dog Cookies

1½ cups whole wheat flower
⅛ cup chopped unsalted seeds and nuts
1 tablespoon vegetable oil
1 egg
1 tablespoon molasses
any or all of the following, to taste:
    grated cheese
    nutritional yeast
    fresh garlic or garlic powder

Combine all ingredients into a firm ball; add milk if more moisture is needed.

Roll the dough out and cut it into your dog's favorite cookie shapes. (My dog prefers cats, rabbits, and squirrels.) Place them on a greased cookie sheet and bake at 300 degrees Fahrenheit for 30 to 40 minutes or until the cookies are crispy.

The King of Dog Cookies

1½ cups cooked rice, oatmeal, or other whole grain cereal
¼ cup whole or skim milk powder
¼ cup vegetable oil
¼ cup wheat bran
¼ cup whole wheat flour, rye flour, or corn meal
any or all of the following, to taste:
    grated cheese
    nutritional yeast
    fresh garlic or garlic powder
    oregano
    fennel seed

Combine all ingredients into a firm ball; add milk if more moisture is needed.

Roll the dough out and cut it into your dog's favorite cookie shapes. Place them on a greased cookie sheet and bake at 300 degrees Fahrenheit for 30 to 40 minutes or until the cookies are crispy.

Please feel free to take great liberties with these recipes. Try different flours, whole grain cereals, spices, seeds, nuts, and cheeses. If you want to make a big batch and keep them in the refrigerator or travel with them, squeeze a vitamin E capsule into the dough as a preservative.

Animal-Origin Chew Toys

Dogs need to chew. Not only is chewing good for your dog's emotional well-being, but it is also good for her health. Chewing prevents boredom and keeps teeth clean, jaws strong, and gums healthy. If your dog lived in the wild, she would spend hours chewing on her prey. Your puppy should always have something to chew on, or (as many dog owners have found) she will find something to chew, and she will not discriminate between the antiques and the old furniture—although many dog owners would argue that their dogs will only chew antiques.

Among the huge variety of chew toys available are animal-origin chew toys, which range from the familiar rawhide chews to the fairly new animal parts, such as hooves, feet, ears, and horns. It seems as if every time I go into a pet store there is a new animal part on the shelf that is being marketed as an all-natural chew toy for my dog. These are parts of animals that would otherwise be thrown away because humans will not eat them. Remember, "all natural" does not always mean nutritious. One of the keys to creating optimal health is to stick with food that has nutritional value.

Lack of nutrition is not the only reason I do not recommend rawhide or animal-part chew toys. They can also endanger your dog's life. Foods with very little nutritional value are harder to digest, which means they sit in the stomach and intestine longer than highly digestible foods. Large chunks of indigestible foods such as rawhide or pig's ears have proved to cause a wide range of illnesses, from mild intestinal problems to complete intestinal blockage and death.

A golden retriever named Sunny is one of many dogs Dr. Beverly Cappel-King has treated for intestinal problems associated with animal-origin chew toys. Sunny was brought to Dr. King with symptoms of vomiting and constipation. When Dr. King palpated her stomach, she could feel something unusual, so she took X rays. The X rays did not show anything, nor did an ultrasound or endoscopy. As a last resort, Dr. King did exploratory surgery and found a piece of rawhide the size of a lime embedded inside Sunny's intestine.

> "Lack of nutrition is not the only reason I do not recommend rawhide or animal-part chew toys. They can also endanger your dog's life."

There have also been many instances of dogs choking on animal-origin chew toys. As the dog chews, these products become soft and sticky, and they are easily caught in the throat. Many rawhide chew toys also contain the chemical propylene glycol, a preservative that is a component of antifreeze. Propylene glycol has a sweet taste that the dogs begin to crave after a few rawhides. You also need to be careful of chew toys like hooves, which can splinter and puncture your dog's intestinal wall. I do not see any reason to take these types of risks when there are safe alternatives that will satisfy your dog's need to chew.

Just as with humans, variety is the spice of life for dogs, so I keep chew toys of all shapes, sizes, and textures around the house. There are a wide variety of safe nonfood chew toys, such as ropes, rubber balls, and fuzzy shapes that squeak. Tennis balls will act like a Brillo pad on your dog's teeth, wearing them down quickly. Reserve them for games of fetch. Avoid synthetic fabrics, plastic toys (which will leach plastic), and brightly colored toys that contain harmful dyes.

A raw marrow bone from your butcher is great for safe, long-term chewing; it will provide good nutrition as well as clean your dog's teeth and keep her jaws strong and her gums healthy. They are inexpensive and will satisfy your dog's chewing needs for days. It is important to serve them raw, because cooking bones is what makes them splinter. A frozen marrow bone is another great treat for your dog on a hot day. If you do not have an outside area where you can leave your dog to chew on her marrow bone, use an old sheet or blanket to protect your carpet and other fabrics from being stained by the fat.

CHAPTER THREE

Vitamins for Your Dog

JUST AS HUMANS DO, dogs need vitamins for growth and maintenance of a healthy body. It would be ideal if your dog could get vitamins from her food, but even the highest-quality nonorganic dog food will not provide enough for maintaining optimal health. Even when you prepare your dog nonorganic home-cooked meals, you need to use supplements, and here is why. Much of our produce is grown in soil depleted of nutrients and sprayed with pesticides. Unless it is organic, the meat we eat comes from animals given hormones and antibiotics. Whether you live in the country or the city, your dog experiences a daily bombardment of physical stressors from pollutants and toxins such as pesticides and car exhaust. When your dog is stressed by environmental or emotional factors, her need for vitamins is much higher.

Unless you are treating your dog for a specific health problem or a stressful environment, the best way to provide daily vitamins is with a multivitamin supplement. Give half the daily dose with the morning meal and half with the evening meal.

For each of the vitamins your dog needs on a daily basis, I will give you dosage recommendations for adult small, medium, large, and giant dogs so that you can choose a good mulitvitamin. Small dogs weigh up to 20 pounds, medium dogs weigh from 20 to 50 pounds, large dogs weigh from 50 to 100 pounds, and giant dogs weigh over 100 pounds.

There are many sources of good dog multivitamins. If you cannot find a vitamin that contains the correct dosages, check the Resources section in the back of this book for mail-order sources of vitamins.

What Are Vitamins?

Vitamins are organic substances found naturally in plants, eggs, fish, fowl, and meat. With the exception of vitamin C, your dog cannot produce her own vitamins and needs you to provide them through food and supplemental sources.

Vitamins A, D, E, and K and the B-complex vitamins are referred to as essential vitamins for dogs, because they need to be provided in the diet and are essential to sustain life. Although your dog produces her own vitamin C, it too needs to be supplemented. These vitamins are divided into water-soluble vitamins, which include the B-complex vitamins and vitamin C, and fat-soluble vitamins, which include A, D, E, and K. The water-soluble and fat-soluble vitamins are processed differently in the body. The water-soluble vitamins (B-complex and C) are absorbed in the small intestine and used as needed, and any excess is excreted in the urine. The fat-soluble vitamins (A, D, E, K) are stored primarily in the liver, and any excess is excreted in the feces. Dogs also excrete vitamin A in the urine, which makes it less toxic to them. This will be discussed in more detail later in this chapter. The important difference between water-soluble and fat-soluble vitamins is that the fat-soluble vitamins (A, D, E, K) are stored in the body, creating a greater risk for toxicity and a lower risk of deficiencies, while the water-soluble vitamins (B-complex, C) are not stored, increasing the potential for deficiencies and decreasing the chance of toxicity. Use the following table as a quick reference on the essential vitamins, their functions within the body, nutritional sources, and the health problems related to excesses and deficiencies of each vitamin.

> "Even when you prepare your dog nonorganic home-cooked meals, you need to use supplements."

Vitamin	Function	Source	Signs of Deficiency	Signs of Excess Intake
A	Beneficial for skeletal growth, skin, epithelial tissue, vision, reproduction, immune system	Yellow, orange, and dark green vegetables and fruits, fish oils, liver, egg, dairy products	Skeletal abnormalities, skin disorders, loss of tissue integrity, night blindness, reproductive failure	Skeletal abnormalities, over-sensitivity to sensory stimuli, cleft palate in puppies
B$_1$ (Thiamin)	Aids in digestion of carbohydrate and protein	Whole grains, liver, pork, legumes, nuts, yeast	Stool eating, lack of appetite, impaired central nervous system, convulsions, muscle weakness	Nontoxic
B$_2$ (Riboflavin)	Aids in digestion of carbohydrate and fat, cell growth	Eggs, yogurt, milk, organ meats, cheese, green vegetables	Stool eating, skin disorders, impaired central nervous system	Nontoxic
B$_3$ (Niacin)	Processes amino acids, carbohydrates, and glucose; aids in utilization of fatty acids	Liver, meat, yeast, milk, egg yolk, whole grains, legumes	Skin disease, diarrhea, madness	Nontoxic
B$_5$ (Pantothenic Acid)	Occurs in all forms of living tissue; aids in synthesis of fatty acids, cholesterol, and steroids, production of cortisone and hormones, utilization of fat and carbohydrate	Liver, kidney, egg yolk, dairy products, yeast, legumes, wheat germ, peanuts	Lowered antibody response, premature graying, low blood sugar, Addison's disease, deterioration of adrenal glands, digestive disorders	Nontoxic

Vitamin	Function	Source	Signs of Deficiency	Signs of Excess Intake
B_6 (Pyridoxine)	Processes amino acids, proteins, hydrochloric acid, and magnesium; helps produce antibodies and red blood cells	Liver, meat, yeast, milk, whole grains, egg yolk	Anemia, dental decay, heart disease, liver disease	Neurological damage
B_{12} (Cobalamin)	Processes amino acids, fatty acids, carbohydrate, and fat; aids in absorption of protein, production of red blood cells	Liver, kidney, meat, fish, poultry, eggs	Anemia, brain damage, fatigue, low red blood cell count, senility	Nontoxic
Biotin	Processes fat, protein, and vitamin C	Liver, kidney, egg yolk, yeast, milk, legumes	Anemia, skin disorders, hair loss, heart disease, weak muscles	Nontoxic
Folic Acid	Aids in production of red blood cells, processes protein, builds antibodies, helps growth and division of cells	Liver, yeast, green vegetables	Anemia, vaccine reactions, watery eyes, lack of appetite	Nontoxic
Choline	Aids in utilization of fat and cholesterol, cell and nervous tissue structure and function	Organ meats, fish, egg yolk, yeast, wheat germ, dairy products, legumes, whole grains	Impaired central nervous system, liver, and thymus gland, heart disease	Diarrhea

(continued)

Vitamin	Function	Source	Signs of Deficiency	Signs of Excess Intake
C (Ascorbic Acid)	Aids in collagen production, absorption of vitamins, growth and maintenance of tissue cells; beneficial for gums, blood vessels, bones, and teeth; works as an antioxidant	Citrus fruit, green vegetables, potatoes, berries	Weak immune system, bladder stones, urinary tract and skin infections, skeletal abnormalities	Nontoxic; diarrhea, low sulfur
D	Aids in absorption of calcium and phosphorus	Fish-liver oils, yeast, egg yolk	Defective bone growth, softening of bones	Calcium deposits, bone resorption, kidney damage
E (Tocopherol)	Works as an antioxidant; enhances immune system, utilization of sex hormones, vitamin D, and cholesterol	Nuts, brown rice, wheat germ, eggs, whole grains, soybean and sunflower oil, seeds, green leafy vegetables	Reproductive failure, low red blood cell count, heart disease, muscle degeneration, anemia, kidney disease	Nontoxic; increased need for vitamins A and D
K	Aids in blood clotting, production of protein	Liver, green vegetables	Hemorrhage, internal bleeding	Anemia

Water-Soluble Vitamins

B-COMPLEX VITAMINS

The B-complex vitamins are grouped together because they work as a team. The team is made up of thiamin (B_1), riboflavin (B_2), niacin (B_3), pantothenic acid (B_5), pyridoxine (B_6), cobalamin (B_{12}), biotin, folic acid, and choline. The effectiveness of one B vitamin is to a large extent dependent upon adequate amounts of other B vitamins. For example, pyridoxine (B_6) is necessary for the absorption of cobalamin (B_{12}). Natural food sources rich in B vitamins never contain only one B vitamin. It is best to supplement the B vitamins together unless you are treating a specific illness with one B vitamin.

The B-complex vitamins help ward off stress, alleviate neurological problems, and are essential for cell maintenance and growth, the production of antibodies and red blood cells, and the absorption of protein, fat, and carbohydrates. Alfred J. Plechner, D.V.M., and Martin Zucker, authors of *Pet Allergies: Remedies for an Epidemic,* have found that hyperactivity and aggressiveness in dogs can sometimes be remedied by a B-complex supplement.

You can give your dog extra B-complex supplement when you know she is going to be stressed or her immune system is compromised. Vaccinations, surgery, and a serious injury or shock to the body are the most extreme cases in which your dog's body needs a lot of extra support from the B vitamins. The B-complex vitamins will also reduce the toxic effects of antibiotics and radiation from X rays or radiation therapy.

Other indications for giving your dog a B-complex vitamin are highly stressful situations such as traveling, separation anxiety, the show ring, nausea during pregnancy, and being a stressed mother. Neurological disorders, such as degenerative myelopathy in German shepherds, can be helped with the B-complex vitamins. Any breed that is susceptible to digestive disorders, such as the boxer and German shepherd, can benefit from extra B-complex vitamins. Toy and short-nosed breeds, such as the bulldog, Pekingese, Pomeranian, and pug, are prone to tooth and gum diseases and can benefit from extra vitamin B-complex.

Sulfa drugs, hormone therapy, cortisone, and drugs for high blood pressure rob your dog's body of some of the B-complex vitamins, so be sure to give your dog a supplement if she is on any of these types of drugs. Sulfa drugs are given for bacterial diseases and are sometimes referred to as an antibiotic, although technically they are not an antibiotic. If your veterinarian has prescribed a drug that begins with sulfa, such as sulfanilamide, it is a sulfa drug; or you may just see a brand name such as Albon, Bactrovet, Primor, or Tribrissen. If in doubt, ask questions.

Nutritional sources of the B-complex vitamins are liver, kidney, dark green vegetables, blackstrap molasses, milk, peanuts, kelp, brewer's yeast, and eggs. The high heat used to process some brewer's yeast depletes it of the B-vitamins, so be sure you are buying unprocessed brewer's yeast if you use it as a nutritional supplement. Unprocessed brewer's yeast is inexpensive and readily available at health food stores. When you give your dog and yourself eggs, try to find a source of organically fed free-range chickens. Free-range chickens get the majority of their nutrients from the pasture and are free of antibiotics and hormones. And yes, raw eggs are good for your dog. The myth that raw eggs are not good for dogs came from the fact that raw egg whites can prevent the absorption of biotin (one of the B-complex vitamins). This is true, but the egg yolk supplies your dog with plenty of biotin to counteract the effects of the egg whites. Feeding the egg raw keeps the food alive and enables your dog to absorb the nutrients more efficiently. Eggs are a great source of protein, B vitamins, vitamin E, vitamin D, vitamin A, magnesium, selenium, amino acids, and zinc. I give my dog an egg for breakfast every Sunday morning, the same day I splurge on a big breakfast.

Vitamin B-complex comes as a tablet and as a powder in a capsule; or you can buy unprocessed brewer's yeast.

Daily dosages for adult dogs are as follows:

	Small Dog	*Medium Dog*	*Large Dog*	*Giant Dog*
Thiamin (B_1)	1 mg	2 mg	3 mg	4 mg
Riboflavin (B_2)	1 mg	2 mg	3 mg	4 mg
Niacin (B_3)	1 mg	2 mg	3 mg	4 mg
Pantothenic Acid (B_5)	1 mg	2 mg	3 mg	4 mg
Choline	1 mg	2 mg	3 mg	4 mg
Pyridoxine (B_6)	1 mg	2 mg	3 mg	4 mg
Cobalamin (B_{12})	1 mcg	2 mcg	3 mcg	4 mcg
Biotin	1 mcg	2 mcg	3 mcg	4 mcg
Folic Acid	1 mcg	2 mcg	3 mcg	4 mcg

VITAMIN C (ASCORBIC ACID)

Unlike humans who must get their vitamin C through diet or supplements, most animals produce their own vitamin C. Dogs produce vitamin C in the liver from the blood sugar glucose. Each day, adult dogs produce approximately 40 milligrams of vitamin C per 2.2 pounds of body weight. That is about 1,800 milligrams for a 100-pound dog, 900 milligrams for a 50-pound dog, and 450 milligrams for a 25-pound dog.

There is an assumption among conventional veterinarians that because dogs manufacture their own vitamin C there is no need to supplement it. However, holistic veterinarians have found that supplementing vitamin C in a dog's diet can clear up a variety of health problems. Dr. Wendell Belfield points out in his book, *How to Have a Healthier Dog,* "Fifteen years of clinical experience, involving over two thousand cases, has told me that dogs definitely benefit from extra vitamin C. When given supplements, they are much less likely to develop hip dysplasia, spinal myelopathy, ruptured discs, viral diseases, and skin problems. They live healthier and longer."

> "We also know that when a dog is stressed she needs additional vitamins for her body to function properly and to protect it from disease."

Vitamin C is a powerful antioxidant that can reduce cancer risk, boost the immune system, stimulate wound repair, and reduce the risk of cataracts. Vitamin C is important for proper bone formation and maintenance and plays a role in preventing heart disease. We also know that when a dog is stressed she needs additional vitamins for her body to function properly and to protect it from disease.

A report published in the *British Journal of Biomedical Sciences* states that in humans a low intake of vitamins A, B$_6$, C, E, beta-carotene, and folic acid have been associated with abnormally low immune system response and greater risk of cancer.

Cataracts, the filming over of the lens of the eye in older dogs, is a common problem in all dogs. Cataracts are caused, at least in part, by oxidative stress to the lens of the eye. Testimony to the power of vitamin C in protecting the eye was shown in a human study that also applies to our pets. The *American Journal of Clinical Nutrition* reported that cataract patients tend to have lower levels of vitamin C in their blood. In a study of 175 cataract patients and 175 cataract-free patients, the cataract-free patients used significantly more vitamin C supplements than those with cataracts.

The body requires vitamin C to form collagen, a substance that functions as the "glue" that holds together skin and connective tissue such as ligaments and tendons. Many holistic veterinarians have used vitamin C to prevent and treat hip dysplasia, an abnormal development of the hip that is very common in all breeds of giant and large dogs. Dr. Belfield has been preventing hip dysplasia for years by supplementing with vitamin C when a dog becomes pregnant and continuing the supplements with the puppies after they are born. He has had many cases in which mothers with hip dysplasia produced litter after litter totally free of hip dysplasia. Many other holistic veterinarians have also successfully used vitamin C in their practices to prevent hip dysplasia. They report that hip dysplasia has virtually disappeared in dogs that are given vitamin C when they are puppies.

An article in the *Journal of the American Podiatric Medical Association* reports that vitamin C levels are higher in healing tissue and return to normal after the healing is complete. Vitamin C, in combination with pantothenic acid (B_5), has been shown to increase skin strength and fibroblastic content of scar tissue. A deficiency of both causes prolonged wound healing.

A poodle puppy named Seymour is alive today because of the healing qualities of vitamin C. Seymour was brought to Dr. Beverly Cappel-King with vomiting, dehydration, and severe intestinal bleeding. A test for the parvo virus, which is often deadly for puppies, came back positive. Dr. King immediately put Seymour on intravenous therapy, which included megadoses of vitamin C to stop the bleeding, potassium for the dehydration, and antibiotics to battle infection. The internal bleeding stopped in about six hours, and Seymour is now a healthy, happy adult.

Most fresh, uncooked fruits and vegetables are great sources of vitamin C. Some that your dog might like include cantaloupe, honeydew melon, kiwifruit, strawberries, asparagus, red pepper, snow peas, broccoli, and cauliflower. Whenever you are preparing these fruits and vegetables for yourself, which I hope is often, you can put some aside for your dog. I recommend you give these to your dog raw, to optimize the nutrients and enzymes.

When supplementing vitamin C, use sodium ascorbate or some other form of buffered vitamin C, because plain ascorbic acid may cause an upset stomach. You can buy it in powder form and add it to your dog's food, or get it in a multivitamin. The daily dosage for an adult dog is the following:

small dogs	500 mg to 1,000 mg
medium and large dogs	1,000 mg to 2,000 mg
giant dogs	2,000 mg to 4,000 mg

For puppies that have not been weaned yet, buy vitamin C pediatric drops or tablets for humans at your health food store. Put the tablet on the puppy's tongue or under the lip, and the tablet will dissolve almost instantly. Use the following daily dosages:

small and medium breeds	50 mg for the first ten days, then from the age of ten days to weaning give 100 mg
large and giant breeds	75 mg for the first ten days, then from the age of ten days to weaning give 150 mg

When the puppy is weaned, gradually switch to powder and slowly increase the dosage until you get to the adult dosage. For the first six months, slowly increase the dosage to the following:

small breeds	250 mg
medium breeds	500 mg
large breeds	1,000 mg
giant breeds	2,000 mg

At six months, slowly increase to the adult dosage. For adult dogs, start at the lowest dose and gradually increase the dosage until you see loose stools. Loose stools or diarrhea is a sign of too much vitamin C, so reduce the amount to the previous dose.

Fat-Soluble Vitamins

VITAMIN A

Vitamin A comes in two forms: preformed vitamin A and provitamin A. Preformed vitamin A is also called retinol and can be found in foods of animal origin, such as liver, egg yolks, and milk. Provitamin A is derived from carotene. Carotene is a pigment found in yellow, orange, and dark green vegetables and fruits and is converted to vitamin A in the liver. Unlike humans, who store their excess vitamin A in the liver, only 30 percent of a dog's excess vitamin A accumulates in the liver until they need it. The remaining 70 percent circulates in the blood, and any excess is excreted through the kidneys and then the urine. The way a dog's body processes vitamin A allows it to tolerate a much higher dose than humans before the amount becomes toxic. The maximum daily dose for both dogs and humans is 50,000 international units (IU) per day. (Humans should not take that much for more than a week or two.)

Toxic levels of vitamin A in adult dogs inhibit the development of collagen in bone. In growing puppies, toxic levels of vitamin A inhibit cartilage production. However, as you can see from the extremely high amounts of vitamin A it would take to be toxic to a dog, that is not something you need to be concerned about unless you are giving your dog very high doses of this vitamin to treat a specific health problem. If you are planning to breed your dog and are treating her for a specific health problem with high doses of vitamin A, discontinue use three months before breeding and do not start the supplements again until after the puppies are born. Vitamin A plays an important role in bone growth and maintenance, healthy skin, wound repair, vision, protection from respiratory ailments, a strong immune system, and the production of sperm in males and normal reproductive cycles in females.

Progressive retinal atrophy (PRA) is a genetic retinal eye disease common to all breeds (including mixed breeds) that causes blindness, but it may be prevented and halted by the addition of vitamin A to the diet. Vitamin A combines with protein and produces rhodopsin or visual purple. Visual purple is what enables your dog to see at night. One of the first symptoms of PRA is poor night vision, which is followed by day blindness and can also lead to cataracts. If your dog is under eight years old and seems disoriented or uncomfortable going out at night or into a dark room, have a veterinary ophthalmologist test her for PRA.

Breeds that are susceptible to skin disorders, such as the cairn terrier, cocker spaniel, golden retriever, and Labrador retriever, may benefit from additional vitamin A in their diet. To test for a vitamin A deficiency pull out one of your dog's hairs. If the hair has a sticky, goopy substance on the end, that is a strong indication your dog has a vitamin A deficiency. Vitamin A deficiency can cause hair loss, scaling, and bacterial and fungal infections of the skin. In susceptible breeds even slightly low levels of this vitamin can precipitate skin problems. Many people with dogs susceptible to skin problems who have gone through round after round of treatments such as medicated shampoos, antibiotics, or steroid hormones with no success have had success with vitamin A. Start with 5,000 IU per day for dogs under twenty pounds and 10,000 IU per day for dogs over twenty pounds, and be patient. You should see improvement within four to six weeks. If you do not see any improvement in that time period, increase the dose. Do not exceed 50,000 IU per day. Improvement from the vitamin A supplementation indicates that your dog needs more vitamin A than the average dog to maintain healthy skin and should remain on the

> "Progressive retinal atrophy (PRA) is a genetic retinal eye disease common to all breeds (including mixed breeds) that causes blindness, but it may be prevented and halted by the addition of vitamin A to the diet."

supplements for life. You have not "cured" the disease—you have given your dog's body the ability to prevent it.

Nutritional sources for vitamin A are dairy products, eggs, liver, fish-liver oils, and yellow, orange, and dark green vegetables and fruits.

Vitamin A comes in liquid and capsule form. As a daily dose give the following:

small dogs	1,500 IU
medium dogs	3,750 IU
large and giant dogs	5,000 IU

VITAMIN D

Vitamin D has many functions in the body, but perhaps its most important role is in building and maintaining bone. It enables calcium and phosphorus, the main ingredients of your dog's skeleton, to build and maintain your dog's skeleton.

With plenty of calcium and phosphorus in the diet, your dog has a very low requirement for vitamin D, which would be met by a high-quality dog food or the nutritional sources named below. Vitamin D can be toxic to your dog with as little as ten times the daily requirement. I do not recommend supplementing vitamin D unless you are sure it is not in your dog's diet or your veterinarian recommends it.

Nutritional sources of vitamin D are fish oils from fish such as cod, bass, mackerel, sardine, tuna, and anchovy; yeast; and egg.

The recommended daily doses for vitamin D are:

small dogs	100 IU
medium dogs	200 IU
large and giant dogs	400 IU

VITAMIN E (TOCOPHEROL)

Vitamin E plays an essential role in the healthy function of all cells in the body. It is widely recognized as a powerful antioxidant, protecting cells from damage. In humans, a diet rich in vitamin E has been proven to reduce the risk of heart disease, some types of cancer, stroke, and viral infections. Vitamin E also plays an important part in the development and function of the immune system. According to a study published in the *Cornell Veterinarian,* vitamin E supplementation has an important influence on the dog's immune system, and dogs supplemented with vitamin E produce antibodies against vaccinations significantly faster than dogs on a vitamin E–deficient diet.

Clearly, vitamin E has a strong influence on the immune system. Although I recommend daily supplementation of vitamin E, it is especially important to give your dog extra in times of stress or illness. It should always be given when your dog has surgery or vaccination(s) or has experienced serious injury or shock. Dogs susceptible to a blood disease called immune-mediated hemolytic anemia (IMHA), including the Akita, Alaskan malamute, American cocker spaniel, basenji, basset hound, beagle, dachshund (miniature), Doberman pinscher, English springer spaniel, golden retriever, Irish setter, Newfoundland, Old English sheepdog, Pekingese, poodle (miniature, standard, and toy), rottweiler, saluki, schnauzer (miniature and giant), shih tzu, Scottish terrier, and West Highland white terrier, can benefit from additional vitamin E in the diet. Larger breeds are more susceptible to heart disease, so vitamin E supplementation is especially important as these dogs approach old age.

Nutritional sources of vitamin E are wheat germ, seeds, soybean oil, sunflower oil, brown rice, seeds, nuts, eggs, whole grains, asparagus, avocados, and green leafy vegetables.

Vitamin E is available in liquid or powder form. The daily dose is as follows:

small dogs	100 IU
medium and large dogs	200 IU
giant dogs	400 IU

VITAMIN K

Vitamin K is necessary for normal blood clotting. Without vitamin K the liver cannot produce the substances that allow the blood to clot. Vitamin K comes in two forms: vitamin K_1, which is found in green plants, and vitamin K_2, which is synthesized by bacteria in the large intestine.

Under normal circumstances there is little need for additional vitamin K, because it is in part produced in the large intestine. However, there are circumstances in which the bacteria in the large intestine are killed, in effect cutting off production of vitamin K. The most common culprit is antibiotics. Give your dog plenty of vitamin K–enriched liver and dark green leafy vegetables when she has been given antibiotics. Even more important is to give your dog a probiotic supplement to restore the bacteria that have been killed. Probiotics are organisms that maintain the health of your dog's intestinal tract. For more detailed information on probiotics, see Chapter 5, Special Nutritional Needs.

The most common blood-clotting disorder in dogs is called Von Willebrand's disease. The different clotting factors in the blood are identified by Roman numerals, such as I, II, III, IV, V, and so on. Von Willebrand's disease involves clotting factor VIII and would not be helped by vitamin K. There are other less-known blood-clotting defects found in dogs. If your dog is diagnosed with one, ask your veterinarian what the clotting factor is. If clotting factor II, VII, IX, or X is involved, your dog may need vitamin K supplements. Factor II deficiency is most common in boxers, English cocker spaniels, French bulldogs, and otterhounds; factor VII deficiency is most common in Alaskan malamutes, basset hounds, beagles, and English bulldogs; factor IX deficiency is found in Airedale terriers, Alaskan malamutes, American cocker spaniels, beagles, bichon frises, black and tan coonhounds, cairn terriers, Chesapeake Bay retrievers, Doberman pinschers, English springer spaniels, French bulldogs, German shepherds, golden retrievers, Great Pyrenees, Labrador retrievers, Manchester terriers, miniature schnauzers, Old English sheepdogs, Pembroke Welsh corgis, Saint Bernards, Scottish terriers, and Shetland sheepdogs. Breeds prone to factor X deficiency are American cocker spaniel, English springer spaniel, and Jack Russell terrier.

Nutritional sources for vitamin K are dark green leafy vegetables and liver.

In summary, the following vitamins should be the minimum nutritional supplementation in your dog's multivitamin: C, A, E, and the B-complex vitamins.

CHAPTER FOUR

Minerals for Your Dog

MINERALS ARE INORGANIC elements that are essential for the growth and maintenance of a healthy body. Amazingly, these elements that are vital to life are only 4 percent of your dog's total body weight. Minerals are found in food, soil, and water. Plants absorb minerals through their roots from the soil and water. Animals get their minerals from eating other animals and plants and drinking water, just as your dog will. The best nutritional sources of minerals are fresh organic fruits and vegetables, free-range organic meat, and fresh spring water. If organic, free-range food is not available or not affordable, you will need to supplement your dog's diet with minerals.

With the exception of organically produced items, the food we eat is depleted of minerals or, even worse, contains the wrong balance of minerals. Today's soil is so overused and loaded with toxins that it has been depleted of most of its nutrients. Dirt in its purest form is loaded with minerals. Unfortunately, most farmers plant crop after crop in the same soil without replenishing the minerals. Plants grown in mineral-deficient soil will be unhealthy, causing the farmers to use chemical fertilizers and pesticides, which further deplete the soil of any nutrients. If the farmers would till in lots of organic compost and let it sit for a year, they would have a rich soil packed with minerals.

Minerals are dependent on each other and many other nutrients for proper absorption and functioning in your dog's body. A mineral deficiency may not always be caused by a lack of the mineral in your dog's diet—it may be caused by your dog's inability to properly absorb the mineral. Absorption problems can be genetic, or they can be caused by an imbalance of another vitamin or mineral. For example, an imbalance of iron, copper, or calcium will interfere with the absorption of zinc.

Minerals are separated into two categories. Macrominerals account for most of the body's mineral content, and microminerals, or trace minerals, are found in the body in very small amounts. The macrominerals include calcium, phosphorus, magnesium, sulfur, potassium, and sodium; the microminerals (trace minerals) include iron, boron, chromium, cobalt, copper, fluoride, iodine, molybdenum, silicon, manganese, selenium, and zinc.

Trace minerals can be toxic even at low doses and are highly dependent on each other for proper absorption. Your best bet is to give them to your dog in a multivitamin-mineral supplement. The recommended daily doses in this chapter can be used as a guideline for finding a good supplement. You will notice that some of the microminerals do not have recommended daily doses. This is because they have not been studied in dogs as they are not considered essential to life, but they are important in a healthy diet.

You also will not necessarily find all the minerals listed here in a dog supplement. I have noted which minerals a healthy dog will get plenty of from home-cooked meals or a high-quality commercial diet and which need to be supplemented. If you cannot find a quality multivitamin-mineral supplement, check the Resources section in the back of this book for a mail-order source.

> "A mineral deficiency may not always be caused by a lack of the mineral in your dog's diet—it may be caused by your dog's inability to properly absorb the mineral. Absorption problems can be genetic, or they can be caused by an imbalance of another vitamin or mineral."

Macrominerals

CALCIUM

Close to 99 percent of the calcium in your dog's body is found in her skeleton. Most of the remainder is in the blood. Calcium keeps bones and teeth strong and fluids balanced. It helps regulate heartbeat and is necessary for normal blood clotting. Without calcium your dog would not be able to utilize magnesium and phosphorus, and to make things even more complicated the ratio of calcium to phosphorus to magnesium is very important. Excess calcium causes decreased phosphorus absorption, and excess phosphorus causes decreased calcium absorption. Calcium without magnesium makes the calcium useless, because it needs magnesium to be absorbed by the body. Your dog's body can easily regulate the balance of these minerals when it gets adequate amounts of all of them in the diet.

Nutritional sources of calcium are leafy green vegetables, beans, blackstrap molasses, soy, sardines, salmon, and nuts. No, I did not leave out milk by mistake. Contrary to popular belief, milk is not a good source of calcium, because there is not enough magnesium in milk for the calcium to be used efficiently.

Calcium is so well known for "building strong bodies" that many people, especially owners of large and giant dogs, make the mistake of oversupplementing calcium, which can be as detrimental as a deficiency. As with the other minerals, stick to a multivitamin-mineral supplement using the following recommended daily dosage:

| small and medium dogs | 100 mg |
| large and giant dogs | 200 mg |

PHOSPHORUS

Phosphorus is found in every cell of your dog's body, with the highest concentration in combination with calcium in the bones and teeth. Phosphorus is necessary for your dog to utilize calcium and therefore, like calcium, is critical for proper growth and maintenance of the skeleton.

Nutritional sources of phosphorus are fish, meats, beans, poultry, and organ meats.

A healthy dog will get plenty of phosphorus from a high-quality diet. Daily doses are:

small and medium dogs	50 mg
large and giant dogs	100 mg

MAGNESIUM

Approximately 60 to 70 percent of the magnesium in your dog's body is in the skeleton. Magnesium is the third member of the calcium-phosphorus team that builds and maintains strong bones and teeth, and it enables your dog's body to use sodium and potassium. Magnesium is important for proper muscle and nerve function and helps the body absorb calcium, vitamin C, vitamin E, and the B-complex vitamins. Magnesium is active in producing enzymes that prevent blood clots, and it helps prevent lead toxicity by drawing lead out of bone and other tissue sites.

> "Convulsive seizures (epilepsy) have been seen in dogs with magnesium deficiency."

Convulsive seizures (epilepsy) have been seen in dogs with magnesium deficiency. The American cocker spaniel, Australian cattle dog, basset hound, Border collie, beagle, Belgian Malinois, Belgian sheepdog, Belgian Tervuren, bichon frise, collie, dachshund, English springer spaniel, German shepherd, golden retriever, greyhound, harrier, Irish setter, Italian greyhound, keeshond, Labrador retriever, Norfolk terrier, Norwich terrier, Pembroke Welsh corgi, petit basset griffon vendeen, pointer, poodle (miniature and standard), pug, Saint Bernard, standard Manchester terrier, and vizsla are all prone to convulsive seizures. If your dog has seizures and is getting her recommended daily dose of magnesium, very gradually add more magnesium to her diet. Too much magnesium will result in gas and loose stools.

Magnesium is also a heart-healthy mineral. Studies done in the 1970s found that dogs recovered from heart failure faster when given magnesium intravenously. Giant and large dogs (over 50 pounds) are more prone to heart problems than are medium and small dogs, with the boxer, cavalier King Charles spaniel, Doberman pinscher, German shepherd, Great Dane, Irish wolfhound, Newfoundland, and Sussex spaniel showing a stronger history of weakness of the heart. Be sure that dogs of these breeds are getting plenty of exercise and their daily dose of magnesium.

Nutritional sources for magnesium are wheat bran, whole grains, leafy green vegetables, milk, meat, beans, bananas, and apricots.

Recommended daily doses are:

small and medium dogs	50 mg
large and giant dogs	100 mg

SULFUR

Sulfur is found everywhere in the body, with the highest concentrations in the skin, hair, and nails. Sulfur's high concentration in the skin makes it a key component in healing wounds. Sulfur deficiency can cause coat discoloration and skin conditions such as eczema and dermatitis. Dogs that are more prone to dermatitis, or hot spots, include the Airedale terrier, Akita, Dalmatian, basset hound, bichon frise, German shepherd, golden retriever, Great Dane, Great Pyrenees, Irish setter, Labrador retriever, Lhasa apso, poodle, pug, Scottish terrier, Sealyham terrier, smooth fox terrier, soft-coated wheaten terrier, and West Highland white terrier. Those of you with dogs of these breeds need to keep an extra eye on your dog's coat for any signs of skin problems, and be sure to keep up with their multivitamin-mineral supplement. Sulfur is absorbed in the intestine and is depleted when intestinal bacteria are destroyed by substances such as antibiotics. Don't forget the spoonful of yogurt or probiotic supplement when giving antibiotics.

Dogs that suffer from skin allergies may need extra sulfur, which I recommend you supplement in the form of methylsulfonyl methane (MSM). See Chapter 10, Natural Healing, for more detailed information.

Nutritional sources for sulfur are meat, fish, dairy products, eggs, and molasses.

A healthy dog will get plenty of sulfur from home-cooked meals or a high-quality commercial food.

POTASSIUM AND SODIUM

Potassium and sodium work together to maintain normal fluid balance in the cells of your dog's body. Normal fluid balance in cells is needed for proper nerve and muscle functioning. A sodium deficiency will result in fatigue, listlessness, loss of equilibrium, exhaustion, drinking less water, poor growth, dry skin, and loss of hair. Commercial dog foods have plenty of potassium and sodium chloride (salt). If you are preparing home-cooked meals for your dog, there will be plenty of potassium in the food and you can add a pinch of salt.

A potassium deficiency would result in restlessness, poor growth, muscular paralysis, dehydration, and lesions of the heart and kidney.

Nutritional sources for potassium are meats, poultry, fish, whole grain cereals, yogurt, bananas, sweet potato, squash, beans, prunes, and dried apricots.

Recommended daily amounts of potassium in a dog's diet are:

small dogs	25 mg
medium dogs	50 mg
large dogs	75 mg
giant dogs	100 mg

Recommended daily doses for sodium are:

small dogs	100 mg
medium dogs	200 mg
large dogs	350 mg
giant dogs	500 mg

"Dogs that suffer from skin allergies may need extra sulfur, which I recommend you supplement in the form of methyl-sulfonyl methane (MSM)."

Microminerals (Trace Minerals)

IRON

Iron teams up with copper, cobalamin (vitamin B_{12}), and protein to form hemoglobin molecules. Hemoglobin molecules are found in the red blood cells and carry oxygen from the lungs to the rest of the body. If your dog is tired all the time, she may be anemic from a deficiency of iron. Part of your weekly health check includes your dog's gums. You are looking for bright, dark pink gums; light pink or almost gray gums are a sure sign of anemia. Anemia is very often the result of a more serious problem such as an infection, so if you suspect your dog is anemic, bring her to your veterinarian for a complete exam.

Nutritional sources for iron are beans, pork, beef, liver, chicken, and turkey.

Current recommended daily amounts of iron in a dog's daily diet are:

small dogs	9 mg
medium dogs	18 mg
large dogs	30 mg
giant dogs	40 mg

Recent studies of humans have found that too much iron is a potent risk factor for heart disease; we do not yet know if the same applies to our dogs. Heart disease is very common in dogs, so be cautious of giving your dog too much iron. If you are feeding home-cooked meals or a commercial food that has iron listed as an ingredient, buy a supplement that does not contain iron.

BORON

Boron works with calcium and magnesium to build and maintain strong bones.

Nutritional sources for boron are fruits and vegetables.

CHROMIUM

Chromium helps manufacture insulin and then helps the insulin maintain the proper level of sugar in the blood. Chromium is also active in the digestion of carbohydrates. Semimoist dog foods became popular because they are easy to keep and serve and because even the fussiest dogs love them. The secret to their success is lots of sugar, which dogs love and become addicted to. Too much sugar will deplete your dog's body of chromium, putting her at risk for diabetes. If you are feeding semimoist foods, slowly wean your dog off of them with home-cooked meals or a commercial dry or canned dog food that fits my guidelines for choosing a commercial dog food (see Chapter 1, Feeding Your Dog for Naturally Great Health).

Nutritional sources for chromium are brewer's yeast, broccoli, ham, turkey, and shellfish.

COBALT

Cobalt is found in cobalamin (vitamin B_{12}), which is a unique relationship because cobalamin is the only vitamin that contains a trace element. Cobalt is involved in the production of red blood cells and the absorption of iron. A cobalt deficiency could cause an iron deficiency, resulting in anemia. Adequate amounts of cobalamin will give your dog enough cobalt.

Nutritional sources for cobalt are meat and shellfish.

COPPER

Copper is another mineral that is important for proper bone growth and maintenance. Copper is involved in putting color in your dog's skin and hair. It is required to convert iron into hemoglobin and is important in keeping the immune system functioning normally. Copper deficiencies result in loss of hair and skin color, anemia, and improper bone formation. The majority of copper is found in the liver, so an excess can cause liver damage.

The Bedlington terrier, West Highland white terrier, and Doberman pinscher are prone to a disease that causes an inability to use and store copper properly, which can result in liver disease and other problems. For these dogs, choose a multivitamin-mineral supplement that does not include copper.

Nutritional sources for copper are whole wheat, calf and beef liver, nuts, beans, seeds, and shellfish.

Daily recommended doses are:

small dogs	0.5 mg
medium dogs	1 mg
large and giant dogs	2 mg

> "If your town adds fluoride to your water, please do not give it to your dog. Fluoride toxicity can cause arthritis, damage to the liver, kidney, and adrenal glands, bone malformations, and cancer."

FLUORIDE

Dogs require very small amounts of fluoride, which they will get through their diet. If your town adds fluoride to your water, please do not give it to your dog. Fluoride toxicity can cause arthritis, damage to the liver, kidney, and adrenal glands, bone malformations, and cancer. You can use a water filter if you are disciplined enough to change the filter frequently. The best and easiest way to give your dog pure water is to buy bottled water or use a reverse osmosis water purification system in your house.

IODINE

Iodine is essential for the production of the thyroid hormone that regulates your dog's metabolism. Since the addition of iodine to salt, the instances of iodine deficiency in dogs have disappeared. All commercial dog foods have salt added—most have too much salt. If you are preparing home-cooked meals for your dog, the pinch of salt you added for sodium will also give your dog her daily requirement of iodine. If your dog has a thyroid problem, you can add an iodine supplement to her diet or sprinkle powdered seaweed on her food.

Recommended daily doses are:

small dogs	0.2 mg
medium dogs	0.4 mg
large dogs	0.7 mg
giant dogs	1 mg

MOLYBDENUM

Molybdenum is active in processing carbohydrates and can protect your dog from excess copper.

Nutritional sources for molybdenum are liver, brewer's yeast, and cereal grains.

SILICON

Silicon is found in your dog's bones, hair, nails, and teeth. It helps heal wounds and protects against skin disorders. If your dog has something foreign in her system, such as worms, an infection from an abscess, or a bacterial infection, silicon will work to eliminate the foreign object from her system. Silicon is a type of sand that is found in dirt and the stems of certain grasses and plants. When your dog eats dirt, grass, or plants, she may be adding silicon to her system to help her eliminate a foreign object. Try to steer her away from grass. Dogs do not digest grass well, and the sharp edges on the blades of grass irritate the throat and intestines. Be sure she has access to pesticide-free dirt and plants; if eating these substances continues for any length of time, bring your dog to your vet.

MANGANESE

Manganese is an antioxidant mineral that is necessary for the utilization of vitamin C, biotin, thiamin (vitamin B_1), and vitamin E. It is also needed for normal reproduction, bone and cartilage growth, collagen formation, fat metabolism, pituitary gland function, and the production of fatty acids.

Nutritional sources for manganese are whole grains, nuts, peas, beets, green leafy vegetables, and eggs.

Recommended daily doses are:

small dogs	0.75 mg
medium dogs	1.5 mg
large dogs	2.6 mg
giant dogs	3.75 mg

SELENIUM

Selenium is a great coworker. It works with vitamin E as an antioxidant to prevent heart disease and cancer and to boost the immune system. It also works with iodine for proper thyroid function. Selenium protects your dog's body from cancer-causing substances, such as the toxic metals mercury and cadmium, by binding with them and flushing them out of the body.

An article in the *Federation Proceedings* reports that dogs with a selenium and vitamin E deficiency have a lower antibody response to vaccines than the dogs who are not deficient. A few days before and after any vaccinations, be sure to add some extra vitamin E and selenium to your dog's diet.

Nutritional sources for selenium are garlic, fish, red meat, red grapes, shellfish, broccoli, eggs, organ meat, and chicken.

Recommended daily doses are:

small dogs	25 mcg
medium, large, and giant dogs	50 mcg

ZINC

Zinc works alone and with copper, the B-complex vitamins, vitamin A, calcium, and phosphorus in a vast number of bodily functions. Zinc is crucial for the production of enzymes, it supports the immune system, improves antibody response to vaccines, regulates white blood cells, helps in protein digestion, and has some antioxidant and antibacterial properties. Zinc is important for a healthy coat, skin, and nails, and it protects your dog's liver from excess poisons such as cadmium, lead, and copper. Zinc teams up with vitamin C in the production of collagen, which makes it another important nutrient when your dog's body is trying to heal a wound.

William H. Miller, V.M.D., assistant professor of medicine at Cornell University's New York State College of Veterinary Medicine, has found that zinc, vitamins A and E, and the essential fatty acids are the nutrients that are most important to the skin. Color abnormalities on solid-colored dogs, such as white tipping, browning out, or red tinges, may be caused by a zinc deficiency. Siberian huskies, Alaskan malamutes, and bull terriers are prone to a genetic condition that causes a decreased capacity for zinc absorption from the intestines. This condition is often missed, because the only symptoms are skin disease and a loss of appetite. The huskies and malamutes will respond quickly to a zinc supplement and will need to be on the supplement for life. Unfortunately, bull terriers are prone to a more complicated form of this condition, and they do not respond to zinc supplementation. I believe there is a missing nutritional link, in addition to zinc, that the bull terriers need. Great Danes, Doberman pinschers, German shorthaired pointers, German shepherds, and Labrador retrievers are also prone to skin problems from a zinc deficiency. The deficiency can be caused by a zinc-deficient diet, malabsorption, parasites, or oversupplementation of nutrients that interfere with the absorption of zinc, such as iron, copper, and calcium.

Nutritional sources for zinc are lamb, pork, liver, eggs, brewer's yeast, wheat germ, and beans.

Recommended daily doses are:

small dogs	10 mg
medium dogs	15 mg
large and giant dogs	30 mg

In summary, the following minerals should be the minimum nutritional supplementation in your dog's multivitamin: calcium, magnesium, chromium, copper, molybdenum, silicon, manganese, selenium, and zinc.

CHAPTER FIVE

Special Nutritional Needs

Dogs, like people, have changing nutritional needs in the varying stages of their lives. Younger dogs are growing and have much more energy, pregnant dogs need proper nutrition to create new life, and older dogs are sedentary and need easily absorbed nutrients. If your dog becomes ill, her body will need the proper nutrients to heal. In this chapter you will learn how to make adjustments to your dog's diet to meet her special nutritional needs.

Puppies

Puppies are irresistible to even the grumpiest of people. They make the sick forget their pain and the elderly feel young. These fun-loving balls of fur need a puppyhood filled with the same pure joy and happiness that they give us. A key to your puppy's happiness, health, and longevity is to build a strong body and a strong immune system with high-quality food and a stress-free environment. You will learn more about the immune system in Part 2, Keeping Your Dog's Immune System Strong.

Your puppy's immune system will get its foundation for health from the mother in the first twenty-four hours after birth. Just as with humans, these critical hours are the only time the mother produces a special milk called colostrum. Colostrum gets the immune system off to a strong start by providing antibodies and other immune-supporting nutrients that will guard against disease as the immune system matures.

Your puppy's first six months of life will be her fastest growth period. She will need the proper nutrition to build a strong, healthy body. Large breeds reach full size at approximately ten to sixteen months; small breeds reach full size at anywhere from six to twelve months. That is a lot of growing in a short time, when you think that humans take twenty years to reach maturity. Your puppy will eat approximately twice what she will eventually be eating as an adult, and during some growth spurts she may exceed that.

If you are buying or adopting a puppy, find out exactly what she has been eating, including proportions and how the food was prepared. If she has been eating commercial food, ask for the brand name and where you can buy the food. Very gradually change your puppy's diet after she becomes comfortable with her new home. Add a small amount of her new food to her old food, gradually increasing the new food and decreasing the old food.

The stress of a new home combined with the stress of new foods on a digestive system that has not matured would put her tiny body on overload. Little things like time changes in her routine and new rules can be very confusing and stressful. You want your puppy's body to be concentrating on growing and maturing, not warding off stress and learning to handle new foods.

You can start with a multivitamin-mineral supplement right away. With the exception of vitamins C and E, do not give your puppy more than is recommended on the label of the multivitamin-mineral supplement, unless you are under the supervision of a veterinarian. More is not better and could be harmful. Vitamin C is a water-soluble vitamin (it is not stored in the body and will not become toxic) and antioxidant that will aid in proper bone formation and boost the immune system. For more on vitamin C, see Chapter 3, Vitamins for Your Dog. If your multivitamin-mineral supplement does not provide the following daily doses, buy a powdered vitamin C to bring her up to these doses.

For weaned puppies, start with a daily dose of the following:

small and medium dogs	100 mg
(up to 50 pounds as adults)	
large and giant dogs	150 mg
(over 50 pounds as adults)	

For the first six months, slowly increase the daily dose to this:

small dogs (up to 20 pounds as adults)	250 mg
medium dogs (20 to 50 pounds as adults)	500 mg
large dogs (50 to 100 pounds as adults)	1,000 mg
giant dogs (over 100 pounds as adults)	2,000 mg

At six months, slowly increase to the final adult daily dose of the following:

small dogs	500 mg to 1,000 mg
medium and large dogs	1,000 mg to 2,000 mg
giant dogs	2,000 mg to 4000 mg

For puppies that are not weaned, Chapter 3, Vitamins for Your Dog, gives instructions and doses for vitamin C. The dosages I have given you are guidelines. Your dog will tell you how much is too much by getting gas or diarrhea (bowel tolerance). If your puppy gets gas or diarrhea, you have given her more than her body needs, so reduce the dosage until she grows into a higher dose.

Vitamin E plays an important role in the development and function of the immune system and is a powerful antioxidant. If your multi-vitamin-mineral does not provide the following daily dosages, you can buy vitamin E in capsule or liquid form at your local health store.

puppies under 20 pounds	100 IU
puppies 20 to 100 pounds	200 IU
puppies over 100 pounds	400 IU

More on vitamin E and dosages for adult dogs can be found in Chapter 3, Vitamins for Your Dog. For stressful situations, either physically or emotionally, such as vaccinations or dog obedience classes, double the daily dose of vitamin E for a few days before and a few days after your puppy is stressed.

At six weeks, your puppy's teeth will begin to come in, and at seven to eight weeks she will start chewing. This is the time to hide the antiques and to keep all kinds of interesting toys on the floor and in her crate or her sleeping area. When your puppy starts to chew, very gradually introduce solid foods. Until your puppy is about one year old, her energy and nutrient needs will be double what she will eventually need as an adult.

If you are going to feed your puppy a commercial dog food, feed her puppy food for one year and then switch to the adult food. Use the feeding amounts on the package as a starting place and adjust the amount for your dog.

If you are preparing home-cooked meals, feed approximate proportions of 30 percent organ meat, 30 percent muscle meat, 20 percent grains, and 20 percent vegetables. Part of the protein requirement can be met with high-protein grains such as buckwheat and quinoa, and for one meal a day give her additional protein from sources such as eggs, cottage cheese, and naturally cultured yogurt. For dogs that have trouble digesting lots of protein, such as Dalmatians, Bedlington terriers, and West Highland white terriers, feed the meat raw (which I highly recommend for all dogs) or cut down on the meat a little and give them protein from other sources such as those mentioned above. Avoid soy, because a puppy's digestive system cannot utilize the amino acids from soy.

Puppies will eat approximately twice what an adult dog of the same weight will eat, which translates to the following:

puppies weighing up to 10 pounds	1 to 2 cups per day
puppies weighing 10 to 25 pounds	2 to 7 cups per day
puppies weighing 25 to 50 pounds	7 to 10 cups per day
puppies weighing over 50 pounds	10 to 14 cups per day

Feed your puppy four times a day until she refuses a meal, then cut back to three times a day until she is not hungry for three meals, and then cut back to two meals a day for life. Two meals a day, rather than one, puts less stress on the digestive system, and your dog will utilize more of the nutrients from each meal.

Feed enough so your puppy does not lick the bowl clean. A little left over means she had her fill. Give her a few minutes to come back to the bowl, and then pick it up. Please do not overfeed or oversupplement your puppy. An overfed, oversupplemented puppy will experience overly rapid growth, which will give you not a bigger dog but a dog plagued by obesity and skeletal problems. If a puppy grows too fast, the bones and joints do not get a chance to form properly, causing problems such as hypertropic osteodystrophy, osteochondrosis, and hip dysplasia. Those are all very painful skeletal abnormalities that involve inflammation and abnormal growth of the bones and joints and will give your puppy a lifetime of painful, chronic skeletal problems. Hip dysplasia is an abnormal growth of the hip that is found in all sizes of dog and is the most common skeletal abnormality in large and giant breeds. A fat puppy will also result in a fat adult. A lean puppy is a healthy puppy.

> "Avoid soy, because a puppy's digestive system cannot utilize the amino acids from soy."

Pregnant and Nursing Dogs

Breeding a dog is a serious undertaking that requires a lot of hard work and money. If you are new to breeding, carefully research the entire process from conception to adoption. If you are considering breeding because you want to be surrounded by adult dogs and puppies, consider foster care for your local animal shelter or breed rescue organization. The shelters and breed rescue organizations throughout the U.S. are overflowing and desperately need people to care for puppies and adult dogs. Most of the shelters and rescue organizations pay all the dog's expenses, including food, toys, and trips to the vet. Your responsibility is to love, train (if you are caring for a puppy), and feed the dogs.

> "A fat puppy will also result in a fat adult. A lean puppy is a healthy puppy."

If, after careful consideration, you decide to breed your dog, it is important that she be in optimal health before conception. A trip to the veterinarian for a complete exam is a good investment in the future of the mother and her puppies. It is especially important to have the following breeds checked by a veterinarian, because they are more prone to complications during birth: Boston terrier, Bouvier des Flandres, Cardigan Welsh corgi, English bulldog, greyhound, Pembroke Welsh corgi, and pug. The health of the mother will be directly reflected in the health of the puppies. An unhealthy mother will produce unhealthy puppies, and after conception will be too late to play catch-up with her health.

With a clean bill of health from your veterinarian, you are ready to prepare your dog for her pregnancy. Two weeks before your dog comes into season, put her on red raspberry leaf tea or powder and keep her on it until six weeks after the puppies are born. Red raspberry leaves tone the uterus and help bring fluid to the birth canal. After birth, the red raspberry leaves help tighten the uterine muscles, preventing infection. Make the tea by putting 1½ teaspoons of red raspberry leaves in a cup of water and bringing it to a boil. Take it off the stove and let it sit overnight. In the morning, strain out the leaves and keep it in the refrigerator.

Use the following daily dosages:

small dogs (up to 20 pounds)	1 tablespoon
medium dogs (20 to 50 pounds)	2 tablespoons
large dogs (50 to 100 pounds)	3 tablespoons
giant dogs (over 100 pounds)	4 tablespoons

If you cannot find red raspberry leaves or are not much of a cook, see the Resources section in the back for supplements you can buy through the mail.

For the first six weeks of your dog's nine-week pregnancy, she can eat her normal diet and probably will not need much more food than usual. At six weeks, her nutritional needs will start to increase, and by the time she has her puppies (whelping), she will be eating approximately 50 percent more than normal. She needs more food and more protein. If you are feeding home-cooked meals, you can follow the guidelines for a puppy. Feed her as much as she will eat without licking the bowl clean and feed her as many times a day as she is hungry. Her increased need for protein can be satisfied by increasing her meat ration, giving her grains with high protein, such as buckwheat and quinoa, and giving her additional protein-enriched foods like eggs, cottage cheese, and naturally cultured yogurt. If you are feeding commercial food, you can switch to puppy food or add some of the above protein-enriched foods to her usual diet. If her appetite seems to decrease before delivery, it may be because the puppies are pushing on her abdomen and it is uncomfortable to eat a lot of food at one time, so try giving her smaller meals. A loss of appetite could also be caused by nausea, which can be helped with a cup of ginger tea and honey. If she does not like the ginger tea, add some homemade chicken or beef broth (not the commercial brands, which are loaded with salt and MSG). Signs of nausea include drooling or repeated swallowing when you offer her food. To make fresh ginger tea, grate 1 tablespoon of fresh ginger into a cup, add boiling water and let it steep for ten minutes. Strain out the ginger, add honey, and serve.

Right after giving birth, she may also lose her appetite for a short time. Try giving her yogurt and raw, uncooked honey for energy. Also offer her some homemade chicken or beef broth to keep her strength up, and be sure she has lots of fluids. It is very important that she always have clean, fresh water available. When the puppies become mobile, keep water right outside their pen so she does not have to leave her puppies for it.

As the puppies' appetites grow, so will their mother's. The second and third weeks of nursing are the most stressful. By then she will be producing milk equivalent to four to seven percent of her body weight per day, which means a 50-pound dog will be producing a whopping two to three and one-half pounds of milk per day, or about one to two quarts of milk. That is a tremendous amount of fluid to keep up with. Keep her on the high-protein diet and, rather than increasing the amount of food you give her at each meal, increase the number of times per day you feed her. Most mothers cannot take in as much food as they need in one or two meals. She may need up to seven meals a day to keep up with milk production for her puppies. If at any time she seems stressed, B-complex vitamins, vitamin E, or a homeopathic remedy can help calm her.

A pregnant and nursing dog will go through many physical and emotional changes in a short amount of time. Women have nine months to slowly adjust to the physical changes of pregnancy, while dogs have a mere nine weeks to produce a litter of puppies. Keep a close eye on her and her needs. She may refuse food in the morning and be ravenous in the afternoon, or your playful, energetic dog may suddenly want to be left alone to sleep in a nice warm, quiet place.

> "The second and third weeks of nursing are the most stressful for the mother. By then she will be producing milk equivalent to four to seven percent of her body weight per day, which means a 50-pound dog will be producing a whopping two to three and one-half pounds of milk per day, or about one to two quarts of milk."

Geriatric Dogs

Like people, as they age dogs eventually start to slow down and are happy sitting under the big oak tree watching life go by. All dogs will age, and they will all age at a different rate, depending on their size, breed, and how they are cared for throughout life. A dog that is in optimal health throughout her life will age more slowly than a dog that is plagued by chronic illnesses. If you have an older dog in poor health, it is not too late to bring her back to health. Many of the symptoms attributed to old age in dogs merely indicate a lack of good nutrition.

As your dog's activity level slows down, her metabolism will decrease and she will not burn as many calories, resulting in weight gain, one of the biggest problems among geriatric dogs. As your dog ages and slows down, her whole body is aging and slowing down, and her digestive tract, heart, kidneys, liver, and brain cannot work as efficiently as they used to. Some small adjustments to your dog's diet and exercise program will give her a better chance for a healthy, pain-free old age.

As your dog's body ages and functions less efficiently, she will not be able to digest food as easily or absorb as many of the nutrients from her food. The lack of nutrients may cause an older dog to become lethargic and can lead to many of the chronic illnesses that so many people, including veterinarians, shrug their shoulders over and attribute to old age. Being elderly is not an illness; it is a stage of life. To adjust for these changes, your dog needs highly digestible, low-calorie foods and a multivitamin-mineral supplement that is easily absorbed. A powdered multivitamin-mineral supplement will be absorbed more easily than a pill. If you cannot find one at your local pet supply store, look in the Resources section in the back of the book. If the multivitamin-mineral supplement is not specifically made for the older dog, give her one-third more than what is recommended for an adult dog. A one-year human trial of vitamin and trace mineral supplements in the elderly showed a significantly decreased infection rate and enhanced immune system function. The same applies to your dog.

Use powdered vitamin C, and once a year up the dose a little to "bowel tolerance" (gas or diarrhea means your dog is getting too much vitamin C) to see if your dog could use some additional vitamin C. Double the vitamin E to daily doses of the following:

small dogs	200 IU
medium and large dogs	400 IU
giant dogs	800 IU

You need to compensate for your dog's less-efficient digestive tract; well-cooked carbohydrates will be easier for her to digest than meat, so cut back a little on her meat and add more carbohydrates. A heaping spoonful of plain yogurt with active cultures with each meal will also aid in digestion by keeping her intestines rich with much-needed bacteria. Digestive enzyme supplements are also available for dogs. Follow the directions on the label for appropriate dosages. Some elderly dogs lose their sense of thirst, so add extra water to her meals and when you cook the grains.

To avoid weight gain, in addition to cutting back a little on her meat, buy the leaner ground meat and add more vegetables if she starts licking the bowl clean or seems to be hungrier than usual. If you are feeding her a commercial dog food, cut back on the food a little and add vegetables if she seems hungry.

To avoid dental problems, which may lead to eating problems, give your dog a marrow bone once or twice a week. They are much less expensive than having your dog's teeth cleaned, and chewing a bone is much more fun for your dog than going to the dentist.

Feeding all the right foods is only half the key to keeping your dog healthy in her elderly years. Exercise will help prevent weight gain, maintain muscle strength, keep the joints flexible, prevent arthritis, and keep the organs strong and functioning. A geriatric exercise program needs to be fun and of shorter duration. Rather than one long walk, take her for two walks a day. The expression "use it or lose it" goes for your dog too, and just like people, dogs need some encouragement to exercise as they age.

Overweight Dogs

If you are at your wit's end trying to keep your dog thin, you can take comfort in the fact that you are far from alone. An estimated 35 to 50 percent of pet dogs are overweight. Obesity is one of the most common health disorders in dogs. That would be an astounding fact if the sole cause of weight problems in dogs was their owner's feeding habits.

> "Obesity is one of the most common health disorders in dogs. That would be an astounding fact if the sole cause of weight problems in dogs was their owner's feeding habits."

Your dog eats practically nothing, is always hungry, and yet is still fat. Does this sound familiar to you? If it does, you and your dog are probably the victims of the multimillion-dollar processed dog food industry that survives on marketing and not on the quality of their products. Many of the commercial dog foods are so loaded with nonnutritional calories that your dog will be obese before she will ever be able to meet her nutritional needs through the food. It would be the nutritional equivalent of you trying to stay thin and healthy on a diet of potato chips.

A neighbor of mine who had struggled with her dog's weight for years finally switched to a high-quality commercial diet, and she was so amazed when her dog became lean and energetic in just a few weeks that she became a distributor of that product. If your dog is overweight and you are feeding a commercial food that does not fit into my nutritional guidelines in Chapter 1, Feeding Your Dog for Naturally Great Health, a simple change to a high-quality food may solve your dog's weight problems. If your local pet supply store does not carry high-quality dog food, the Resources section in the back of this book lists many affordable sources.

Before you put your dog on a diet, bring her to your veterinarian to be sure there is not a medical reason for her weight gain. If your dog gets a clean bill of health and you are feeding her a high-quality food but she is still overweight, then you are feeding her too much and/or she does not get enough exercise.

What seems like an occasional treat or just a few table scraps can add up quickly when a dog is only thirty or forty pounds to begin with. The smaller the dog, the more true this is and the harder it is to keep her slim. The secret is to cut down on the calories your dog consumes and to keep her moving.

Obesity will shorten your dog's life by years by putting stress on all her organs and her skeleton. A study of the development of obesity in dogs at the University of Mississippi Medical Center found that as dogs become obese they develop high blood pressure that becomes dramatically worse during exercise. Not surprisingly, these dogs were not able to exercise as much as they could when they were lean. Along with heart disease, obesity in dogs causes diabetes, lung disease, and arthritis. For overweight dogs, there is no such thing as routine surgery. They are at a higher risk for complications, including death, during and after surgery. Lean dogs live longer, healthier lives with significantly fewer trips to the veterinarian.

Your dog's new diet and exercise program should be introduced very slowly, starting with my first rule for nutritional health: do not feed your dog anything that does not have nutritional value for her.

If your dog has mastered the begging technique and you entertain a lot, ask your guests as they settle in by the hors d'oeuvres not to feed your dog. If you are used to scraping your dishes into your dog's dish after dinner, skip the fat and limit the leftovers to food that is good for her. If eliminating all nonnutritional consumption does not take the weight off, shave some more calories by giving her

> "Inadequate nutrition causes slow wound healing, decreased immune response, a higher infection rate, and a longer recovery rate. When your dog is healing she will use nutrients faster, so you need to increase her supplement levels."

fewer treats or low-calorie treats, such as a carrot or an ice cube. If cutting the calories of the between-meal snacks does not work, very slowly reduce the size of her meals. If she seems hungry during any of the adjustments in her diet, add more finely chopped fresh vegetables to her meal.

If you do not exercise your dog at all, start with short walks and very gradually lengthen them as she loses weight. If you already have her on an exercise program, slowly increase her exercise to at least twenty minutes per day. Never force your dog to exercise.

Every time you are tempted to give your dog junk food or one too many treats, give her a hug, a good pat, and a lot of praise instead. Sharing love is more gratifying than sharing food.

Dogs Recovering from Illness

The most potent medication you can give your dog when she is recovering from an illness is a daily dose of good nutrition. Nutrients are what the body uses to restore diseased or damaged tissue.

Whether your dog has a minor ailment or is recovering from major surgery, it is important to provide her body with the nutritional tools it needs to repair itself. Inadequate nutrition causes slow wound healing, decreased immune response, a higher infection rate, and a longer recovery rate. When your dog is healing she will use nutrients faster, so you need to increase her supplement levels. A study of nutrition and wound healing found that vitamin C levels are higher in healing tissue and return to normal after the healing is complete.

Each day your dog's body relies on a certain amount of nutrition to keep her body running smoothly. For example, if she gets diarrhea with daily doses of vitamin C higher than 1,000 mg, that means her body uses approximately 1,000 mg of vitamin C in addition to what her body naturally produces. If she has surgery and the entire 1,000 mg of vitamin C goes to repair the wound, it leaves the rest of the body depleted of vitamin C.

Have you ever noticed that some dogs are always sick? If your dog becomes ill and does not have the nutritional tools to bring her body back into balance, she will become less and less able to ward off disease, and the illnesses will mount.

If your dog is scheduled for surgery, start boosting her immune system and strengthening her body a week before the surgery. If emergency surgery is necessary or your dog is fighting a disease, start building her nutritional forces as soon as she is able to keep food down.

> "Antibiotics destroy the friendly bacteria in the intestines, interfering with your dog's ability to digest food and absorb the nutrients that she needs to become healthy."

Don't ever force an ill dog to eat, or you will risk causing her to vomit, which will only make things worse and can cause serious problems such as choking or pneumonia. Drooling and swallowing repeatedly when you offer her food are signs of nausea. Take the food away and try again later.

A week before and two weeks after surgery or during an illness, increase the multivitamin-mineral supplement by one-third and double her dose of vitamin E.

After surgery, your dog is healing the surgical wound and detoxifying from the anesthesia and other drugs. The body removes anesthetics through the lungs, kidneys, and liver. If your dog has to stay in the hospital overnight, ask your veterinarian if you can come in and feed her. She may eat more readily with you there, and you will be able to keep her on her usual high-quality diet with the proper supplements.

Vitamin C plays a major role in wound healing, so after surgery increase her vitamin C, watching for loose stools, which are an indication that you are giving her more than she needs. If she has had major surgery, do not be surprised if she needs twice her usual daily dose. As the wound heals, her need for extra vitamin C will decrease, so a week after surgery slowly decrease the dosage until you are back to her usual daily dose.

Stress is another factor that suppresses the immune system. If your dog has to stay in the hospital overnight, she will be in a very stressful situation with bright lights, people coming and going, and other stressed dogs that also cannot sleep. B-complex vitamins, vitamin E, or a homeopathic remedy will be beneficial for these types of stressful times.

The most frequent prescriptions the veterinarian writes are for antibiotics. If your dog is on antibiotics, be sure she is also receiving a daily dose of probiotics. Probiotics are friendly bacteria that maintain the health of your dog's intestinal tract. Antibiotics destroy the friendly bacteria in the intestines, interfering with your dog's ability to digest food and absorb the nutrients that she needs to become healthy. Yogurt that contains active cultures is a good source of probiotics. You can also buy a probiotic supplement in the refrigerated section of your health food store.

If you have the time to tend to her and a clean, warm, quiet, and safe place where she can recover, then the optimal place for your dog to be is at home. She should be free of drafts or disturbances and have access to fresh air and sunlight. If you are caring for her at home and she is not eating, you may need to stimulate her appetite with something that has a strong odor, is very tasty, and is easy to digest, like homemade turkey or chicken broth. Feed as many small meals as she will eat and do not be afraid to pamper her by hand feeding, warming the food, or pureeing the food so it is easier for her to eat. Every bite counts when a dog is recovering from illness. Give her only highly nutritious, protein-enriched foods and don't forget the fresh water. Keep water near her at all times, and if she is not very mobile, really spoil her by bringing the water to her. You may have to put a little on her mouth to entice her to drink. And the last, but certainly not the least, important ingredient for a speedy recovery is lots of tender, loving care.

PART TWO

Keeping Your Dog's Immune System Strong

Chapter Six

The Importance of a Strong Immune System

Support of the immune system is one of the most important roles that proper nutrition plays in your dog's health. The immune system protects your dog from illness and supports the repair of her body when it is injured. Our environment is always teeming with microscopic organisms that have the potential to infect your dog with any number of minor to life-threatening diseases. How your dog's immune system responds to these organisms determines her health.

Have you noticed that when a cold or flu is going around some people always get it and others never get sick? Those who stay well have an active, healthy immune system to protect them. Those who get sick from infectious diseases have an immune system that is in less-than-optimal condition.

The immune system is a complex network within the body that produces millions of cells each day. Each cell's mission is to seek out and destroy foreign invaders, called antigens. An antigen, which is short for "antibody generating," is a foreign invader in the body, such as a pollen, virus, fungus, bacteria, or parasite. Elimination of antigens is accomplished primarily by white blood cells that use the lymphatic and blood vessels to move through the body. One drop of blood contains 5,000 to 10,000 white blood cells; two-thirds of them are a part of the immune system.

The major players in the immune system's defense strategy against infection are called natural killer cells, T-cells, and B-cells. The natural killer cells mount the first and most rapid attack against the antigens. The next line of defense is white blood cells called T-cells, which are produced by the thymus gland, a primary gland of the immune system. If the T-cells need backup, they can call on helper T-cells, which are able to call on the last and most powerful line of defense, the B-cells.

B-cells are white blood cells that produce and secrete proteins called antibodies. The antibodies bind to the antigen, inactivating it so that scavenger cells can digest it. Although the white blood cells are the primary workers in the immune system and the thymus gland is the primary producer of the white blood cells, the bone marrow, spleen, tonsils, and adenoids also play important roles in the functioning of the immune system.

Your dog will begin her life with the antibody immunity she gets from colostrum, a special milk her mother will produce for twenty-four hours after her birth. She will continue to get some antibodies from her mother's milk, but when she is weaned it is time for her own immune system to take over. As your dog grows in a stress-free environment with proper nutrition, she builds on the immunity she received from her mother by producing antibodies that will successfully fight off infections introduced through the environment or vaccinations. Keeping your dog's immune system strong requires proper nutrition as well as an awareness on your part as to what will weaken her immune system. Some breeds are more susceptible to immune system stress than others. Akitas, Scottish terriers, shar peis, and West Highland white terriers are prone to immune system disorders, so it is especially important to avoid situations that will weaken their immune systems.

> "Our environment is always teeming with microscopic organisms that have the potential to infect your dog with any number of minor to life-threatening diseases. How your dog's immune system responds to these organisms determines her health."

What Weakens the Immune System?

Anything that enters your dog's body that is foreign, such as a vaccination, toxin, virus, bacteria, or allergen, will trigger her immune system into action. The immune system is designed to masterfully handle millions of "invasions" a day, but it does have a stress point. It can become weak if it is overexposed to toxic substances, if it is repeatedly suppressed by stress, or if it is malnourished.

There are warning signs that will alert you if your dog's immune system is weakened. Recurring infections, recurring skin problems, arthritis, fatigue, slow-healing wounds, allergies, and chronic diarrhea are all signs that the immune system is weak and vulnerable to more serious illnesses. You can keep your dog's immune system strong with good nutrition and careful monitoring of her environment and by providing additional nutritional support for those times when her immune system will be stressed.

VACCINATIONS

Most dog owners dutifully bring their dogs to the veterinarian every year for "shots," not knowing what the vet is injecting into the dog or why. I cannot tell you exactly how this practice of yearly vaccinations began, but I can tell you that this schedule is not based on scientific evidence. In fact, the evidence is that we are drastically overvaccinating our dogs and cats.

According to Dr. Ronald Schultz, a respected expert on clinical immunology and vaccinology from the Department of Pathobiological Sciences at the University of Wisconsin, there is no scientific justification or immunologic requirement for annual revaccinations. There is mounting consensus among veterinarians that annual revaccinations are causing serious side effects in our dogs, such as anaphylaxis (hypersensitivity to vaccines), allergic reactions, aggression, impaired immune function, and a long list of chronic diseases. Veterinarians concerned about this are now doing yearly antibody titer tests before they vaccinate. An antibody titer test is a simple blood test that measures your dog's antibodies to a specific disease, such as the distemper or parvo virus. If the antibody titer remains in the protective range, there is no need to revaccinate your dog.

Vaccines are a very small dose of the disease you are trying to prevent. The injection of the infectious organism into your dog causes the immune system to mount a defense by producing antibodies. Antibodies are the protein substance that is produced by the immune system to destroy specific foreign invaders. For example, when your dog receives her rabies vaccination, specific rabies antibodies are produced that will kill the rabies virus if it enters the body.

A dog's immune system will only produce so many rabies antibodies. If she receives a rabies vaccination when she already has plenty of rabies antibodies, her immune system will still be able to destroy the rabies virus if she is exposed to it, but she will not produce additional antibodies. Not only was your money wasted on the vaccine, but your dog's immune system was put under tremendous stress from battling the rabies virus, weakening it and leaving your dog vulnerable to other illnesses.

> "There is mounting consensus among veterinarians that annual revaccinations are causing serious side effects in our dogs, such as anaphylaxis (hypersensitivity to vaccines), allergic reactions, aggression, impaired immune function, and a long list of chronic diseases."

Vaccinations are not all bad. They are a useful addition to preventive medicine when given with care and only when needed. Please do not give a stressed or sick dog a vaccination. "Sick" in this case means anything but optimal health. If your dog is fighting fleas, skin problems, or allergies, she is not in optimal health. Leave her immune system alone to fight that battle and bring her in for a vaccination when she is strong and healthy. There are many factors, such as thunderstorms, the show ring, or new people and pets in a household, that can cause your dog emotional stress. If your dog cowered under the bed all night because of a thunderstorm, postpone her vaccination for a day or two.

For longer-term stress, such as going to a show or someone new in your dog's life, give her a few days to rest and get used to her new routine. If you adopt a dog, wait until she gets used to her new home before you take her to the vet. Be especially careful if you adopt a puppy, because a puppy's immune system is not fully developed and the additional stress of a trip to the vet along with a vaccination could weaken her immune system for life. Imagine being a mere eight weeks old. You have recently been weaned and taken away from your mother, and some stranger comes and takes you away from your home. You are then thrust into a big noisy thing that moves, knocks you to and fro, and makes you feel nauseated. Finally the car stops and this stranger brings you into a strange house with a big furry cat that is hissing at you and two little people that will not let you go hide, take a nap, and figure this all out. In addition to the stress of a new home, your new dog will be getting used to new food and water. The last thing your puppy needs on top of all those new stressors is a vaccination.

Each dog adjusts to new experiences differently. Some dogs are more high-strung than others. Keep an eye on your dog, and when she seems comfortable with her surroundings and easily fits into her new routine, make an appointment with the vet for vaccinations.

Puppies should go through an initial or first vaccination series. The types of vaccines your puppy needs will vary, depending on her lifestyle and the part of the country you are in. For example, if she will be staying in a kennel while you are away, you might want to vaccinate for kennel cough or, if there have been incidences of leptospirosis (a potentially deadly bacterial disease) in your area, vaccinate for leptospirosis. Unless your veterinarian works with your local shelter, she may not know if there have been any recent outbreaks of disease among the wildlife that could affect your puppy. Talk to your local shelter or animal control officer about any recent outbreaks of disease in the wildlife or local pet population. State law requires that all dogs must have a current rabies vaccination, and many states go as far as to bar veterinarians from treating dogs whose owners refuse to give them a rabies vaccination. Most towns have expensive fines for dogs without a current rabies vaccination. This is because rabies is deadly to animals and people. If nothing else, do have your dog vaccinated for rabies. The state also mandates the frequency of the rabies shots and at what age puppies must be vaccinated. Your veterinarian will have information on when to vaccinate a puppy for rabies.

Parvo virus and distemper are common throughout the U.S. and potentially deadly in dogs. All puppies should be vaccinated against these two diseases and then, starting at one year old, have yearly antibody titer tests done.

If possible, avoid combination vaccines. These are single shots containing more than one vaccine. If you make an appointment for your dog's "shots," many veterinarians will automatically give what is commonly known and seen on your receipt as a DHLPP. Those initials look harmless, until you translate them to distemper, hepatitis, leptospirosis, parainfluenza, and parvo. Those are five different diseases that your dog's immune system suddenly has to battle. Have you ever had a flu shot? A flu shot contains one virus, and most people spend at least twenty-four hours with a sore arm and minor flu symptoms. Imagine getting a shot with the flu, measles, chicken pox, hepatitis, and tetanus. Space vaccines by a minimum of one week, and preferably wait four weeks between vaccinations. Puppies should have their vaccinations at anywhere from six weeks old to twenty weeks old (five months). The reason for waiting twenty weeks would be to give the immune system time to mature, but this must be weighed against the risks of your puppy contracting the disease. If you have your puppy vaccinated earlier than twenty weeks, she will need to receive each vaccine twice, because the antibodies that a puppy receives from her mother (maternal antibodies) during the first six weeks of life can interfere with the effectiveness of the vaccine. If your puppy is isolated from contact with other dogs and wildlife, then it is safe to hold off on vaccinations until she is twenty weeks old. By twenty weeks, the maternal antibodies will not interfere with the effectiveness of the vaccine, so you only have to give each vaccine once.

A typical parvo and distempter vaccination schedule for a puppy would be the following:

first distemper	ten weeks
first parvo	fourteen weeks
second distemper	eighteen weeks
second parvo	twenty-two weeks

In one year, start yearly antibody titer tests. If you adopt an older dog and do not know her vaccination history, have antibody titer tests done. For a list of labs that do antibody titer tests, see the Resources section in the back of the book. It is very important to ask for a vaccine titer. The lab can educate your veterinarian about protective ranges and whether you need to revaccinate.

EMOTIONAL STRESS

Emotional stress can affect a dog's immune system, and the owner is often the source of emotional stress. Most dogs are very sensitive to their owner's emotions. If you are upset or stressed, then chances are good that your dog will become stressed. Have you ever noticed your dog's reaction when there is a high level of stress in the room? She will be highly attentive and worried, or she may hide under something or leave the room. I know several dogs that will not leave their owner's side when the owner is sick. These dogs are emotionally stressed by their owner's illness. If your dog suffers when you suffer, mustering up some strength for a happy reassurance that you will be okay would be very calming for her and probably for you as well. What could be more stress-reducing than patting your dog?

Dr. Beverly Cappel-King is seeing a strong connection between bone cancer in dogs and stress. In nearly every incidence of bone cancer that she treats, the family has recently gone through a highly stressful event, such as divorce, illness, or a loved one leaving. A four-year-old Doberman named Hilda is one example out of many. Hilda and her owner are inseparable. Except for the few hours a day when Hilda's owner is at work, they are together. Hilda's owner decided to get a second job; three months later, Hilda came in from playing and was limping on her left front leg (a common place for bone cancer in Dobermans). Hilda was diagnosed with bone cancer. Her owner immediately quit her second job and made Hilda the center of her life. She even went as far as to call ahead when she took Hilda with her to visit friends and asked them not to comment on the limping but instead tell Hilda how beautiful she was. Dr. King gave Hilda antioxidants, herbal remedies, vitamins, minerals, and homeopathics to build up her immune system. Six months later, X rays showed a clean bone. Hilda and her owner have had three and a half years of cancer-free health and happiness. Dr. King attributes Hilda's recovery more to her owner's positive, loving energy than to the remedies she gave Hilda.

"Dr. Beverly Cappel-King is seeing a strong connection between bone cancer in dogs and stress."

Every breed and every individual dog responds differently to stress. Some dogs are relaxed most of the time (bloodhounds and golden retrievers come to mind), and some dogs are in a near-constant state of stress (Border collies and some toy breeds come to mind). Notice what causes stress in your dog and try to minimize those situations when possible.

Stress increases the production of adrenaline, which inhibits the production of your immune system's first line of defense, the white blood cells. The thymus gland, which produces many of the immune system's white blood cells, will begin to shrink if it is constantly suppressed by stress. A shrunken thymus gland will not produce an adequate number of white blood cells, resulting in suppression of the immune system and leaving your dog susceptible to illness.

High levels of stress have also been proven to trigger autoimmune diseases such as arthritis, hemolytic anemia, lupus, and various skin diseases. In an autoimmune disease, the immune system becomes confused, attacking healthy tissues in the body.

Sudden, extreme stress causes the fright-or-flight instinct to kick in, which shuts down the immune system. The body was elegantly designed by nature to shift resources to running or attacking in the face of danger, but if this shift is made too often, it can be a killer itself. If your dog was facing an attacking bear in the woods, the fright-or-flight stress response could save her life, but just as with people, chronic stress means the immune system is shut down too much of the time.

If your dog is highly stressed by events such as a thunderstorm, separation anxiety, or a ride in the car, the fright-flight instinct causes her heart to beat as fast as it can so she can run away from the thunderstorm, away from the car, or away from her fear of being alone. The only way her heart can work that hard is by borrowing resources from other parts of her body that are not needed for running, such as blood from her stomach or thymus gland. The parts of her body that are not essential for running, such as the immune system and the digestive system, will be suppressed or put on hold.

Imagine what happens to a dog's health if she is terrified of riding in the car or of being at the vet, and her immune system shuts down. The vet gives her the DHLPP vaccination (five diseases) and then the dog is put back in the car. Finally home, the dog jumps out of the car and runs onto a lawn that was recently treated with pesticides. She drinks from a bowl that was downwind from the pesticide spray and also contains chlorine and benzene. She takes a nap in the grass, and as she sleeps her immune system comes back to life and finds five diseases, along with a heavy onslaught of pesticides and the usual water contaminants to battle. Even an immune system that was healthy and strong before the visit to the vet could not cope with that much stress. You may not notice immediate symptoms from this type of stress reaction, but it will take a toll on your dog's body, setting the stage for heart, kidney, and liver disease as well as cancer and arthritis.

If your dog is in a constant state of stress from hyperactivity or oversensitivity, there are natural remedies that have a calming effect, such as the B-complex vitamins, magnesium, and homeopathic remedies. Valerian and kava are natural remedies that can be used on occasion to treat stress. For more information, see these chapters: Chapter 3, Vitamins for Your Dog; Chapter 4, Minerals for Your Dog; Chapter 8, Understanding Homeopathy.

ENVIRONMENTAL THREATS
TO THE IMMUNE SYSTEM

There are more than 75,000 different chemical compounds in use today, and a year from now thousands more will have been added to the list. Each year, approximately twenty billion tons of chemicals, radioactive waste, and pollutants are released into our environment. The majority of these toxins have never been tested for their long-term effects on you and your dog. If you buy into the often-said "they wouldn't sell it if it weren't safe . . ." think back to DDT, asbestos, leaded gasoline, PCBs, thalidomide, and fen-phen, to name a few government-approved products that are now banned because they made people seriously ill. Rachel Carson, author of *Silent Spring,* summed up the accumulating effects of toxins: "The fact that the suburbanite is not instantly stricken has little meaning, for the toxins may sleep long in the body, to become manifest for months or years later in an obscure disorder almost impossible to trace to its origins." In 1979, the United States Surgeon General issued a warning as to the serious consequences of our already polluted environment when he said, "There is virtually no major chronic disease to which environmental factors do not contribute, directly or indirectly."

> "Many toxins cannot be eliminated from the body, so they sit in fatty tissues for decades, harming cells and creating an environment for cancer."

Toxins are not natural to your dog's body and will trigger the immune system into action. Many toxins cannot be eliminated from the body, so they sit in fatty tissues for decades, harming cells and creating an environment for cancer. Short of wearing a space suit, you cannot possibly avoid all environmental toxins, so you need to give yourself and your dog the extra protection of a healthy lifestyle. Proper daily nutrition and some extra support for the immune system when your dog is unavoidably stressed is good health insurance.

THE PLAGUE OF PESTICIDES

Pesticides are used in such abundance both agriculturally and in residential communities that they are one of the biggest environmental threats to your dog's immune system. In the United States, a staggering 800 million pounds of pesticides are used each year on foods and crops, and an additional 70 million pounds are used on urban lawns. With approximately 870 million pounds of pesticides used every year, you would think that insects would be extinct. On the contrary, according to the Natural Resources Defense Council, since 1940 pesticide use has increased tenfold, while crop losses to insects have doubled.

Pesticides are in and around nearly every home in the United States. They are killing more than pests—they are killing us and our pets. We like to think that the poisons in pesticides are only poisonous to insects and weeds, but that is not true. It just takes a correspondingly higher dose to kill us because we are bigger.

Our dogs spend most of their lives sleeping and playing on the ground and carpet, where the highest concentrations of pesticides are found. A nine-home study found pesticides in all the homes, with the highest concentrations in the carpet dust. If you do not use pesticides on your lawn or in your home, your dog is still at risk. Pesticides move through the air and the ground, so if your neighbors use pesticides or if you live near a farm, you and your dog are being exposed. Pesticide runoff from lawns pollutes the sidewalks and roads. When your dog goes for her daily walk with you, she picks up pesticides through her nose and the pads of her feet, where they will be absorbed directly into her bloodstream.

Studies of human populations have found that people exposed to pesticides have higher incidences of cancer, birth defects, nervous system disorders, and liver and kidney disease, with children having higher incidences of illness from pesticides than adults. There is no reason why those same studies would not also apply to our dogs, with the rates of illness in children being more applicable. A dog's size and lifestyle of playing close to the ground would more closely mimic those of a child than an adult. The *Journal of the National Cancer Institute* reports that the incidence of leukemia in children is six and one-half times higher in homes where pesticides are used. That statistic alone should be reason enough for you to ban all pesticides from your home.

Pesticide poisoning can cause immediate symptoms, or the toxins can slowly weaken the immune system, causing your dog to become sick after years of exposure. Symptoms of pesticide poisoning can include all or one of the following: headaches, nausea, fever, respiratory illness, seizures, vomiting, diarrhea, incontinence, behavior problems, anxiety, hyperactivity, fatigue, heart, liver, and kidney disease, immune system disorders, and cancer.

You cannot eliminate your dog's exposure to pesticides, but you can keep it at a minimum. Start in your own back yard with organic gardening. You will be amazed at how easy and inexpensive it is and how much healthier your plants and lawn will be. To ward off pests, I spray a mixture of hot (spicy) oil, dish soap, and water on my fruit trees, and they thrive. Throw away all the toxins inside your house as well. From the flea to the mouse, there are effective, inexpensive, natural ways to eliminate them from your house. Your local library or bookstore will have plenty of material on natural pest control. Finally, be aware of where your dog walks and plays. Avoid neighborhoods, playgrounds, or golf courses where a lot of pesticides are used. Wildlife habitats are tucked away in many parts of the country and are wonderful for a nice long walk in any season and weather.

ALLERGENS

An allergen is anything that causes an allergy. It can literally come from anything in your dog's environment, including the air, food, furniture, bedding, plants, detergents, animals, and chemicals. Allergens can be inhaled, ingested, or absorbed through the skin, and if they cause an allergic reaction, the most common symptom is itchy, red skin. Dogs, like people, can also develop sneezing, red, runny eyes and nose, and postnasal drip. Symptoms of postnasal drip are wheezing or trouble breathing. Allergies are a useful red flag that your dog's immune system is weakened.

Allergies occur when the immune system overreacts to a foreign substance or allergen, such as pollen. The allergen stimulates the release of a substance called histamine, which triggers irritation, inflammation, and itchiness in the skin.

Early detection of an allergic reaction will make a big difference in treating it. The more advanced an allergic reaction, the longer the battle is to bring the immune system back to balance. Many dog owners let allergies go until their dogs have scratched themselves bald and their immune systems are highly oversensitive. At the first sign of an allergic reaction, put on your detective cap and figure out what is causing it and, if possible, eliminate it from your dog's environment. While you look for the culprit, start building your dog's immune system and keep notes on when the allergies seem to flare up. Notice if they are better when you are away from home, whether they are seasonal, or if they seem worse when your dog wakes up in the morning or at the end of the day. It may take a year of seasonal changes with the environment changing both inside and outside your home to pinpoint the exact cause of the allergies. Be persistent, keep an allergy diary nearby, and look to the light at the end of the tunnel: an allergy-free dog.

> "Allergies are a useful red flag that your dog's immune system is weakened."

Allergies are only one of the many causes of skin problems, so if you have put forth your best effort and cannot clear up the skin problems, they may be caused by something else, including genetics, hypothyroidism, or a nutrient absorption problem. Your best bet is to find a holistic veterinarian to work with you and your dog to bring the body back into balance and strengthen the immune system. For more information on allergies, see Chapter 10, Natural Healing.

AIR POLLUTION

The mention of "air pollution" usually brings to mind the yellowish haze often seen over New York City or Los Angeles. Few people consider that when they shut all the windows in their house and turn on the heat or air conditioning they could be breathing air more toxic than in downtown Manhattan at rush hour. The Environmental Protection

Agency studied levels of air pollution indoors and outdoors for five years and found that indoor air pollution is 100 to 200 times higher than outdoor air pollution. Unless you faithfully clean your filters, ducts, and vents, you and your dog could be breathing asbestos, pollens, pesticides, cleaning chemicals, tobacco, smoke, rodent feces, dust mites, mold, mildew, and bacteria.

> "Few people consider that when they shut all the windows in their house and turn on the heat or air conditioning they could be breathing air more toxic than in downtown Manhattan at rush hour."

If you are building a new home, remodeling, or just sprucing up your house, keep a careful eye on labels and choose products that are toxin-free. New carpets, paint, or wood can contain toxins that are lethal to you and your dog's immune system. If you are buying new carpet, look for the "green label" stating that the rug has met voluntary emissions criteria. Have the retailer air out the carpet before installation, and air out your house for a few days after the carpet is installed. The rubber latex contained in carpet backing and carpet adhesives very often emits toxic fumes, which can cause lethargy, headaches, vomiting, skin irritations, nausea, and red, watery eyes. If the health problems persist, the best thing you can do for yourself and your dog is to have the carpet removed.

It has become common to hear of business and home owners who have experienced serious health problems after having carpet installed. Many of these people had their carpet tested in a laboratory, with findings of extremely high levels of toxic fumes. In one instance, a mouse died after only forty minutes of exposure to air blown over the carpet and another three mice died after twenty-four hours.

If you have ever painted with oil or latex-based paint, you have smelled the fumes from the approximately 300 toxic substances that can come from the paint. The fumes will linger long after the smell is gone, causing you and your dog headaches, nausea, runny, watery eyes, and throat and lung irritation. There are good-quality paints with lower levels of toxins. Look for paints that are labeled as a clean air choice.

Pressed woods, such as plywood, particle board, and fiberboard, can also be a threat to you and your dog's health. A toxin called urea formaldehyde is used in the glue of many pressed woods and will cause coughing; nausea; red, watery eyes; and throat, lung, and skin irritation. Choose woods such as softwood plywood, wafer board, or strand board that contain glue made with the less toxic phenol formaldehyde.

The Environmental Protection Agency estimates that in the United States we spend over one billion dollars on medical costs for cancer and heart disease caused by indoor pollutants. When you consider these same indoor pollutants are twice as toxic to a dog half the size of an adult, it is staggering to think of the medical costs dog owners must pay out of their pockets due to illness from indoor pollution.

If you see your dog rubbing her eyes or face with her paws or on the furniture or the ground, she is probably feeling a burning in her eyes or throat from any one of these products. Immediately bring her out to fresh air and rinse her eyes with clean, fresh water. If possible, make any moves or renovations at a time when you can keep your windows open for a few days to air the house out after you are finished. If you are painting, put your dog outside or at a friend's house while you are painting and for a few hours after you have finished, and for yourself leave the windows open while you paint.

> "New carpets, paint, or wood can contain toxins that are lethal to you and your dog's immune system."

The air may be cleaner outside, but it is far from pollution-free. Twice as many people die each year from airborne pollution as from auto accidents. In the most polluted cities in the U.S., which are primarily in California, lives are shortened by an average of one to two years from airborne pollution. In a report titled "Acid Rain and Transported Air Pollutants," the Congressional Office of Technology Assessment concluded that air pollution may cause 50,000 premature deaths in the U.S. every year. The list of air pollutants is endless, ranging from the obvious pollens and auto exhaust to unsuspected substances such as latex antigens. You did read that right: a study of air pollution and latex allergy found latex antigens in abundance in urban air samples. The study concluded that the latex antigens came from automobile tires.

You and your dog must breathe the air, so you both need to be sure you are getting the cleanest air possible. Exercise together at a time of day when the air pollution is at its lowest and stay away from busy roads. If your dog rides in the back of a truck with an enclosed cab, be very careful of poisoning from the exhaust. Always have fresh air available, and if you open a window on the cab cover be sure it is not over the exhaust pipe. If you stop for gas and the window to the cab is over the gas tank, close the window and open the back of the cab so your dog has plenty of fresh air. If you are stuck in traffic, open the window. Studies show that toxins from car exhaust are two to four times higher inside the car than outdoors. Small concentrations of the chemicals in automobile exhaust can cause lethargy and skin, eye, and lung irritation, and higher concentrations will cause headaches, fatigue, and cancer.

> "If your dog comes upon antifreeze, she will lap it up as if it is candy, when in fact it is a poison and will cause her to be seriously ill and possibly die."

POISONS

When you take your dog for a walk the world looks very innocent. You do not see the hidden dangers that your dog's nose will find in an instant. A dog's habit of eating strange and disgusting things such as feces, grass, or dirt is caused by an attempt to satisfy a nutritional void. The likelihood is slim that what she finds is nutritional, and most likely it is poisonous. Dogs may also be harming themselves if the feces they eat came from a sick animal or the grass or dirt has been poisoned with pesticides, antifreeze, oil, or a whole host of other toxic substances that people pour onto the ground.

Propylene glycol, a preservative in rawhide that is also an ingredient in antifreeze, is sweet and highly addictive. If your dog comes upon antifreeze, she will lap it up as if it is candy, when in fact it is a poison and will cause her to be seriously ill and possibly die. Not many dogs can resist a dead animal, if only just to play with it and roll in it. That dead animal may be diseased or it may have been killed with a poison.

If your dog picks up a piece of wood to chew, be sure it is not pressure-treated wood. Pressure-treated wood contains arsenic.

Indoors can be lethal to a puppy that is still chewing. Dog-proof your home just as you would child-proof it, keeping anything toxic that could be ingested or used as a toy out of reach. This includes cleaners, medications, pesticides, and paint.

Poisons abound in our environment. Feed your dog a well-balanced diet and keep a careful eye on what she puts in her mouth.

Nutrition for a Strong Immune System

To maintain a strong immune system, your dog needs high-quality food, clean water, plenty of fresh air and exercise, and a good multi-vitamin-mineral supplement. Your dog's immune system will need extra nutritional support if she is subjected to anything that could suppress her immune system, such as vaccinations, stress, or any of the environmental dangers listed above.

If you are spending more time at your vet's office than at home and have to take out a second mortgage to pay for medication for your dog, then her immune system probably needs to be restored to health. I would recommend you consult a holistic veterinarian, who will treat the underlying cause rather than treating only the symptoms. Many holistic veterinarians can diagnose and treat your dog using the results of blood work. Holistic veterinarian Dr. Beverly Cappel-King brought a cat with feline infectious peritonitis back to health without ever meeting the cat or her owner in person. She diagnosed and treated the cat through blood work and keen observations of the cat by the owner during phone consultations.

If your dog has milder symptoms of a weakened immune system, such as lethargy, occasional bouts of diarrhea, or occasional skin problems, you can restore her immune system by following my nutritional guidelines, paying particular attention to the nutrients for a strong immune system and avoiding anything that will stress and weaken her immune system.

Just as with people, as your dog ages there is a natural decline in the efficiency of the immune system. In a one-year study of thirty-five people between the ages of sixty-one and seventy-nine, some took a placebo and some took a multivitamin-mineral supplement. Those who took the supplement had less decline in their immune function than those who took the placebo. In a similar study of the elderly, those who took a multivitamin had fewer days of illness due to infectious disease.

Good nutrition will delay and minimize the inevitable decline in immune function that occurs as your dog ages. Be sure that your geriatric dog is getting the nutrients listed below in a form that is easily absorbed, such as a powder or pill that will quickly dissolve in water.

Below, I will give you the key nutrients and their daily dosages for maintaining a strong immune system. If your dog is geriatric, is highly stressed, or has a weakened immune system, increase her multivitamin-mineral supplement by one-third and follow the guidelines below for nutrients that are not found in a multivitamin-mineral supplement. For more information, see Chapter 3, Vitamins for Your Dog, and Chapter 4, Minerals for Your Dog.

> "If you are spending more time at your vet's office than at home and have to take out a second mortgage to pay for medication for your dog, then her immune system probably needs to be restored to health."

PROTEIN

Protein is just as important to your dog as it is to you, and your dog needs an even higher percentage of protein in her diet than you do. A protein-deficient diet will cause a significant weakening of your dog's immune system. As with everything, moderation is the key. Too much protein can cause kidney damage.

Buckwheat, quinoa, red meat, and eggs are high in protein and should be included in your dog's diet on a daily basis if the immune system is weakened or stressed. It is ideal to vary your protein sources.

Limit eggs to two to four a week, depending on the size of your dog, and at each meal try to combine different types of protein, such as grains and red meat.

GARLIC

Garlic strengthens the immune system and has antibiotic, antiviral, and antiparasitic properties. Garlic has a long, illustrious career as a healing agent. The Egyptians worshipped it, monks ate it in the Middle Ages to fend off the plague, and during World War I it was used on wounds to prevent infection. Garlic has been found to inactivate cancer-causing substances and aids in destroying parasites. One-half to two cloves of garlic per day, depending on the size of your dog, will help to maintain a strong immune system. If your dog is stressed or the immune system is weakened, stick to the daily maintenance dose. Too much garlic can upset the stomach. Because of potential blood-thinning properties, it is not advisable to give your dog garlic before surgery.

BETA-CAROTENE

Beta-carotene is a powerful antioxidant that protects cells within the immune system from free radical damage and helps immune system cells communicate more efficiently. Beta-carotene improves production of natural killer cells, the first line of defense for the immune system. If your dog's body is deficient in vitamin A, beta-carotene has the unique ability to convert to vitamin A. However, since beta-carotene loses its antioxidant properties when it converts to vitamin A, it is best to give your dog a multivitamin-mineral supplement that contains both beta-carotene and vitamin A along with plenty of fresh foods that are rich in beta-carotene, such as dark green leafy vegetables and yellow and orange fruits and vegetables.

The recommended dosage for all dogs is 15 IU.

VITAMIN A

Vitamin A is important in the production of the immune system's phagocyte cells and T-cells. T-cells are the white blood cells that identify the foreign substances in your dog's body, and the phagocyte cells are one of the many types of white blood cells that the T-cells can call on to engulf the foreign substances (antigens). Vitamin A also aids in the fight against bacteria in the tears, saliva, and sweat. It is important for healthy mucous membranes, which are found in the nose, mouth, and digestive system, and it is a potent weapon in the body's fight against bacterial infections.

Vitamin A comes in liquid and capsule form. Small dogs should be getting a daily dose of 1,500 IU, medium dogs 3,750 IU, and large and giant dogs 5,000 IU.

VITAMIN E

Vitamin E is an antioxidant that enhances T-cell function and has proven to boost antibody response to vaccinations. Vitamin E is one of the most important antioxidants for protecting and supporting the immune system.

Vitamin E is available in liquid or powder form. The daily dose for small dogs is 100 IU, medium and large dogs 200 IU, and giant dogs 400 IU. For stressful situations or a weakened immune system, double the dose.

B-COMPLEX VITAMINS

The B-complex vitamins aid in the production of antibodies and the normal functioning of cells.

Again, daily dosages for adult dogs are as follows:

	Small Dog	Medium Dog	Large Dog	Giant Dog
Thiamin (B_1)	1 mg	2 mg	3 mg	4 mg
Riboflavin (B_2)	1 mg	2 mg	3 mg	4 mg
Niacin (B_3)	1 mg	2 mg	3 mg	4 mg
Pantothenic Acid (B_5)	1 mg	2 mg	3 mg	4 mg
Choline	1 mg	2 mg	3 mg	4 mg
Pyridoxine (B_6)	1 mg	2 mg	3 mg	4 mg
Cobalamin (B_{12})	1 mcg	2 mcg	3 mcg	4 mcg
Biotin	1 mcg	2 mcg	3 mcg	4 mcg
Folic Acid	1 mcg	2 mcg	3 mcg	4 mcg

VITAMIN C

Vitamin C is an antioxidant that plays a key role in the production of interferon and infection-fighting white blood cells. Interferon, another part of the immune system's defense team, is produced in response to viruses or tumors. The infection-fighting white blood cells, the backbone of the immune system, engulf foreign substances that enter the body. Many holistic veterinarians have had miraculous results giving critically ill dogs megadoses of vitamin C. The vitamin C helps restore the immune system, thus restoring the ability to fight the disease. Vitamin C also inhibits the secretion of histamines, making it a natural antihistamine and a necessary nutrient in the battle against allergens. Physical and emotional stress depletes your dog's body of vitamin C, so keeping up with the daily doses of vitamin C will go a long way in keeping her immune system strong.

> "Many holistic veterinarians have had miraculous results giving critically ill dogs megadoses of vitamin C."

The daily dosage of vitamin C for an adult dog is: small dogs 500 mg to 1,000 mg, medium and large dogs 1,000 mg to 2,000 mg, and giant dogs 2,000 mg to 4,000 mg.

For a weakened immune system, slowly increase the dose to "bowel tolerance" (loose stools or diarrhea is a sign of too much vitamin C, in which case reduce to the previous dosage).

TRACE MINERALS

Copper

A copper deficiency will dramatically lower your dog's resistance to infection and disease by decreasing the white blood cell and antibody production.

Daily recommended doses are: small dogs 0.5 mg, medium dogs 1 mg, and large and giant dogs 2 mg.

Zinc

Zinc is important in all phases of immune function. A study on the effect of dietary zinc deficiency on immune function published in the *International Journal of Immunopharmacology* found that dietary zinc deficiency resulted in depressed T-cells, natural killer cells, and antibody functioning. The study also found zinc deficiencies were related to several forms of cancer, including head, neck, and lung cancer.

Recommended daily doses are: small dogs 10 mg, medium dogs 15 mg, and large and giant dogs 30 mg.

Iron

An iron deficiency will inhibit your dog's use of oxygen, which in turn inhibits the function of the immune system. The entire immune system is dependent upon oxygen to work efficiently. Iron is another nutrient where moderation is the key. Too much iron can generate free radicals, which will injure cells on your dog's artery walls, causing heart disease. A blood test will tell you if your dog has an iron deficiency. Your veterinarian will provide you with iron supplements, or you can feed your dog plenty of organic foods rich with iron, such as beans, pork, beef, liver, chicken, and turkey.

The recommended amount of iron in a dog's daily diet is: small dogs 9 mg, medium dogs 18 mg, large dogs 30 mg, and giant dogs 40 mg.

Manganese

Manganese is an important coworker of many of the vitamins that play key roles in maintaining the strength of the immune system. Manganese is necessary for utilizing the B-complex vitamins, vitamin E, and vitamin C. A manganese deficiency has been found to suppress the production of antibodies.

Recommended daily doses are: small dogs 0.75 mg, medium dogs 1.5 mg, large dogs 2.6 mg, and giant dogs 3.75 mg.

Selenium

Selenium is an antioxidant that works with vitamin E to increase the body's antibody production in response to antigens (foreign substances) and enables white blood cells to destroy bacteria and viruses. According to a study on selenium and cellular immunity, selenium deficiency can lead to impaired immune function and reduced T-cell counts. Many medical doctors who use alternative medicine use selenium to fight a wide range of viruses, including AIDS and herpes.

Recommended daily doses are: small dogs 25 mcg and medium, large, and giant dogs 50 mcg.

A healthy immune system will give you a healthy dog. To maintain a healthy immune system, your dog needs a daily diet of high-quality nutrition and extra nutritional support for those days when she has added stress to her immune system. Just as your dog's body needs more calories if she expends more energy, your dog's immune system needs additional nutrition on the days it has to work harder.

PART THREE

A Flea-Free Household Naturally

CHAPTER SEVEN

Natural Flea Control for Your Dog

RIGHT NOW, you probably feel less affection for the flea than you do for the mosquito. You think of fleas as blood-sucking creatures that were put on this earth to torment you and your dog. A flea is a parasite, so in a way you are right. Parasites are organisms that survive on another organism without contributing anything. I felt tortured and tormented by fleas until one wonderful hot summer came and went without one flea bath, daily vacuuming, or a trip to the vet. We had a flea-free summer. Not once did my dog look at me with those sad, "please help me" eyes, after biting and scratching for ten minutes.

My miracle cure was garlic. Knowing the great health benefits of garlic, I had recently started giving my dog garlic with every meal. Feeding your dog garlic is one of the many ways you too can have a healthier, flea-free dog.

Fleas are tiny, brown, wingless insects that thrive on blood and can jump 100 times their height to get to the source of the blood. Pet owners collectively spend millions of dollars every year on an endless quest to rid their furry friends of this minuscule menace. These tiny insects not only cause endless aggravation, they also can cause your dog to become seriously ill. Dogs that are allergic to flea saliva experience severe itching and welts from each flea bite. The allergic reaction is triggered by a chemical in the flea's saliva that prevents the dog's blood from clotting until the flea has finished its meal. If left untreated, the dog will chew her skin raw, creating open sores and the possibility of infection. The dog's skin is not the only thing that suffers. The immune system becomes weaker and oversensitized with every bite, leaving the dog vulnerable to additional chronic health problems. On the outside the dog is biting and scratching, and on the inside the immune system is working overtime to fight the allergic reaction and to heal the sores caused by the itching and biting.

> "Pet owners collectively spend millions of dollars every year on an endless quest to rid their furry friends of this minuscule menace."

To add insult to injury, fleas do not travel alone: they carry tapeworm, another parasite. Fleas are two parasites in one tiny package. As your dog is biting and licking, she undoubtedly will ingest a few fleas. The tapeworm inside the flea has a free ride into your dog's small intestine, where it lives and prospers. If your dog is infested with fleas, she probably has tapeworm. To know for sure, bring a stool sample to your vet and ask her to check your dog for worms. You may also see tapeworms around the anus or in the stool. Tapeworms are thin, segmented worms that can reach several feet in length. However, when you see them outside your dog, they usually look like small grains of rice.

Tapeworms attach themselves to the small intestine with hooks and suckers and, like the flea, live off your dog's blood. The tapeworm has an outer coating that prevents it from being digested in the small intestine. If your dog has tapeworm, or any other worm, there are natural wormers you can buy from a holistic vet or a health food store, or check the Resources section in the back of the book. For prevention of worms, use garlic or black walnut hulls.

Fleas rarely infest a really healthy animal. I find it interesting that the companies that make millions selling dog food that does not begin to meet your dog's nutritional needs also make millions selling pesticides to kill fleas and further compromise your dog's health. It is a vicious circle that can be stopped.

The key to a flea-free household is not to see how many fleas you can kill in a season. The key is to make your dog an undesirable food source. If you walk into a restaurant that smells terrible, you will not stay around for a meal; you will find another restaurant. In this section, I will explain how the flea lives and why it wants to live on your dog's body. I will discuss why the chemicals and pesticides you have used for years do not work and are hazardous to you and your dog and how you can rid your dog of fleas naturally.

The Life Cycle of the Flea

Your dog is exposed to fleas the minute she walks out the door for a walk around the block or a romp in the yard. A flea's ideal environment is warm, dark, and moist, with food readily available, making your dog a perfect host. The flea's only nutritional need is blood. It prefers to live on your dog's belly or back or near the tail. It may prefer the back end, because there is less activity, although really happy dogs with long tails must be a challenge. One female flea can produce 20,000 eggs in three months. The female flea will stay on your dog to lay her eggs or she will find a nice warm, dark, moist environment off your dog in which to lay them. Preferred living quarters off your dog are carpets, furniture, curtains, and bedding. If she decides to lay her eggs on your dog they will fall off inside and outside your house. In a week to two weeks, the eggs hatch into larvae and spin a cocoon, where they will stay from one week to a year. They stay in the cocoon if it is not warm or moist enough and if there is no food source, such as you or your dog. While in the cocoon, the fleas are protected from insecticides and low temperatures. Normally fleas take from three to six weeks to go from egg to

> "The key to a flea-free household is not to see how many fleas you can kill in a season. The key is to make your dog an undesirable food source."

larvae to adult. If you want to find out if your house is infested with fleas, take your family, including pets, on a vacation. If you have a problem with fleas, on your first night home you will wake up itching and scratching. Sound familiar? I have known people who walked into their homes after being away and could watch the fleas jumping onto their bare legs. The fleas were hungry because their food source had been gone.

The remarkable ability of the flea larvae to stay in their protective cocoon for so long is probably the biggest reason that the fight against fleas can be so difficult. You have to be patient and persistent.

Flea Collars, Shampoos, Sprays, Powders, and Pills

In simplest terms, flea collars, shampoos, sprays, powders, and "spot-on" drugs are used externally on your dog to kill the adult fleas.

The new spot-on drugs, such as Advantage and Frontline, are chemicals that a veterinarian puts on your dog's skin, where they are absorbed into the sebaceous glands. The sebaceous glands secrete oil into your dog's coat to keep it healthy and shiny. When the fleas come into contact with the chemicals, their nervous system is destroyed and they die.

Flea control chemicals that come in pill form, such as Program, are insect development inhibitors. Insect development inhibitors prevent the flea eggs from developing into adult fleas by interfering with the synthesis of chitin. Chitin is the primary substance used to form the arthropod exoskeleton. An arthropod is an animal that does not have a spinal column or backbone, and an exoskeleton is the hard shell that protects and holds together the animal's body.

What the collars, shampoos, sprays, powders, spot-on drugs, and pills all have in common is that they are all pesticides. According to veterinarian Michael W. Lemmin, "Popular flea collars often contain powerful nerve gases. They can also kill some pets, and can do damage to children and adults handling the pet wearing the poisonous flea collar." These pesticides are toxic to the fleas and are also toxic to you and your dog. Carbaryl (sevin), a pesticide used in many external flea control products, adversely affects human sperm, the nervous system, motor function (the ability to move), and the production of the hormone melatonin.

Western Michigan University published a study finding that chlorphyrifos (Dursban), another pesticide commonly used in external flea control products, causes birth defects of the brain, eyes, ears, palate, teeth, heart, feet, nipples, and genitalia of humans. I do not care how flea-infested your home is, it is not worth that kind of risk. Even if you are not pregnant or about to be, it should be clear that these pesticides are not good for you. There is abundant evidence from hundreds and probably thousands of studies done worldwide that the types of pesticides we are using on our pets have the potential to cause—in our pets, our children, and ourselves—a variety of cancers (especially leukemia), skin problems such as rashes, disruption of the reproductive system, damage to glands such as the thyroid, liver damage, disorders of the nerves and the brain, heavy-metal toxicity, blood poisoning, and acute symptoms such as seizures, vomiting, asthma, and allergies. That is quite a list. Are these pesticides you would bathe in, spray all over your body, ingest, or wear around your neck? I hope not. Please do not expose your dog to them.

> "While in the cocoon, the fleas are protected from insecticides and low temperatures."

The effectiveness of flea collars, shampoos, sprays, powders, spot-on drugs, and pills is also very limited. Flea collars kill the fleas when they go under the collar on the way to the dog's eyes for water. Unless your dog has a severe infestation, the fleas will be getting enough moisture from the skin and will not be traveling to your dog's head. The shampoos kill the adult fleas on your dog, until she jumps out of the bathtub and picks up more. You have to keep the sprays, powders, and spot-on drugs on your dog at all times, which is unpleasant and toxic for you, your children, and your dog. The pills only work if the female flea bites your dog. Knowing there are thousands of fleas waiting for your dog to

"Western Michigan University published a study finding that chlorphyrifos (Dursban), another pesticide commonly used in external flea control products, causes birth defects of the brain, eyes, ears, palate, teeth, heart, feet, nipples, and genitalia of humans. I do not care how flea-infested your home is, it is not worth that kind of risk."

come out and play, the FDA recommends that the pills be used along with external flea control. They are asking you to expose your dog to pesticides both internally and externally.

There are herbal flea control products that can be used until my program of nutritional flea control starts to work. I do not ever recommend flea collars. Aromatic essential oils from plants such as rosemary, in doses strong enough to repel fleas on a flea collar, can be irritating to your dog's skin. I do not like putting anything so close to a dog's eyes, nose, ears, and mouth on a constant, twenty-four-hour basis, and since their effectiveness is so limited, why bother?

Herbal flea shampoos will leave a fragrance on your dog that is undesirable to fleas. Look for shampoos containing pine cedar, citronella, juniper, bergamot, geranium, lavender, or eucalyptus. You can kill all the fleas on your dog by working the shampoo up into a nice lather and massaging your dog for about fifteen minutes. Your dog will enjoy the massage, it's great for her skin, and you will drown the fleas. For those of you with bathtubs, here is a tip for avoiding a battle at bath time: before you put your dog in the bathtub, fill a plastic pitcher full of water that is as warm as you can get it without it being hot. Have you ever noticed that your dog does not really start fighting until you turn the water on? Preparing the warm water before your dog is in the bathtub avoids the stress of the running water until you can get your dog relaxed. Once you get your dog in the bathtub start pouring this water on her, add shampoo, and give her a good massage. The very warm water causes the dog to become totally relaxed, and your only problem will be keeping your dog standing. A woman who had to put on her bathing suit and close the shower curtain to bathe her excitable golden retriever tried this and has retired her bathing suit.

Natural Flea Control

The way to prevent a severe case of fleas is to catch them early when there are only a few. Be sure to include a quick check for fleas in your weekly health check. Look on the stomach, in the leg pits, on the back, and near the tail. As you look for fleas, also look for flea feces. Flea feces, also known as flea dirt, is black and about the size of a poppy seed. To confirm that it is flea dirt and not dirt from your backyard, put some on a paper towel and put a few drops of water on it. If it dissolves into red blood, it is flea dirt.

If you find fleas on your dog, the first task is to rid your dog and house of fleas. The second task will be to make your dog undesirable to the fleas so you will not be constantly battling the fleas. Your best defense is a good offense, so concentrate on prevention.

If you do find some fleas on your dog, bathe her with a natural herbal shampoo containing any combination of citronella, pine cedar, eucalyptus, juniper, bergamot, geranium, rosemary, or lavender. Massage the shampoo into the hair and skin for fifteen minutes to be sure all the fleas are dead. If your dog is allergic to the flea saliva and has chewed her skin raw, bring her to your veterinarian. There she will receive a steroid shot, which will keep her from itching and biting, giving the skin a chance to heal and buying some comfortable time for your dog until you can bring her back to health. Oatmeal shampoo is also good to help relieve the itching.

If your dog only has a couple of fleas, you do not have to worry about a house infestation. You will know your house is infested if the fleas are biting you as well as your dog.

If your home is infested with fleas, here is a recipe for getting rid of them: mix 1½ pounds of diatomaceous earth, 1½ pounds of natural borax, and 1 cup of salt. The diatomaceous earth contains tiny particles with sharp spines that puncture the outer covering, or exoskeleton, of the flea. The borax and salt absorb all the moisture from the flea and make the cracks and crevices dry and undesirable. Diatomaceous earth does not kill the eggs or larvae in their cocoon, so it will take a few weeks to months of weekly treatments and vacuuming to rid your house of all the adults, larvae, and eggs.

Buy the diatomaceous earth and natural borax at a garden store, not a pool store. The diatomaceous earth at the pool store has a high crystalline silica content that is dangerous to you and your dog. Look for diatomaceous earth with a crystalline silica content that is less than 3 percent. Pour some of the mixture into your vacuum cleaner bag and thoroughly vacuum all carpeting. Clean your dog's bedding, your bedding, and curtains. Sprinkle the mixture into any cracks and crevices that your dog cannot get into, such as closets, a spare bedroom, or behind furniture. If the infestation is really bad, you can sprinkle it onto your carpeting and upholstery, let it sit for a day or two, and then vacuum it up. Needless to say, it is best if you are elsewhere while the powder sits. These powders are not poisonous, but it is not wise to breathe any type of powder for hours on end.

> "If your dog only has a couple of fleas, you do not have to worry about a house infestation. You will know your house is infested if the fleas are biting you as well as your dog."

If you do not have time for all that, there is a company (see the Resources section at the back of the book) that will come to your home and apply a sodium-polyborate powder (similar to the diatomaceous earth, borax, and salt mixture), which rids your home of fleas in two to six weeks; your home is guaranteed to be flea-free for one year.

Next, we want to make your dog undesirable to the fleas with our nutritional program. As with all new things you introduce to your dog, introduce each facet gradually, carefully watching for any adverse reactions.

Unprocessed brewer's yeast (not nutritional yeast) is readily available at your health food store and some pet stores. It is packed full of B vitamins, which will enhance your dog's overall health. Vitamin B_1 (thiamine) will repel fleas, mosquitoes, and ticks. As with all the supplements, give half the daily dose with the morning meal and half with the evening meal. Give 1 tablespoon per day for a small dog (under 20 pounds), 2 tablespoons a day for a medium dog (20 to

50 pounds), 3 tablespoons a day for a large dog (50 to 100 pounds), and 4 tablespoons a day for a giant dog (over 100 pounds).

If your dog shows any adverse reactions to brewer's yeast, such as itching or diarrhea, give her a yeast-free B-complex supplement. For B-complex supplement dosage, see Chapter 3, Vitamins for Your Dog.

Garlic, one of my favorite nutrients for humans and pets, is intolerable to fleas. Give your dog a half to two cloves a day, depending on size, using whole fresh cloves, liquid, or powder. Fresh cloves can be irritating to the stomach, so if you use them, be sure to give them with plenty of food. The fleas are repelled by the odor of the garlic, so the odorless garlic that comes in pill form will not work. If you too are repelled by the smell of garlic, don't worry, you will not smell it unless your dog gives you a big kiss or yawns in your face right after she has eaten. Garlic is also excellent for your dog's overall health. It boosts the immune system, relieves respiratory problems, strengthens the heart, is antibacterial and antiviral, and works as an intestinal cleaner and parasite preventative.

Black walnut hulls come in capsule form at most health food stores and will repel fleas, ticks, and mosquitoes. Give small and medium dogs (up to 50 pounds) one capsule a day, large dogs (50 to 100 pounds) two capsules a day, and giant dogs (over 100 pounds) three capsules a day. Double the dose if you live in an area or will be traveling to an area where Lyme disease or heartworm is a threat. Lyme disease is carried by ticks, and heartworm is carried by mosquitoes. If you are not sure whether Lyme disease or heartworm is a threat, call a local veterinarian or the state's veterinary medical association.

If you are looking for the convenience of one-stop shopping and quicker meal preparation for your dog, there are very tasty organic supplements that work very well. See the Resources section at the back of the book.

As an additional precaution against bringing fleas into the house, run a flea comb through your dog before she comes in the house. The flea comb pulls any fleas out of the hair, and it will also keep your dog's hair mat-free, which is an important part of maintaining your dog's health. Most veterinarians and pet stores carry flea combs.

None of these supplements are instant answers to your flea problem. They will take, on average, four to six weeks to work. If your dog is in poor health and exposed to a lot of fleas, it will take longer. Keep your focus on the light at the end of the tunnel, which is a flea-free household forever. If you endure cold winters and only have to worry about fleas a few months out of the year, start your dog on flea prevention two months before flea season starts.

PART FOUR

Homeopathy for Dogs

CHAPTER EIGHT

Understanding Homeopathy

HOMEOPATHIC REMEDIES CAN heal many of your dog's health problems quickly, without invasive methods or drug side effects. You can use homeopathy to treat your dog for a wide variety of common ailments. For more complicated problems, it is best to seek out an experienced homeopathic practitioner. Many homeopaths treat both people and animals, and many holistic vets use at least some homeopathy.

Homeopathy is a type of medicine developed in the 1800s by a German scientist named Dr. Samuel Hahnemann. He is particularly known for creating an extensive *Materia Medica* (Latin for "materials of medicine"), or list of homeopathic remedies and the symptoms they could cause or cure. In the late 1800s, veterinary homeopathy was established by Baron von Boenninghausen, and by the early 1900s, homeopathic remedies formulated specifically for animals became available.

Homeopathic remedies may be of plant, animal, or mineral origin, and they are prescribed for every conceivable type of illness, including mental and emotional illnesses.

Dr. Hahnemann found that a substance that caused an ailment in a normal or large dose could also cure those symptoms when given in doses so small that not even a molecule of the original substance could be found in it. For example, arsenic is a poison in normal doses, but in homeopathic doses it can be given to treat a wide variety of symptoms, many of which resemble some stage of arsenic poisoning. An internal dose of the plant arnica causes what Dr. Hahnemann describes as "conditions upon the system quite similar to those resulting from injuries,

> "In the late 1800s, veterinary homeopathy was established by Baron von Boenninghausen, and by the early 1900s, homeopathic remedies formulated specifically for animals became available."

falls, blows, contusions." In homeopathic doses, arnica is one of the most commonly used remedies for treating bruises, sprains and strains, and muscle soreness.

In Dr. Hahnemann's words, "Every medicine which, among the symptoms it can cause in a healthy body, reproduces those most present in a given disease, is capable of curing the disease in the swiftest, most thorough and most enduring fashion." That elaborate description is now commonly known as "like cures like."

One way to describe how homeopathy works is that it helps stimulate the body to marshall its resources to heal very specific symptoms. For that reason, a homeopathic doctor will ask extremely detailed questions about the symptoms of an ailment. For example, is it better or worse at different times of the day, or when it is hot or cold, or with or without pressure? Does the patient avoid sunshine or darkness, crave hot or cold drinks, or have great sensitivity to loud noises? All of the hundreds of remedies described in Hahnemann's *Materia Medica* list these types of symptoms, and a good homeopath is familiar with most of them.

In nearly 200 years of testing homeopathic remedies, Dr. Hahnemann and his successors also found that the more they diluted the remedies and then activated (by shaking) the remedies, the more potent they became. The remedies are diluted to either a 10 times potency, which is noted as "x" on the label, or a 100 times potency, which is noted as "C" on the label. A "1x" on the label of a liquid remedy would mean that one drop of the remedy was added to nine drops of alcohol and shaken. It would become "2x" if one drop of the "1x" remedy were added to nine drops of alcohol and shaken. A "C" potency is one drop of the remedy added to 99 drops of alcohol and shaken.

Homeopathic remedies come in sugar pills, alcohol-based tinctures, or, for external applications, creams.

Working with a Homeopath

The homeopath evaluates the whole animal, so the more information regarding your dog's life that you can provide, the more precise a remedy can be chosen. Successful treatment with homeopathic remedies relies on a detailed description of the illness. Some of the questions you might be asked include these:

- When did you first notice the symptoms?
- Have there been any changes in your dog's nature or attitude?
- Were there any special circumstances when the problem started, such as a change in diet, moving, death in the family (including another dog), new rugs, or a new lawn care company?

In the case of diarrhea, vomiting, or nasal or anal discharge, for example, specific descriptions are needed. It will be unpleasant, but you need to be able to describe the color and consistency of discharges, along with anything in the liquid such as blood, food, objects, or grass.

It is important to know if weather, heat, cold, rest, or motion seems to affect the symptoms. Have water intake or appetite increased or decreased? Does your dog have an unusual need for warmth or cold? Have sleeping habits changed?

It can be helpful if you know the mother's history. Did she have any serious illnesses or trauma before or during pregnancy?

Discuss all your thoughts, no matter how insignificant they may seem, and don't be afraid to start your sentence with "I thought this was really weird . . ." That may be just what your homeopath was looking for.

Using Homeopathic Remedies

Homeopathic remedies cost very little, they work quickly, and you never have to struggle to get a pill down your dog's throat. For an acute or immediate problem, remedies can be given every hour to two hours depending on symptoms, or they can simply be added to your dog's drinking water.

Homeopathic remedies come as either a very small sugar pill or a liquid, which can be placed under the lip or on the tongue. The tablets dissolve in a matter of seconds. If at all possible, do not give the remedies fifteen minutes before or one hour after feeding.

The dosages for people are also applicable to dogs. Read the label and follow the dosage instructions. You can stop using the remedy when the symptoms begin to change. Only resume using it if the symptoms reappear. More is not better with homeopathic remedies. In the Resources section at the back of the book you will find some very useful homeopathic products made specifically for pets, which can narrow your choices from a confusing array of hundreds of possible remedies to a few that are known to work well for specific ailments in dogs.

Homeopathic Remedies for Common Ailments

There are a wide variety of common dog ailments that you can treat yourself with homeopathic remedies. For example, if your dog is playing and suddenly starts limping, it is a pretty good guess that she has a bruise or strain. (If the leg is obviously broken or dislocated—if she is not putting any weight on it after an hour or so or is whining or crying—take her to the vet.) Arnica, rhus tox, and ruta are wonderful homeopathic remedies for bruises, sprains, and strains; they can be put on externally as a cream or given internally as a liquid or sugar pill.

PHYSICAL SYMPTOMS

Here are some remedies to keep in your dog's medicine cabinet (and most likely yours as well!) to treat simple, non-life-threatening symptoms.

Aconite can be used to treat a sudden onset of fever, inflammation, or infection in the initial stages.

Apis Mellifica is for allergic reactions that cause swelling, such as bee stings or hives. Use with any swelling that is shiny red in appearance and will momentarily indent when you press on it.

Arnica Montana should always be within arm's reach. Arnica montana is used for injuries, bruising, muscle soreness, fever, hemorrhage, and a high sensitivity to pain to the point where your dog does not want to be touched. Recovery from surgery can be accelerated by giving your dog arnica before and after surgery. In addition to being sold in tablet form for internal use, arnica is available in lotion, ointment, or gel for external use on injuries that are not too painful to touch.

> "There are a wide variety of common dog ailments that you can treat yourself with homeopathic remedies."

Bryonia is useful for both diarrhea and constipation.

Calendula Officinalis works as an antiseptic as well as for relieving pain. You can use calendula cream to treat minor cuts and scrapes or to prevent infection and promote healing, and you can also use it as a homeopathic remedy internally for promoting healing in somewhat more serious wounds.

Hepar Sulphuris is useful for inflammation, bacterial infections, hot spots, and when there is evidence of pus (thick, yellowish-white fluid) with sensitivity and a tendency toward repeated infections.

Hypericum Perforatum is useful as a cream in treating nerve damage, such as is incurred in that awful moment when your dog hesitates as you go through the door and gets her tail or toe caught. It is most useful when there is a shooting pain present.

Ledum Palustre should be used internally if the wound had dirt in it or your dog was bitten by a wild animal and tetanus is a concern. Ledum can be used for any type of puncture wound and before, during, and after surgery.

Nux Vomica is helpful if your dog has bloating and gas that is worse after eating. The dog that needs nux vomica may also be constipated with ineffective urgings or have indigestion and irritability. These dogs sometimes also have diarrhea and vomiting.

Pyrogenium works well with pets with infected wounds, some abscesses, and septic conditions, especially if accompanied by a high fever.

Rhus Toxicodendron is useful for aches and pains in the joints, commonly diagnosed as arthritis, rheumatism, or old age, as well as sprains or strains. If damp weather tends to cause lameness in your dog, give rhus toxicodendron preventively whenever the humidity is high. Rhus tox can also be used for rashes.

Ruta Graveolens is useful for sprains, strains, and the dislocation of a joint. Sprains are a result of torn or stretched ligaments or tendons, while strains are caused by stretched or torn muscles. Sprains and strains are usually the result of sudden, quick movements and cause temporary pain and swelling around a joint. The symptoms of a sprain or strain (lameness or painful, swollen joints) will also be seen if there is a broken bone. If the lameness is severe or your dog cannot put weight on the joint, she may have a broken bone.

Symphytum is very useful if your pet has broken a bone and has already had it set. It has often been observed to dramatically speed up bone healing. Three to four doses of this remedy during the course of the healing process will be sufficient. Please do not overtreat with this remedy.

Thuja Occidentalis is used to counteract the side effects of vaccinations. If you cannot avoid multiple vaccines, give one daily dose for each vaccine. For example, if your dog has had three vaccines, give one dose of thuja for three days. Never vaccinate your dog if she is under stress or ill.

EMOTIONAL AND BEHAVIORAL SYMPTOMS

Many dogs and cats have emotional and behavioral problems that, despite all your patience and loving care, you cannot seem to cure. Many veterinarians have seen dramatic results with homeopathic remedies. Dr. Stephen Day, author of *The Homeopathic Treatment of Small Animals: Principles and Practice,* treated a cocker spaniel that had been sick and depressed since his lifelong companion, a ten-year-old female, had died. Conventional treatment had cured each symptom, only to find another one appearing. Dr. Day treated the dog with ignatia for the sadness and grief. After a few treatments, the dog had a full recovery and is now back to his old self.

Here are some simple remedies for treating short-term emotional and behavioral symptoms at home:

Aconitum Napellus is good for dogs who love to go for a ride in the car, but when it comes to a long car trip to a strange place, they become uneasy. To help ease the fear of traveling, give a tablet one hour before traveling and another tablet just before you leave. If your dog becomes nervous again during your trip, give as needed. Aconite can be used any time your dog has experienced a sudden shock or is anxious and restless.

Baryta Carbonica is useful for the dog that is overly shy and timid without aggressiveness.

Chamomilla is used when there is irritability due to pain. It is used during recovery from an illness, for teething, or for a mother in

> "Many dogs and cats have emotional and behavioral problems that, despite all your patience and loving care, you cannot seem to cure. Many veterinarians have seen dramatic results with homeopathic remedies."

pain after giving birth. Chamomilla does not affect the source of the pain—it helps alleviate the grumpiness from being in pain. Chamomilla should also be on your shopping list with the bowls, leash, and collar when you adopt a new puppy. It does wonders to stop incessant chewing.

Cocculus can be used if your dog loves the car, boat, plane, or train but suffers from motion sickness.

Gelsemium alleviates fear in anticipation of an event or after a fright if your dog is shaky or lethargic. This is for those dogs who start shaking before the TV weatherperson knows a thunderstorm is coming or who somehow know you are taking them to the veterinarian.

Ignatia has many uses. The cocker spaniel that Dr. Day treated with ignatia for loss of a loved one is one example. Ignatia can also be used when stress appears at the time of the event, rather than in anticipation. Ignatia is also used for symptoms such as separation anxiety, stress at the groomer or vet's office, and nervousness in the show ring.

Platina Metallicum is useful for female dogs obsessed with sex.

Pitric Acid is useful for male dogs who are overly obsessed with sex.

A remedy for extreme situations, such as trauma, stress, fear, and unconsciousness and should never be far from your dog. There are combination homeopathic remedies made specifically for pets in distress. A Bach flower remedy called **Rescue Remedy** is very effective for dogs in distress as well as people. Bach flower remedies are flower essences that assist in physical healing by keeping the emotional state in balance. Rescue Remedy is a combination of the five flower remedies rock rose, impatiens, clematis, star of Bethlehem, and cherry plum.

These remedies are invaluable in an emergency situation to buy some time until you can get medical help for your dog. They can help keep your dog from going into shock, which can mean the difference between death and a full recovery. These same remedies can also be used for stressful situations that are not emergencies, such as fear of thunderstorms, show ring jitters, and separation anxiety.

PART FIVE

The Five Most Common Dog Diseases

CHAPTER NINE

Natural Prevention and Treatment of Common Dog Diseases

THESE DAYS, our dogs rarely die from old age—they die prematurely from kidney failure, liver disease, heart disease, cancer, and gastric bloat and torsion. The expected life span for dogs has decreased over the years, while the life span of people has been climbing. While advanced medical technology and better nutrition have made major contributions to the increased life span of people, advances in veterinary medicine have not been accompanied by better nutrition for dogs. I was in an animal hospital a few months ago that was selling a dry dog food that had peanut hulls as one of the ingredients. Clearly, we cannot depend on the conventional veterinarians to educate us about the nutritional needs of our dogs, so we must educate ourselves and bring that knowledge back to our veterinarians.

Following my nutritional guidelines for keeping your dog at optimal health in all phases of life and life situations will prevent or significantly delay the onset of these illnesses.

In this chapter, you will find out more about the top five causes of death in dogs, what causes these illnesses, and how you can nutritionally support your dog to prevent them.

Kidney Failure

Like you, your dog has two kidneys located behind and below the rib cage. The kidneys are involved in the formation and excretion of urine and the balance of water and electrolytes. The kidneys extract water, mineral salts, toxins, and other waste products from the blood and send them to the bladder for elimination. The kidneys then take the purified water, mix in the perfect balance of electrolytes such as sodium, calcium, potassium, and phosphorus, and put it back into the bloodstream.

A dog is considered to be experiencing kidney failure when 65 to 75 percent of both kidneys are not functioning. Kidney disease (as compared to kidney failure) is rarely diagnosed in dogs, because the loss of kidney function is usually not symptomatic until the dog experiences kidney failure.

Kidney failure can be caused by a poor diet; toxins such as pesticides; anything that affects the flow of blood such as high or low blood pressure and heart disease; all infections including those of skin, teeth, and gums; an imbalance of electrolytes; dehydration; any kind of trauma such as an accident; or a severe illness such as cancer. Over time, a diet too high in acid, phosphorus, sodium, or protein or a diet low in potassium can cause kidney failure.

Breeds prone to kidney failure are the chow chow, Doberman pinscher, German shepherd, Samoyed, American cocker spaniel, basenji, beagle, Brittany spaniel, Norwegian elkhound, standard poodle, and Lhasa apso.

Breeds prone to abnormally developing kidneys, which can lead to kidney failure, are the soft-coated wheaten terrier, miniature dachshund, miniature schnauzer, shih tzu, standard dachshund, and Doberman pinscher.

Kidney failure is a critical condition that must be treated by a veterinarian immediately. Long-term successful treatment of kidney

> "Clearly, we cannot depend on the conventional veterinarians to educate us about the nutritional needs of our dogs, so we must educate ourselves and bring that knowledge back to our veterinarians."

failure is labor-intensive for you and your veterinarian. It requires a strong commitment of time and money to keep a dog healthy after it has had kidney failure. Special meals have to be prepared, in combination with daily supplements and frequent trips to the veterinarian. Nothing can be taken for granted with a dog that has had kidney failure.

A six-month-old springer spaniel named Mandy was in total kidney failure and given a few weeks to live by a conventional veterinarian. Mandy came to Dr. Beverly Cappel-King with breath that smelled like a mixture of bad fish and ammonia, vomiting, and diarrhea. She was so weak she could barely walk. Dr. King's diagnosis was that Mandy was in kidney failure as a result of renal dysplasia, a congenital kidney disease. She immediately put Mandy on intravenous therapy that included fluids, vitamin C, and B-complex vitamins. Over the next two weeks, Dr. King also used homeopathic remedies, special supplements, an herbal formula called Essiac to help flush out the liver and kidneys, Chinese herbs, and some acupuncture to stimulate the kidneys. She gave Mandy's owners instructions for home-cooked meals and a dandelion and parsley tea, which they gave her two or three times a day to help flush her kidneys. Mandy made a full recovery and has been maintaining healthy kidneys for a year and a half.

Dr. King carefully monitors Mandy, and the owners are vigilant in keeping her on a strict diet, which includes liver (liver is easy to digest), small portions of other meats, eggs, cheese, and lots of grains and vegetables. Dandelion and parsley are added to Mandy's food to keep her kidneys flushed. Mandy also drinks a variety of fluids to keep her kidneys flushed. When she gets tired of drinking home-made chicken broth, clam broth, and water from tuna fish, they offer her melted ice cream. Aside from being a fluid when it is melted, ice cream is high in fat, does not have a lot of protein (which Mandy has to stay away from), and is high in carbohydrates and sugar, which give her energy.

Mandy also takes kidney supplements that contain raw kidney, high doses of the B-complex vitamins, vitamin A, and vitamin C, along with an essential fatty acid supplement.

The key to preventing kidney failure is to keep your whole dog healthy. If your dog is exposed to a lot of pesticides, the kidneys will be stressed as they work to detoxify the blood. If you have a dog that is prone to kidney problems, be sure to read Chapter 6, The Importance of a Strong Immune System (building a strong immune system), and Chapter 1, Feeding Your Dog for Naturally Great Health (making home-cooked food).

If you have a dog like Mandy who is born with abnormal kidneys, early detection is important. Symptoms of failing kidneys are vomiting, diarrhea, lethargy, dry coat, lack of appetite, increased thirst and urinating, and breath that smells like ammonia and/or rotten fish.

> "Symptoms of failing kidneys are vomiting, diarrhea, lethargy, dry coat, lack of appetite, increased thirst and urinating, and breath that smells like ammonia and/or rotten fish."

Heart Disease

The heart is a complex muscle that gives your dog life by pumping nutrient- and oxygen-enriched blood throughout her body. The heart, human and animal, has four chambers, called the right atrium and right ventricle and the left atrium and left ventricle. The right and left chambers are separated by a wall of muscle. Each of the four chambers has a valve that controls the flow of blood into and out of the heart. The valves open, letting blood flow through, and then close tightly to force the blood forward and at the same time prevent any backflow of blood. The degeneration of the valves is called valvular heart disease, heart murmur, leaky valve, or congestive heart disease and is the most common type of heart disease in dogs.

Other common types of heart disease in dogs are cardiomyopathy, pericardial disease, bacterial infections, and arrhythmias. Cardiomyopathy is a deterioration of the heart muscle that leaves the heart unable to pump blood through the dog's body efficiently. Cardiomyopathy is rarely seen in mixed-breed dogs. Over 90 percent of recorded cases have occurred in the boxer, cocker spaniel, Doberman pinscher, golden retriever, German shepherd, Great Dane, Irish wolfhound, and Saint Bernard.

Pericardial disease is an accumulation of fluid between the heart and the pericardial sac, which surrounds the heart. Pericardial disease is usually caused by an infection or cancer of the sac or the outer surface of the heart. The most common sources of bacterial infections in dogs are diseased teeth or gums. If your dog has rotting teeth and gums, it is only a matter of time before the infection in her mouth will spread throughout her body, infecting her organs, including the heart. Raw marrow bones once or twice a week are an inexpensive way to keep your dog's gums and teeth healthy and clean.

An arrhythmia is an irregular heartbeat, usually seen as an unusually fast or slow heartbeat. A heart beating too fast or too slow can result in severe weakness and collapse. You can check your dog's heartbeat by lightly pressing your fingers over your dog's heart, which is located in her chest just below her front legs. The heartbeat can also be felt on the femoral artery, which is inside the back leg at the very top where it meets the body. Your dog's heart rate can vary tremendously, depending on her size, age, and activity level. A large dog that is sleeping will have a heart rate of about 30 beats per minute, while a small, excited dog's heart rate can climb to over 200 beats per minute. Heart rate at a normal activity level can be anywhere from 60 to 140 beats per minute.

Heart disease can either be congenital or acquired. Congenital heart disease occurs when a puppy is born with a defect in the heart that may or may not be hereditary and most commonly occurs in purebred dogs. If caught early, many types of congenital heart disease can be corrected with surgery.

Acquired heart disease develops over time and can be caused by a slow degeneration of the heart, an infection invading the heart, a weak immune system, or stress. With proper nutrition and exercise, acquired heart disease can be prevented or the onset delayed.

Most heart problems, acquired or congenital, involve an erratic flow of blood, which can be detected by an experienced person simply listening to your dog's heart with a stethoscope. As the heart disease progresses and the heart functions less efficiently, there will be a buildup of fluid in the lungs, and abdominal cavity, beneath the skin, and in the space between the lungs and the chest wall. The severity of the buildup of fluids is an indication of how much the heart disease has progressed. Symptoms of heart disease, such as coughing, shallow, rapid breathing, intolerance to exercise, and fainting, are primarily caused by the fluid buildup. Early detection is the key to the prevention of serious heart problems.

> "Symptoms of heart disease, such as coughing, shallow, rapid breathing, intolerance to exercise, and fainting, are primarily caused by the fluid buildup. Early detection is the key to the prevention of serious heart problems."

Breeds prone to congenital heart disease are the beagle, Border terrier, Chihuahua, English bulldog, Great Dane, keeshond, miniature poodle, Newfoundland, Samoyed, toy poodle, and wirehaired fox terrier. If you adopt a puppy of any of these breeds, have your veterinarian listen to her heart carefully so you can catch any problems early.

Breeds prone to acquired heart disease are the American cocker spaniel, beagle, boxer, cavalier King Charles spaniel, Chihuahua, Doberman pinscher, German shepherd, Great Dane, Irish wolfhound, miniature schnauzer, Newfoundland, rottweiler, Saint Bernard, Samoyed, standard schnauzer, smooth fox terrier, Sussex spaniel, and wirehaired fox terrier.

If heart disease is diagnosed early it can be treated, with adjustments in your dog's exercise routine, a low-salt, home-cooked diet, and some heart-healthy supplements. If your dog has advanced heart disease, the most successful treatment involves a combination of conventional and complementary medicine. It is best to do as much as you can naturally before you give drugs to an already sick dog.

A cocker spaniel named Beau is a perfect example of the dramatic effect natural supplements can have on your dog's health.

Beau was in heart failure when he went to a conventional veterinarian. His lungs and abdomen were full of fluid and he could not tolerate the slightest exertion. The doctor put him on the drugs digitalis, vasotex, and lasix, which made Beau feel a little better, but he still could not go up or down the stairs or romp with his friends. The owner brought Beau to Dr. Beverly Cappel-King, and she prescribed the natural supplements CoQ10, vitamin E, dimethylglycine (DMG), L-carnitine, and taurine. She also gave the owners instructions for making low-salt, home-cooked meals. Beau had a miraculous recovery and is now running up and down the stairs and playing and running with his friends.

It is important to closely monitor a dog with heart disease and work closely with your veterinarian. If the disease has not progressed too far, you can usually treat your dog with natural supplements alone with great success, which is preferable to expensive drugs that always have negative side effects.

If your dog is on a diuretic drug such as lasix to control fluid buildup, she will need extra minerals to replace those flushed out by the diuretics. You can add a liquid mineral supplement from your health food store, or find one at your pet store that she can chew, or look in the Resources section in the back of the book.

To maintain a healthy heart, your dog needs the same things you do: a slim, trim body, daily exercise, clean air and water, good nutrition, a toxin-free environment, and a daily vitamin-mineral supplement. If you follow my nutritional guidelines for food and a multivitamin-mineral supplement in Part 1, Creating Optimum Nutrition for Your Dog, then you are most of the way toward providing your dog with a good foundation for a healthy heart.

If your dog is chronically stressed either emotionally or physically or exposed to environmental toxins, follow my recommendations for nutritional support for the immune system (Chapter 6, The Importance of a Strong Immune System). As your dog ages, follow my recommendations for geriatric dogs (Chapter 5, Special Nutritional Needs), increasing her multivitamin-mineral supplement and adjusting her exercise regimen. If your dog has heart disease, develops heart disease, or is at high risk for heart disease, the following are some nutrients that are essential to the proper functioning of the heart.

For more information on vitamins, see Chapter 3, Vitamins for Your Dog and for more information on minerals, see Chapter 4, Minerals for Your Dog.

VITAMIN C

Vitamin C is an antioxidant that keeps the blood clean and the arteries clear and reduces blood pressure. If your dog has heart disease, be sure the vitamin C is sodium-free and check to see if your dog can tolerate additional vitamin C with the "bowel tolerance" test. If your dog is not already receiving the following recommended daily dose, start with these, and if her stools remain normal, gradually increase the dose. If she develops diarrhea or gas, the dose is too high. Return to the last dose that did not cause gas or diarrhea and use that as your daily dose of vitamin C for your dog.

Approximate daily dosages are: small dogs 500 mg to 1,000 mg, medium and large dogs 1,000 mg to 2,000 mg, and giant dogs 2,000 mg to 4,000 mg.

VITAMIN E

Dr. Wendell Belfield, author of *How to Have a Healthier Dog,* believes that vitamin E is the key to a healthy heart. Dr. Belfield has found that many symptoms of heart disease, such as coughing and intolerance to exercise, greatly improved with vitamin E supplementation. If your dog has heart disease, it is important that you give her vitamin E every day. Dr. Belfield has also found that dogs whose owners skipped a few days of their vitamin E supplements had the symptoms of heart disease return very quickly. I have found that the easiest way to remember my dog's supplements is to fit them into my daily routine. He gets his supplements right after each meal.

Vitamin E is also great for the prevention of heart disease. Because of the high incidence of heart disease in dogs, I recommend all dogs receive vitamin E supplements every day in their multivitamin-mineral. If you need to give more, vitamin E is available in liquid or powder form. Recommended daily doses for all dogs are: small dogs 100 IU, medium and large dogs 200 IU, and giant dogs 400 IU.

B-COMPLEX VITAMINS

Low levels of the B vitamins B_{12}, B_6, and folic acid will result in dangerously high levels of homocysteine in your dog's blood. Homocysteine is an amino acid that is a waste product of methionine, another amino acid that is important in maintaining your dog's metabolism. High levels of homocysteine will damage your dog's blood vessels, causing her heart to have to work much harder to pump blood throughout her body. As with all things, animate and inanimate, if the heart is forced to continuously work beyond its normal capacity it is going to wear out sooner. The B-complex vitamins work intricately together and are all essential for your dog's health, so I recommend that you supplement with a B-complex rather than individual B vitamins.

Check to be sure your daily multivitamin-mineral supplement gives your dog the dosages recommended in Chapter 3, Vitamins for Your Dog.

MAGNESIUM

Vitamin E is at the top of the list for heart-healthy vitamins, and magnesium is at the top of the list for heart-healthy minerals. Magnesium is involved in almost every process within your dog's body, including the absorption of nutrients, the maintenance of blood vessels, and normal heart rhythm and valve function. Proper nutrition is useless if your dog cannot properly absorb the nutrients from her food. Without strong, clean blood vessels your dog's heart will not be able to efficiently pump blood throughout her body. A magnesium deficiency can also be the cause of arrhythmias (irregular heartbeat). Magnesium, like vitamin C, can cause diarrhea if it is not in a chelated form, meaning bound to another substance.

> "I have found that the easiest way to remember my dog's supplements is to fit them into my daily routine. He gets his supplements right after each meal."

Magnesium needs calcium to be properly absorbed, so buy magnesium in combination with calcium in the chelated forms of magnesium glycinate, magnesium citrate, or magnesium gluconate.

Be sure your dog's multivitamin-mineral supplement includes magnesium at the following daily doses: small and medium dogs 50 mg, and large and giant dogs 100 mg. If she has heart disease, try an additional supplement in the same dosage.

COENZYME Q10 (CoQ10)

Coenzyme Q10 is a safe, nontoxic nutrient that is vital to life. Without CoQ10, your dog's cells would not work properly. CoQ10 strengthens the heart and the immune system and lowers blood pressure. Stress and illness deplete your dog's body of CoQ10, and as she ages she will produce less CoQ10. The highest concentrations are in the heart and the liver, which means that if those organs are diseased they will more readily deplete your dog's body of CoQ10. CoQ10 comes as a powder in a capsule or in a gel capsule. I recommend the gel capsules, which are more potent. If your dog has heart disease or is prone to heart disease, give her daily dosages of: small and medium dogs 10 mg, and large and giant dogs 30 mg.

The best nutritional sources for CoQ10 are beef heart and liver.

GARLIC

Garlic helps keep your dog's blood and blood vessels clean, and it helps reduce blockages that may already exist.

Garlic has also been proved to lower blood pressure. If you walk into a doctor's office, the first thing the nurses do is take your blood pressure, but nobody takes a dog's blood pressure because there's no quick, easy way to do it. I am sure it is an important risk factor for dogs just as it is with people.

Garlic is heart healthy and will also help your dog eliminate any parasites, both internally and externally. One half to two cloves a day, depending on the size of your dog, will drive away fleas and kill internal worms (it does not kill heartworm).

If you give your dog fresh garlic cloves, which I recommend, mix them in with her meal. Fresh garlic can be irritating to an empty stomach. The other forms of garlic, such as powder, flakes, or the aged garlic found in the health food store in capsules, are all beneficial too, but fresh, raw garlic has the most benefit.

Cancer

Standing in the veterinarian's office with a sick dog and hearing the word "cancer" generates more fear in dog owners than any other diagnosis. We tend to remember the people we knew who died of cancer rather than the many survivors. Cancer does not have to be a death sentence if caught early. If you do not want to go the conventional route with chemotherapy and radiation (they have not been proved to cure cancer in dogs), holistic veterinarians use natural remedies to bring your dog's body back into balance and give it the strength to fight the cancer.

> "Cancer does not have to be a death sentence if caught early."

A golden retriever named Butter is one of the many dogs that holistic veterinarian Dr. Beverly Cappel-King has successfully treated for cancer.

Butter had bone cancer of the upper jaw. It had invaded the palate and the jaw by the left upper canine tooth so severely that the tooth had been moved out of place. The cancerous mass was bigger than a quarter and caused severe swelling, so that Butter could not chew on that side and his lip did not close properly. Dr. King put Butter on shark cartilage, a proanthocyanidin bioflavonoid (such as grapeseed extract or pycnogenol), the herbal formula Essiac, vitamins, homeopathic remedies, and a special diet of homemade food. In six months, Butter went into remission, and over a year later Butter's tumor is gone and she is a healthy, happy dog. Butter's owner reports that the process of caring for Butter and making her meals created an even stronger bond between them. They are inseparable, and both of them have found a whole new love for life.

Unfortunately, not every dog who gets cancer has the benefit of Dr. Cappel-King's treatment. One in four dogs develops cancer, and approximately 50 percent of dogs over ten years old die from cancer. The most common locations for cancer in dogs are the skin, mouth, bones, mammary glands, lymph nodes, and other organs involved in the formation of blood. The most common types of cancerous tumors in dogs are adenocarcinomas (cancer of the glandular tissue), lymphomas (cancer of lymphocytes, which are critical to the immune system), and osteosarcomas (bone cancer).

> "A dog with a healthy immune system is the least likely to get cancer, and boosting the function of the immune system is the best way to control cancer."

Some of the symptoms of cancer are an abnormal growth or lump, a sore that does not heal, lack of appetite or energy, difficulty eating, swallowing, urinating, or defecating, and stiffness or lameness. These are all symptoms that tend to be ignored for a few days or a few months by owners because "otherwise the dog seems fine." It is important to bring your dog to the veterinarian if you see any changes in health or appearance, especially with older dogs.

Breeds prone to one or two types of cancer are the beagle, boxer, briard, bull terrier, Chinese crested, collie, Dalmatian, Doberman pinscher, German shepherd, German shorthaired pointer, golden retriever, Great Dane, greyhound, keeshond, Labrador retriever, Mexican hairless, miniature poodle, pug, Saint Bernard, Samoyed, standard poodle, standard schnauzer, toy poodle, vizsla, weimaraner, and whippet.

Breeds prone to numerous types of cancer are the American cocker spaniel, Border terrier, Boston terrier, English bulldog, English springer spaniel, and Scottish terrier.

Exactly how cancer gets out of control is still debatable, but we know a lot about its causes. In very simple terms, cancer occurs when damaged cells multiply out of control and destroy healthy cells in the process. Cancer occurs most often in older dogs and is caused by a combination of factors, such as poor diet, exposure to toxins, and stress, that, over time, leads to an overload of damaged cells and a deterioration of the immune system. A dog with a healthy immune system is the least likely to get cancer, and boosting the function of the immune system is the best way to control cancer.

Chemotherapy and radiation may kill a cancer in the short term, but in the long term the dog's body is severely weakened and her chances of survival are diminished.

The best prevention program for cancer is to give your dog healthy, natural food, a daily vitamin-mineral supplement, clean water, plenty of exercise, a pesticide-free environment, and of course plenty of love. If you have a breed that has a higher risk of cancer, be sure she is getting the following cancer-fighting vitamins and minerals daily. If she is on my daily multivitamin-mineral program, she is getting what she needs of these nutrients.

VITAMIN C

The pioneer of vitamin C studies and two-time Nobel Prize winner Linus Pauling was adamant in his conviction that vitamin C plays an important role in both the prevention and treatment of cancer. Almost thirty years ago, scientists at the National Cancer Institute found that vitamin C is lethal to cancer cells.

Vitamin C boosts the immune system, is a powerful antioxidant, and has been proven to reduce the risk of cancer and improve the health of cancer patients. I recommend that all dogs have a vitamin C supplement every day.

Again, the daily dosage for an adult dog is: small dogs 500 mg to 1,000 mg, medium and large dogs 1,000 mg to 2,000 mg, and giant dogs 2,000 mg to 4,000 mg.

VITAMIN E

Vitamin E is a powerful antioxidant that protects cells from damage, boosts the immune system, and has proven anticancer effects. I recommend that all dogs get a vitamin E supplement every day. The daily dose for small dogs is 100 IU, medium and large dogs 200 IU, and giant dogs 400 IU.

BETA-CAROTENE

Beta-carotene is a powerful antioxidant that boosts the immune system and will reduce your dog's risk of cancer. Beta-carotene also has the unique ability to convert to vitamin A, another anticancer nutrient, as the body needs it.

If your dog is prone to cancer, be sure to give her the yellow, orange, and dark green vegetables and fruits, which are rich in beta-carotene.

A beta-carotene supplement should always be given with a vitamin E supplement, as they work together. The recommended dosage for all dogs is 15 IU.

SELENIUM

Selenium is a trace mineral that acts as an antioxidant. It stimulates the immune system and has strong anticancer effects. Population studies have shown that people living in areas where the soil is depleted of selenium have higher rates of cancer, while populations living in selenium-rich soil have lower rates of cancer.

Check your dog's multivitamin-mineral supplement to be sure she is getting enough selenium: small dogs 25 mcg, and all dogs over 20 pounds 50 mcg.

Liver Disease

The liver is your dog's largest organ. It is located between the diaphragm and the stomach and does at least 500 different jobs involving metabolism, digestion, detoxification of drugs and toxins, temperature and circulation regulation, removal of waste from the blood, and the storage and dispersal of nutrients.

Liver disease, like kidney disease, does not tend to show obvious symptoms until the disease has progressed to a serious condition. Symptoms of liver disease are jaundice, which is seen as a yellowing of the whites of the eyes and tea-colored urine, accumulation of fluid in the abdomen, a loss of appetite, weight loss, and excessive thirst.

The most common forms of liver disease in dogs are chronic hepatitis, a viral infection that causes inflammation of the liver, and hepatic necrosis, a deterioration of liver cells or tissues. Liver disease can be a symptom of another illness such as a virus, cancer, an infection, or an intestinal disorder. It can also be caused by an immune-mediated response, drugs, toxins, nutritional deficiencies, or nutrition absorption problems. In most cases, liver disease is the result of the cumulative effects of being exposed to a combination of liver stressors over a long period of time.

Breeds prone to liver disease are the Australian cattle dog, Bedlington terrier, Bernese mountain dog, boxer, cairn terrier, Chihuahua, Doberman pinscher, golden retriever, Irish wolfhound, keeshond, Labrador retriever, Maltese, miniature schnauzer, Pomeranian, pug, Saint Bernard, Samoyed, Shetland sheepdog, shih tzu, toy poodle, West Highland white terrier, and Yorkshire terrier.

If treated aggressively and naturally with the help of a good holistic vet, even a seriously diseased liver can be restored to health.

A Doberman named Sam and his owner are proof. Sam has a condition that is common in the Doberman pinscher, West Highland white terrier, and Bedlington terrier, in which the body is unable to metabolize copper. As a result, the copper builds up in the liver, poisoning it and causing it to fail. Sam was brought to Dr. Beverly Cappel-King in liver failure and was immediately put on oral doses of zinc to remove the copper from the liver. Sam was also taken off food for a couple of days and put on an intravenous solution that contained glucose and an electrolyte solution. Sam's therapy also included the herb milk thistle (silymarin), B-vitamins, a small amount of vitamin E, and some glandular supplements containing adrenal and liver extracts, along with a copper-free vitamin-mineral

> "If treated aggressively and naturally with the help of a good holistic vet, even a seriously diseased liver can be restored to health."

supplement. Over the next couple of weeks, Sam's liver returned to its normal size; he put on some weight, and the luster in his coat returned. A few months later, he took a turn for the worse and Dr. King found that there was a tumor in Sam's liver. She put him back on the regimen that had restored his liver a few months earlier, along with high doses of antioxidants. The antioxidants help flush out the liver, they protect the tiny blood vessels called capillaries from breaking down and bleeding, and they improve circulation. Dr. King also put Sam on a combination of herbs that have proven successful in her practice in treating cancer. The tumor shrank over a period of four months and Sam became a healthy, happy dog. He lived for four more years until he died at the ripe old age of fourteen.

Keeping your dog in optimal health will keep her liver in optimal health. If your dog has to take medications over a long period of time, has had a high exposure to toxins, or has spent her life on a low-quality diet, there is no doubt that her liver has suffered.

Milk thistle and alpha lipoic acid are both nutrients that can help restore the health of the liver.

Milk thistle is a member of the daisy family and contains a flavonoid called silymarin, which enhances liver function, stimulates production of new cells, and has antioxidant properties that protect the liver cells from damage. Daily doses for milk thistle are: small dogs one-half capsule, medium and large dogs one capsule, and giant dogs two capsules. For maintenance of a healthy liver, I recommend milk thistle (silymarin) for a month each year for all dogs over six years old.

Alpha lipoic acid is an antioxidant that is a potent promoter of glutathione. Glutathione (GSH), a major antioxidant and detoxifying agent, is found in highest concentrations in the liver, which is the primary organ in charge of detoxifying the body. If your dog has been or is on any kind of medications for an extended period of time, I recommend supplementing with alpha lipoic acid at the following daily doses: small dogs 50 mg, medium dogs 100 mg, large dogs 200 mg, and giant dogs 300 mg.

Gastric Bloat and Torsion

Gastric bloat and torsion, also know as gastric dilation/volvulus (GDV), is a life-threatening condition that is primarily found in large and giant deep-chested dogs. Gastric bloat is the result of air and gas building up in the dog's stomach, causing the stomach to swell and, in most cases, causing the torsion or twisting of the stomach. The swelling and twisting of the stomach cuts off blood circulation to the stomach and other organs by putting pressure on them. If this happens, your dog will go into shock and all the organs, including the heart, will start to shut down from lack of blood. Another danger with gastric bloat and torsion is that of the stomach rupturing and spilling toxins and bacteria into the bloodstream.

> "If you suspect that your dog may be experiencing gastric bloat and/or torsion, know that it is an emergency situation and needs to be treated immediately."

The one common denominator in the many theories about what causes gastric bloat and torsion is that it is linked to diet. A team of researchers from Purdue University found that dogs who eat smaller meals, dogs who are slow eaters, and calm, relaxed dogs have less risk for bloat than stressed dogs who quickly gulp a big meal. The researchers found that, contrary to popular belief, vigorous exercise is not a precipitating factor but stress is. They also found that dogs described as happy are less likely to experience bloat than dogs that are described as fearful.

Breeds that are more prone to gastric bloat and torsion are the basset hound, Bernese mountain dog, bloodhound (leading cause of death), borzoi, Bouvier des Flandres, boxer, briard, bullmastiff, Chinese shar-pei, chow chow, Doberman pinscher, English setter, German shepherd, Great Dane, Gordon setter, greyhound, Irish setter, Labrador retriever, mastiff, Saint Bernard, Scottish deerhound, standard poodle, and weimaraner.

Dogs suffering from gastric bloat and torsion will suddenly be panting, whining, and restless. Their breathing will become labored and they will start arching their back. They may also drool and try to vomit, and the stomach will become visibly distended and firm. If you suspect that your dog may be experiencing gastric bloat and/or torsion, know that it is an emergency situation and needs to be treated immediately.

Here are some guidelines that may reduce the risk of gastric bloat and torsion:

- Feed a high-quality diet.
- Feed several smaller meals rather than one large one.
- Do not feed an excited or stressed dog.
- Do not feed one hour before or after vigorous exercise. (Although the Purdue researchers found this not to be a cause, many breeders do feel it is an important factor.)
- Do not let an excited or stressed dog drink large quantities of water.

PART SIX

Natural Remedies for Common Ailments

CHAPTER TEN

Natural Healing

IT IS INEVITABLE that your dog will have minor ailments and accidents. Here you will learn what to keep in your medicine cabinet for those occasions. You will also learn what to do in case of trauma and shock and how to prevent or delay the progression of some of the more common ailments that all dogs, including mixed breeds, are highly prone to.

Accidents

For minor accidents, such as cuts, scrapes, and burns, clean the wound thoroughly and use a zinc ointment on the wound for faster healing. Zinc is important for healthy skin and has antibacterial properties. Try to keep your dog from licking the wound long enough for the zinc to be absorbed into the skin. If you cannot keep your dog from licking, wrap the wound and change it twice a day. I have found that the self-sticking bandaging gauze works well and does not tear the hair out when you take it off. If that fails, your veterinarian will have a neck brace or cone that will prevent your dog from getting to the wound. If you watch your dog for a while after the wound is bandaged and gently tell her "no" when she starts to lick or chew, that is often enough. Unless she is very uncomfortable she will probably leave it alone once she knows what you want from her.

For more serious wounds and burns, go to the vet. She will be able to clean and bandage the wound in a way that will prevent infection.

If your dog is badly injured and you can keep her from going into shock, it will speed her recovery. A dog that is in a stupor with pale gums and tongue, slow pulse, and glazed eyes is in shock. Make her as comfortable as possible, cover her with a blanket (progressed shock will cause your dog to become cold), talk very calmly to her, tell her what is going on, and get her to a veterinarian as soon as possible. If your dog has a serious accident, immediately give her a homeopathic remedy for trauma and shock or Rescue Remedy (see Chapter 8, Understanding Homeopathy, for details). I keep Rescue Remedy in my house and car for any type of traumatic event and give it to people and animals. The dosage instructions on the label apply to people and pets. If your dog has been in a serious accident, it will also be very traumatic for you, so remember to take some of the Rescue Remedy yourself.

> "If your dog is in pain, try to avoid aspirin, Tylenol, and anti-inflammatory drugs such as ibuprofen."

For serious injuries that will take time to heal, support your dog's body by increasing her multivitamin-mineral supplement by one-third and doubling her dose of vitamin E. Increase her vitamin C to "bowel tolerance" and when you change the bandage reapply the zinc ointment on the wound.

If your dog is in pain, try to avoid aspirin, Tylenol, and anti-inflammatory drugs such as ibuprofen. Aspirin and ibuprofen-type drugs very often cause stomach upset in dogs, and aspirin has blood-thinning properties, which can prevent blood from clotting. Tylenol is sometimes used to reduce a high fever but has not been shown to be highly effective for relieving pain in dogs. For external pain, calendula is a homeopathic ointment that works as an antiseptic and relieves pain and will promote healing. Use calendula instead of the zinc ointment if your dog is in pain. For internal pain, use the herb kava.

If your dog is stressed, use liquid valerian, kava, or a homeopathic remedy to calm her. Valerian and kava are herbal remedies that have a calming effect. Kava is also an effective analgesic, or painkiller. You can find both at your local health food store. They come in liquid form as tinctures or in capsules. In the liquid form they can be put directly on the tongue; if you get them in the capsule form, pull the capsule apart, empty out enough to create the proper dose, and wrap it in food or put it down her throat as you would any other pill. Most tinctures contain alcohol and some dogs detest the taste of alcohol, so a capsule in food would be the easiest and least stressful approach for those dogs. With herbs, use one-fourth the recommended dose for small dogs, and for medium, large, and giant dogs use half the recommended dose for people. The dosages for homeopathic remedies are the same for people and pets.

If your dog is put on antibiotics, be sure to give her a heaping spoonful of plain yogurt that contains active cultures (lowfat for overweight dogs) with each meal or buy a probiotics supplement in the refrigerated section of your health food store.

For more information on homeopathic remedies and Rescue Remedy, see Chapter 8, Understanding Homeopathy; on vitamins (vitamins C and E), see Chapter 3, Vitamins for Your Dog; on minerals (zinc), see Chapter 4, Minerals for Your Dog; and on recovering from illness and probiotics, see Chapter 5, Special Nutritional Needs.

Allergies

The most common symptom of allergies is itchy, red skin. More severe allergies can cause dogs, like people, to start sneezing and to have red, runny eyes, a runny nose, and postnasal drip. Symptoms of postnasal drip are wheezing and labored breathing.

Breeds prone to allergies are the American cocker spaniel, beagle, bichon frise, Boston terrier, boxer, Chinese shar-pei, Dalmatian, English springer spaniel, German shepherd, golden retriever, Labrador retriever, Lhasa apso, Ibizan hound, Irish setter, miniature poodle, toy poodle, miniature schnauzer, petit basset griffon vendeen, pharaoh hound, pointer, pug, Scottish terrier, Sealyham terrier, smooth fox terrier, soft-coated wheaten terrier, standard poodle, West Highland white terrier, and wirehaired fox terrier. West Highland white terriers seem to have a very high incidence of allergies. When I spoke to Dr. Beverly Cappel-King about dog allergies, she was treating at least fifty Westies for allergies.

One of the most important steps in ridding your dog of allergies is to get all the chemicals out of her life. Eliminate all lawn pesticides, chemical flea spays, collars, and shampoos and any chemical cleaners that you use.

High-quality chemical-free foods, preferably in the form of home-cooked meals, will alleviate allergies in many dogs. A lot of dogs are allergic to beef and dairy products, so experiment with different types of meat, such as fish, liver, lamb, pork, venison, or rabbit, and, if you need to, eliminate all dairy products.

Vitamin C and quercetin have antihistamine properties and are excellent for allergies.

Daily doses for quercetin are: small dogs, 100 mg to 150 mg three times daily; medium and large dogs, 150 mg to 300 mg three times daily; and giant dogs 500 mg two to three times daily.

For skin allergies, you can try methylsulfonyl methane (MSM), an organic sulfur supplement that comes in tablet or powder form. Recommended daily doses are: small dogs, 250 mg; medium dogs, 500 mg; and large and giant dogs, 1,000 mg.

If your dog has flea allergies (bites herself raw from one flea bite) and they are seasonal, be sure to start your dog on flea control a month before flea season starts.

Try to avoid using steroids for any length of time. They are an immune suppressant and cause weight gain, brittle bones, and increased urination.

For more information on allergies, see Chapter 6, The Importance of a Strong Immune System; on high-quality commercial dog food and home-cooked meals, see Chapter 1, Feeding Your Dog for Naturally Great Health; on vitamin C, see Chapter 3, Vitamins for Your Dog; on flea allergies and natural flea control products, see Chapter 7, Natural Flea Control for Your Dog, and the Resources section in the back of the book.

Arthritis

The most common form of arthritis in dogs is commonly referred to as "old age" arthritis. Old age arthritis is a degenerative disease that causes inflammation and pain in the joints. It is common in all breeds of dogs, including mixed breeds. Large and giant dogs are more prone to arthritis than medium and small dogs. The added weight of larger dogs causes more wear and tear to their joints.

> "Large and giant dogs are more prone to arthritis than medium and small dogs. The added weight of larger dogs causes more wear and tear to their joints."

If your dog gets up very slowly or seems stiff or lame when she walks, she may have arthritis. Those can also be symptoms of other illnesses, such as Lyme disease or hip dysplasia, so have your dog diagnosed by a veterinarian before you treat her.

Vitamin C plays a major role in healthy tissue and will help to protect cartilage from further deterioration. If your dog has arthritis and her daily multivitamin-mineral supplement does not meet my recommended daily doses for vitamin C, buy a powder supplement and increase her dose to "bowel tolerance." Once or twice a year gradually increase her vitamin C to "bowel tolerance," which will tell you if her need for vitamin C has increased. If she is sick or stressed, she will need more vitamin C.

Alfalfa and yucca are great anti-inflammatory nutrients. Both are available for pets (see the Resources section). Read the label for dosage instructions.

If your dog is suffering from arthritis, you can double the recommended daily dose of vitamin E and selenium, which will help prevent loss of muscle tone.

Glucosamine is great for building cartilage and connective tissue back on the joints. Start with 500 mg per day for all sizes of dogs and, if needed, increase to 500 mg twice a day. Glucosamine can take a few months to have its effect, so be patient.

It is also important to give high-quality chemical-free foods. Home-cooked meals are preferable, as long as you avoid vegetables from the nightshade family (tomato, potato, peppers, eggplant), as these vegetables can sometimes aggravate arthritis.

For more information on vitamins (vitamins C and E), see Chapter 3, Vitamins for Your Dog; and on minerals (selenium), see Chapter 4, Minerals for Your Dog.

> "It is also important not to let your dog ride in the car with her head out the window, because the dust and debris will be driven into her eyes at a high rate of speed, causing inflammation and damage to the eyeball."

Cataracts

All breeds of dogs, including mixed breeds, are highly prone to cataracts. Cataract is a degenerative disease in elderly dogs that causes the lens of the eye to become cloudy, causing a partial or total loss of vision. If you look into the eyes of a dog with cataracts, you will see an almost white film in the eye.

A lifestyle free of toxins, a diet of fresh, chemical-free foods, and a multivitamin-mineral supplement containing plenty of antioxidants will prevent or delay the onset of cataracts. I recommend daily supplementation of the antioxidant vitamins E and C for all dogs, to help prevent cataracts.

Orange and yellow vegetables, such as cantaloupe, carrots (you can shred them), yams, and squash, contain high levels of carotenoids, nutrients that protect the eyes from ultraviolet light and keep blood vessels strong.

Alpha lipoic acid is an antioxidant that has been successfully used to prevent cataracts in laboratory animals, and it improves blood flow through the tiny blood vessels in the eyes. If your dog has been diagnosed with cataracts, use alpha lipoic acid in the following daily dosages: small dogs 50 mg, medium dogs 100 mg, large dogs 200 mg, and giant dogs 300 mg.

It is also important not to let your dog ride in the car with her head out the window, because the dust and debris will be driven into her eyes at a high rate of speed, causing inflammation and damage to the eyeball.

For more information on vitamins, see Chapter 3, Vitamins for Your Dog; and on minerals, see Chapter 4, Minerals for Your Dog.

Constipation

A healthy, well-exercised dog has at least two bowel movements a day. Walking your dog at about the same time in the morning and the evening will easily produce that.

> "A healthy, well-exercised dog has at least two bowel movements a day."

If your dog goes twenty-four hours without a bowel movement, then she is constipated and needs some help. Psyllium seed husk is a natural, gentle form of fiber and bulk that is easy to add to your dog's food because it has no taste. Buy it in pure form at your natural health food store and feed one teaspoon for every twenty pounds of your dog's weight. For example, a 10-pound dog would get ½ teaspoon, a 40-pound dog would get 2 teaspoons, and a 60-pound dog would get 3 teaspoons per day. Add at least 2 cups of water for every teaspoon of psyllium. Too much psyllium, especially without adequate liquid, can cause a serious bowel impaction, so please do not overdose your dog on fiber!

If the psyllium is not helpful and the constipation continues for more than a couple of days, it is time to seek veterinary help.

Diarrhea

If your dog has continuous diarrhea for longer than twenty-four hours, it is important to bring her to your veterinarian to determine the underlying cause.

Occasional short bouts of diarrhea can be treated with a diet that is easy to digest and has plenty of liquids. Use organic liver, tofu, or cottage cheese for protein, add well-cooked brown rice, minced or shredded vegetables, and plenty of homemade chicken or beef broth.

If your dog has chronic or frequently recurring bouts of diarrhea and your veterinarian cannot find a medical reason, it is most likely a nutritional problem. Very slowly switch her to home-cooked meals, using well-cooked grains and raw meat and vegetables. The home-cooked meals will be easier to digest, because the raw food contains live enzymes that help with digestion.

If your dog is on antibiotics, give her probiotics (available from the refrigerated section in your health food store) or a heaping spoonful of plain yogurt with active cultures (lowfat for overweight dogs) with each meal. The active cultures in the yogurt are probiotics and will keep the good intestinal bacteria alive and prevent diarrhea. Give probiotics while your dog is on the antibiotics and continue them for one week after your dog is off the antibiotics.

For more information on home-cooked meals and fresh foods, see Chapter 1, Feeding Your Dog for Naturally Great Health; and on probiotics, see Chapter 5, Special Nutritional Needs.

Digestive Problems

Digestive problems can be caused by a large number of factors, such as diabetes, a foreign object in the intestines, allergies, and kidney or liver disease. Digestive problems can also be caused by a lack of digestive enzymes, malabsorption, food allergies, nutrient deficiencies, or nutrient imbalances. The symptoms of digestive problems are as varied as the causes. They range from diarrhea, constipation, lack of appetite, or an overabundant appetite to all types of skin and skeletal problems. If your dog is older and has digestive problems, she probably just needs food that is easier to digest. If your dog has chronic digestive problems, see your veterinarian to rule out any life-threatening conditions.

Once again, feeding home-cooked meals, including raw meat and raw vegetables along with a multivitamin-mineral supplement, will solve the vast majority of digestive problems. For severe digestive problems, stick to foods that are easily digested.

If after a couple of months on home-cooked meals your dog is still experiencing digestive problems, add some digestive enzymes to her food. You can find digestive enzymes at a health food store. Some pet stores may have digestive enzymes for dogs; alternatively, see the Resources section in the back of the book. If you buy digestive enzymes for people, use one-fourth the recommended dose for small and medium dogs and half the recommended dose for large and giant dogs.

For more information on home-cooked meals and fresh foods, see Chapter 1, Feeding Your Dog for Naturally Great Health; on vitamins, see Chapter 3, Vitamins for Your Dog; and on minerals, see Chapter 4, Minerals for Your Dog.

> "Once again, feeding home-cooked meals, including raw meat and raw vegetables along with a multi-vitamin-mineral supplement, will solve the vast majority of digestive problems."

Hip Dysplasia

Hip dysplasia is an abnormal development of the hip, which causes the hip joint to rub on the socket, causing pain, inflammation, and a deterioration of the bones. In severe cases, the hip will slip in and out of place. Symptoms such as abnormal gait, lameness, and difficulty getting up will manifest by the time the dog is two years old.

Breeds prone to hip dysplasia are the Afghan hound, Airedale terrier, Akita, Alaskan malamute, American cocker spaniel, American Eskimo, Australian cattle dog, Australian shepherd, bearded collie,

Belgian Malinois, Belgian sheepdog, Bernese mountain dog, bloodhound, Border collie, Bouvier des Flandres, briard, bullmastiff, Canaan
dog, collie, coonhound, Chesapeake Bay retriever, Chinese shar-pei,
chow chow, clumber spaniel, Dalmatian, Dandie Dinmont terrier,
Doberman pinscher, English bulldog, English setter, English springer
spaniel, flat-coated retriever, German shepherd, German shorthaired
pointer, German wirehaired pointer, giant schnauzer, golden retriever,
Gordon setter, Great Dane, Great Pyrenees, harrier, Hungarian puli,
Irish setter, Irish water spaniel, Irish wolfhound, komondor, kuvasz,
Labrador retriever, Maltese, Neapolitan mastiff, Newfoundland, Norwegian elkhound, Old English sheepdog, otterhound, petit basset griffon vendeen, pointer, pug, Rhodesian Ridgeback, rottweiler, Russian
wolfhound, Saint Bernard, Samoyed, Shetland sheepdog, Siberian
husky, shiba inu, standard poodle, Tibetan mastiff, vizsla, weimaraner,
Welsh springer spaniel, and wirehaired pointing griffon.

Vitamin C is important in the prevention of hip dysplasia. For
details, see the section on vitamin C in Chapter 3, Vitamins for
Your Dog.

Once a dog has hip dysplasia, the best you can do is to make her
comfortable and attempt to stop the progression. Regular exercise can
help postpone the degeneration of the hip for years, because the muscles
will support the hip joint.

To care for a dog with hip dysplasia, see the above instructions for
arthritis. Although hip dysplasia and arthritis originate from different
causes, the end results of bone deterioration and loss of cartilage in the
joints are the same. The needs of a dog with hip dysplasia, as with
arthritis, are strong bones, strong muscles to support the bones, and
maintenance of the fluid and cartilage in the joints.

Seizures

Most dogs that get seizures have a magnesium deficiency and/or low
thyroid (hypothyroidism).

Breeds prone to seizures are the American cocker spaniel, Australian cattle dog, basset hound, beagle, Belgian Malinois, Belgian sheepdog, Belgian Tervuren, bichon frise, Border collie, collie, dachshund, English setter, English springer spaniel, German shepherd, golden retriever, greyhound, harrier, Irish setter, Italian greyhound, keeshond, Labrador retriever, miniature poodle, Norfolk terrier, Norwich terrier, Pembroke Welsh corgi, petit basset griffon vendeen, pointer, pug, Saint Bernard, standard Manchester terrier, standard poodle, toy poodle, and vizsla.

Under the supervision of a veterinarian you should be able to significantly cut down on seizure medication by adding magnesium supplements to your dog's diet. Dr. Beverly Cappel-King puts all dogs with seizures on magnesium and consistently sees a decrease in the frequency and intensity of their seizures.

Go to "bowel tolerance" (gradually increase dosage until the dog experiences diarrhea or gas) and then cut back until the diarrhea stops. Start with doses of: small dogs 10 mg, medium dogs 20 mg, large dogs 50 mg, and giant dogs 75 mg.

A simple blood test can tell you if your dog has hypothyroidism (underactive thyroid) or hyperthyroidism (overactive thyroid). Ask your veterinarian for the natural, rather than synthetic, thyroid supplements such as Armour (also called desiccated thyroid or USP thyroid), and be sure your dog is getting her daily dose of selenium. Selenium works with the thyroid hormone, enabling it to work more efficiently.

> "Under the supervision of a veterinarian you should be able to significantly cut down on seizure medication by adding magnesium supplements to your dog's diet."

For more information on magnesium and selenium, see Chapter 4, Minerals for Your Dog.

Skin Problems

Skin problems, such as rashes, bald spots, and constant scratching, are the number one chronic condition in dogs. Dr. Beverly Cappel-King finds that the majority of skin problems are caused by hypothyroidism, or low thyroid. A simple blood test can tell you if your dog has thyroid problems. Ask your veterinarian for the natural, rather than synthetic, thyroid supplements such as Armour (also called desiccated thyroid or USP thyroid), and be sure your dog is getting her daily dose of selenium. Selenium works with the thyroid hormone, enabling it to work more efficiently.

Skin problems are sometimes caused by an inability to absorb certain nutrients. Alaskan malamutes, bull terriers, and Siberian huskies are prone to a genetic condition in which they have a decreased capacity for zinc absorption from the intestines.

The huskies and malamutes will be fine if put on a zinc supplement. Your veterinarian will give you the proper dosages and will adjust the dosages as your dog ages. Bull terriers are prone to a more complicated form of this condition, and they usually do not respond to zinc supplementation.

Doberman pinschers, German shorthaired pointers, German shepherds, Great Danes, and Labrador retrievers are also prone to skin problems from a zinc deficiency. The deficiency can be caused by a zinc-deficient diet, parasites, or oversupplementation of nutrients that interfere with the absorption of zinc, such as iron, copper, and calcium.

Skin problems can also be caused by allergies. In this chapter, see the earlier section on allergies for more information.

If your dog is flea-free and does not have a medical reason for the skin problems such as hypothyroidism, a zinc deficiency, or allergies, then the skin problems are most likely caused by nutritional and/or environmental factors.

Start feeding your dog home-cooked meals, including plenty of fresh, live foods and a multivitamin-mineral supplement every day. Eliminate all the toxins from her life, including all chemicals and pesticides.

Within a few months, depending on the severity of the problems, you will have a vibrant, energetic dog with a beautiful shiny coat.

For more information on vitamins, see Chapter 3, Vitamins for Your Dog; and on minerals, see Chapter 4, Minerals for Your Dog.

Tooth and Gum Disease

Plaque and tartar buildup leads to tooth decay and gum disease. If left untreated, the bacteria can cause kidney and heart valve infections. If your dog has bad breath, there is a good chance she has gum disease.

Keep your dog's teeth clean and gums healthy with marrow bones once or twice a week and raw meat at least once a day. The enzymes in raw meat give your dog's teeth a daily cleaning, while the marrow bone will get the tough spots and keep her jaws strong. If the marrow bones at your butcher or local grocery store are too big for your dog, ask the butcher to cut them. Don't be afraid to give a little dog a fairly big bone.

Vomiting

If on rare occasions your dog vomits some yellow bile, vomits a small object such as a piece of bone or stick, gets carsick, or vomits from stress, you do not need to be overly concerned. Just be sure she has plenty of fresh, clean water close by when it happens.

Vomiting blood or foul-smelling material, projectile vomiting, and continuous vomiting or retching are serious conditions that need to be treated by a veterinarian.

If your dog vomits occasionally, seems lethargic, and has a dull, dry coat, there is an underlying disorder such as diabetes, worms, or a liver or kidney problem that needs to be treated.

If your dog has frequent bouts of vomiting and your veterinarian does not know the cause, it is most likely something in her food and/or environment. Slowly switch your dog to a chemical-free commercial food or home-cooked meals along with a multivitamin-mineral supplement. If there is no improvement in a month, eliminate all dairy products and try different forms of protein, such as lamb, venison, and liver. It is also important to eliminate all chemicals from your dog's life, including flea products, lawn applications, and housecleaning products.

For more information on home-cooked meals, fresh foods, and commercial dog food, see Chapter 1, Feeding Your Dog for Naturally Great Health.

PART SEVEN

The Dog Hit Parade

CHAPTER ELEVEN

Breed-Specific Health Problems

THE PROCESS OF adopting a dog starts with deciding whether you want a mixed-breed dog or a purebred dog. Mixed-breed dogs, also known as mutts, mongrels, and Heinz 57s, are just as the names imply—a mixture of breeds. Mixed-breed dogs have a significantly larger genetic background than purebred dogs, so they are not as prone to health problems as purebred dogs are. Purebred dogs are "man-made" dogs, whose genetic background is limited by the breed and the specific line within the breed that is created by the breeder. Purebreds easily become inbred, which exaggerates both positive traits and weaknesses, such as a predisposition to illness.

Mixed-breed dogs, although generally healthier than purebred dogs, have high incidences of the most common health problems. If you have a mixed-breed dog and can connect her to a specific breed or breeds, such as a German shepherd mix or a Labrador retriever and golden retriever mix, then you can familiarize yourself with the health problems for the breed(s) to which your dog is related.

The breed-specific health problems listed in this chapter range from very rare to very common. They include birth defects and developmental abnormalities, as well as diseases that develop over the years from a combination of genetic predisposition, poor nutrition, and immune-suppressing agents, such as yearly revaccinations and environmental toxins.

The importance of becoming familiar with your dog's potential health problems begins when you start looking for that very special dog to join your family, and it continues into your dog's geriatric years.

If you are interested in a purebred puppy, these lists give you the general health information for each breed so you can ask the breeder specific questions about the health of the puppy's ancestors.

One of the keys to successfully treating an illness is early detection. If you are trying to diagnose an illness, bring the list for your breed(s) to your veterinarian. There may be an uncommon health problem that is specific to your breed that your veterinarian has not considered.

The lists also give you the tools for the most successful treatment, which is prevention. In this book, you will learn how to keep your dog in optimal health through nutrition. I will also tell you which nutrients help prevent many of the more common illnesses dogs are prone to. For example, if your dog is prone to heart disease, you will learn what nutrients you can give your dog throughout her life to keep her heart healthy.

> "The importance of becoming familiar with your dog's potential health problems begins when you start looking for that very special dog to join your family, and it continues into your dog's geriatric years."

Purebred Giant (Over 100 Pounds)

Anatolian Shepherd (Karabash)

Anesthetic Sensitivity   A serious condition in which the dog is very sensitive to anesthesia. In many cases the dog is also sensitive to medications and flea control products that contain pesticides.

Eye Abnormality   The Anatolian shepherd is prone to a rolling in of the eyelid(s).

Gastric Bloat and Torsion   Gastric bloat is a swelling of the stomach from excess gas and is usually followed by gastric torsion, a twisting of the stomach. Gastric torsion will result in death if not treated immediately.

Hip Dysplasia   An abnormal development of the hip joint(s).

Hypothyroidism   A common disease of thyroid hormone deficiency. The thyroid regulates your dog's metabolism. A large number of skin problems in dogs are caused by thyroid disease.

Borzoi (Russian Wolfhound)

Blood-Clotting Disorder   The borzoi is prone to a blood-clotting disorder due to coagulation factor I deficiency.

Calcinosis   Hard lumps of calcium salt deposits in the skin.

Cataract   In elderly dogs the lens of the eye becomes cloudy, causing a partial or total loss of vision.

Gastric Bloat and Torsion   Gastric bloat is a swelling of the stomach from excess gas and is usually followed by gastric torsion, a twisting of the stomach. Gastric torsion will result in death if not treated immediately.

Hip Dysplasia   An abnormal development of the hip joint(s).

Hygroma   A thick-walled, fluid-filled sac, usually found on the elbows.

Progressive Retinal Atrophy (PRA)   A slow deterioration of the retina, leading to blindness.

Teeth Abnormalities   The number, placement, or development of the teeth is not normal.

Thyroid Disease   The borzoi is prone to thyroiditis and hypothyroidism. Thyroiditis is an inflammation of the thyroid, which very often leads to hypothyroidism. Hypothyroidism is a common disease of thyroid hormone deficiency. The thyroid regulates your dog's metabolism. A large number of skin problems in dogs are caused by thyroid disease.

Von Willebrand's Disease   Abnormal blood-clotting defect involving both platelet and coagulation function (factor VIII).

Bullmastiff

Cleft Palate   A birth defect in which the roof of the mouth does not grow properly, leaving a hole from the roof of the mouth into the nose.

Eye Abnormalities   The bullmastiff is prone to abnormally growing eyelashes, a rolling in of the eyelid(s), a protruding of the third eyelid(s), malformed retina(s), and a developmental condition in which the iris, which regulates the amount of light entering the eye, does not form properly.

Gastric Bloat and Torsion   Gastric bloat is a swelling of the stomach from excess gas and is usually followed by gastric torsion, a twisting of the stomach. Gastric torsion will result in death if not treated immediately.

Glaucoma   Pressure on the retina from excess fluid in the eyeball, which causes partial or total loss of vision.

Hip Dysplasia   An abnormal development of the hip joint(s).

Hypothyroidism   A common disease of thyroid hormone deficiency. The thyroid regulates your dog's metabolism. A large number of skin problems in dogs are caused by thyroid disease.

Neck Vertebrae Malformation   An abnormal development of the vertebrae in the neck, causing nerve damage. Some dogs walk with a pronounced flexion of the knee, similar to a high-stepping horse.

Osteochondritis Dissecans　Inflammation of the cartilage in the joints. A form of arthritis.

Osteochondrosis　An abnormal development of joint cartilage. Most commonly found in the shoulder, knee, and elbow.

Progressive Retinal Atrophy (PRA)　A slow deterioration of the retina, leading to blindness.

Teeth Abnormalities　The number, placement, or development of the teeth is not normal.

Vaginal Hyperplasia　An increase in the number of cells in the tissues of the vagina, possibly indicating a precancerous condition.

Great Dane

Acne　Pimples and blackheads on the chin and lips of young dogs.

Ataxia　A progressive loss of coordination.

Bone Disease　The Great Dane is prone to diseases of the bone caused by a metabolic dysfunction.

Calcinosis　Hard lumps of calcium salt deposits in the skin.

Cancer　The Great Dane is prone to bone cancer.

Cataract　In elderly dogs the lens of the eye becomes cloudy, causing a partial or total loss of vision.

Cerebellar Hypoplasia　Underdevelopment of a part of the brain called the cerebellum. The cerebellum gives your dog coordination, posture, and balance.

Cervical Spondylosis　A degenerative disease of the neck vertebrae.

Deafness　A partial or total loss of hearing.

Degenerative Myelopathy　A progressive deterioration of the spinal cord.

Demodectic Mange   A skin disease in which canine mites are living in the skin, causing itching, loss of hair, and skin infections. Usually found on the face and front legs.

Dermoid Cyst   A skinlike growth, usually seen on the back.

Eye Abnormalities   The Great Dane is prone to abnormally growing eyelashes, rolling in or out of the eyelid(s), abnormal growing retina(s), and protruding third eyelid(s).

Gastric Bloat and Torsion   Gastric bloat is a swelling of the stomach from excess gas and is usually followed by gastric torsion, a twisting of the stomach. Gastric torsion will result in death if not treated immediately.

Glaucoma   Pressure on the retina from excess fluid in the eyeball, which causes partial or total loss of vision.

Heart Disease   The Great Dane is prone to a developmental abnormality of the mitral valve and cardiomyopathy, or weakened heart muscles.

Hemeralopia   A disorder of the retina causing blindness during the day with partial sight in dim light.

Hip Dysplasia   An abnormal development of the hip joint(s).

Histiocytoma   A tumor that forms beneath the skin.

Hygroma   A thick-walled, fluid-filled sac, usually found on the elbow.

Hypertrophic Osteodystrophy   A painful inflammation of the bones along with development of bony growths, found in fast-growing giant breeds.

Lick Granuloma (Acral Lick Dermatitis)   Inflammation or infection of the skin from excessive licking. Usually found on the leg or paw.

Muscular Dystrophy   A progressive muscle disorder that causes a wasting of the muscles. It is an inherited disease, with symptoms of slow growth, difficulty eating and swallowing, and weakness.

Neck Vertebrae Malformation   An abnormal development of the vertebrae in the neck, causing nerve damage. Some dogs walk with a pronounced flexion of the knee, similar to a high-stepping horse.

Osteochondritis Dissecans Inflammation of the cartilage in the joints. A form of arthritis.

Osteochondrosis An abnormal development of joint cartilage. Most commonly found in the shoulder, knee, and elbow.

Progressive Retinal Atrophy (PRA) A slow deterioration of the retina, leading to blindness.

Thyroid Disease The Great Dane is prone to thyroiditis, lymphocytic thyroiditis, and hypothyroidism. Thyroiditis and lymphocytic thyroiditis are autoimmune diseases that lead to hypothyroidism, a common disease of thyroid hormone deficiency. The thyroid regulates your dog's metabolism. A large number of skin problems in dogs are caused by thyroid disease.

Von Willebrand's Disease Abnormal blood-clotting defect involving both platelet and coagulation function (factor VIII).

Zinc-Responsive Dermatosis Skin disease caused by a zinc deficiency.

Great Pyrenees

Blood-Clotting Disorders The Great Pyrenees is prone to blood-clotting disorders due to coagulation factor IX or XI deficiency.

Cataract In elderly dogs the lens of the eye becomes cloudy, causing a partial or total loss of vision.

Deafness A partial or total loss of hearing.

Demodectic Mange A skin disease in which canine mites are living in the skin, causing itching, loss of hair, and skin infections. Usually found on the face and front legs.

Eye Abnormality The Great Pyrenees is prone to a rolling out or in of the eyelid(s).

Hip Dysplasia   An abnormal development of the hip joint(s).

Hot Spots   A bacterial skin infection that progresses into severe inflammation from excessive licking and chewing.

Hypothyroidism   A common disease of thyroid hormone deficiency. The thyroid regulates your dog's metabolism. A large number of skin problems in dogs are caused by thyroid disease.

Osteochondritis Dissecans   Inflammation of the cartilage in the joints. A form of arthritis.

Osteochondrosis   An abnormal development of joint cartilage. Most commonly found in the shoulder, knee, and elbow.

Progressive Retinal Atrophy (PRA)   A slow deterioration of the retina, leading to blindness.

Swimmer Puppies   A developmental condition caused by a weakness of the muscles puppies use to pull their legs together. Newborns are unable to put their feet under them to walk.

Teeth Abnormalities   The number, placement, or development of the teeth is not normal.

Thrombocytopenia   An abnormal decrease in the number of blood platelets. Blood platelets play a role in blood clotting. Symptoms are tiny hemorrhages in the skin and mucous membranes.

Vaginal Hyperplasia   An increase in the number of cells in the tissues of the vagina, possibly indicating a precancerous condition.

Greater Swiss Mountain Dog

Osteochondritis Dissecans   Inflammation of the cartilage in the joints. A form of arthritis.

Osteochondrosis   An abnormal development of joint cartilage. Most commonly found in the shoulder, knee, and elbow.

Platelet Disorders   The Greater Swiss mountain dog is prone to functional abnormalities of the blood platelets and an abnormal decrease in the number of blood platelets. Blood platelets play a role in blood clotting.

Irish Wolfhound

Cataract   In elderly dogs the lens of the eye becomes cloudy, causing a partial or total loss of vision.

Eye Abnormality   The Irish wolfhound is prone to a rolling in of the eyelid(s).

Heart Disease   The Irish wolfhound is prone to cardiomyopathy, or weakened heart muscles.

Hip Dysplasia   An abnormal development of the hip joint(s).

Hygroma   A thick-walled, fluid-filled sac, usually found on the elbow.

Hypertrophic Osteodystrophy   A painful inflammation of the bones along with development of bony growths, found in fast-growing giant breeds.

Hypothyroidism   A common disease of thyroid hormone deficiency. The thyroid regulates your dog's metabolism. A large number of skin problems in dogs are caused by thyroid disease.

Liver Abnormality   The Irish wolfhound is prone to an abnormal formation of blood vessels in the liver.

Osteochondritis Dissecans   Inflammation of the cartilage in the joints. A form of arthritis.

Osteochondrosis   An abnormal development of joint cartilage. Most commonly found in the shoulder, knee, and elbow.

Von Willebrand's Disease   Abnormal blood-clotting defect involving both platelet and coagulation function (factor VIII).

Komondor

Cataract   In elderly dogs the lens of the eye becomes cloudy, causing a partial or total loss of vision.

Eye Abnormality   The komondor is prone to a rolling in of the eyelid(s).

Hip Dysplasia   An abnormal development of the hip joint(s).

Hypothyroidism   A common disease of thyroid hormone deficiency. The thyroid regulates your dog's metabolism. A large number of skin problems in dogs are caused by thyroid disease.

Skin Disease   The komondor is prone to all types of skin disease.

Kuvasz

Cataract   In elderly dogs the lens of the eye becomes cloudy, causing a partial or total loss of vision.

Eosinophilic Panosteitis   An inflammatory bone disease found in fast-growing puppies, accompanied by increased eosinophils, a type of white blood cell.

Eye Abnormality   The kuvasz is prone to a rolling in of the eyelid(s).

Hip Dysplasia   An abnormal development of the hip joint(s).

Hypertrophic Osteodystrophy   A painful inflammation of the bones along with development of bony growths, found in fast-growing giant breeds.

Hypothyroidism   A common disease of thyroid hormone deficiency. The thyroid regulates your dog's metabolism. A large number of skin problems in dogs are caused by thyroid disease.

Osteochondritis Dissecans   Inflammation of the cartilage in the joints. A form of arthritis.

Osteochondrosis   An abnormal development of joint cartilage. Most commonly found in the shoulder, knee, and elbow.

Von Willebrand's Disease   Abnormal blood-clotting defect involving both platelet and coagulation function (factor VIII).

Mastiff

Corneal Dystrophy   An inherited degenerative condition in which the cornea of the eye becomes cloudy or opaque.

Eye Abnormalities   The mastiff is prone to a rolling in or out of the eyelid(s) and abnormal development of the retina(s).

Gastric Bloat and Torsion   Gastric bloat is a swelling of the stomach from excess gas and is usually followed by gastric torsion, a twisting of the stomach. Gastric torsion will result in death if not treated immediately.

Hypothyroidism   A common disease of thyroid hormone deficiency. The thyroid regulates your dog's metabolism. A large number of skin problems in dogs are caused by thyroid disease.

Osteochondritis Dissecans   A inflammation of the cartilage in the joints. A form of arthritis.

Osteochondrosis   An abnormal development of joint cartilage. Most commonly found in the shoulder, knee, and elbow.

Progressive Retinal Atrophy (PRA)   A slow deterioration of the retina, leading to blindness.

Vaginal Hyperplasia   An increase in the number of cells in the tissues of the vagina, possibly indicating a precancerous condition.

Neapolitan Mastiff

Cataract   In elderly dogs the lens of the eye becomes cloudy, causing a partial or total loss of vision.

Dermoid Cyst   A skinlike growth, usually seen on the back.

Eye Abnormality   The Neapolitan mastiff is prone to a rolling in or out of the eyelid(s).

Hip Dysplasia   An abnormal development of the hip joint(s).

Hypertrophic Osteodystrophy   A painful inflammation of the bones along with development of bony growths, found in fast-growing giant breeds.

Hypothyroidism   A common disease of thyroid hormone deficiency. The thyroid regulates your dog's metabolism. A large number of skin problems in dogs are caused by thyroid disease.

Osteochondritis Dissecans   Inflammation of the cartilage in the joints. A form of arthritis.

Progressive Retinal Atrophy (PRA)   A slow deterioration of the retina, leading to blindness.

Newfoundland

Cataract   In elderly dogs the lens of the eye becomes cloudy, causing a partial or total loss of vision.

Dermoid Cyst   A skinlike growth, usually seen on the back.

Elbow Dysplasia   An abnormal development of the elbow joint(s).

Eye Abnormalities   The Newfoundland is prone to a rolling in or out of the eyelid(s) and protruding third eyelid(s).

Heart Disease   The Newfoundland is prone to cardiomyopathy, or weakened heart muscles, developmental abnormalities of the heart, and valve disease.

Hip Dysplasia   An abnormal development of the hip joint(s).

Immune-Mediated Hemolytic Anemia (IMHA)   Anemia resulting from an immune system–mediated destruction of the red blood cells.

Osteochondritis Dissecans   Inflammation of the cartilage in the joints. A form of arthritis.

Osteochondrosis   An abnormal development of joint cartilage. Most commonly found in the shoulder, knee, and elbow.

Thrombocytopenia   An abnormal decrease in the number of blood platelets. Blood platelets play a role in blood clotting. Symptoms are tiny hemorrhages in the skin and mucous membranes.

Thyroid Disease   The Newfoundland is prone to thyroiditis, lymphocytic thyroiditis, and hypothyroidism. Thyroiditis and lymphocytic thyroiditis are autoimmune diseases that lead to hypothyroidism, a common disease of thyroid hormone deficiency. The thyroid regulates your dog's metabolism. A large number of skin problems in dogs are caused by thyroid disease.

Von Willebrand's Disease   Abnormal blood-clotting defect involving both platelet and coagulation function (factor VIII).

Rottweiler

Addison's Disease   A disease in which the adrenal glands secrete an insufficient amount of cortisone, a steroid hormone.

Cataract   In elderly dogs the lens of the eye becomes cloudy, causing a partial or total loss of vision.

Diabetes Mellitus   A disease caused by an insufficient production or use of insulin.

Elbow Dysplasia   An abnormal development of the elbow joint(s).

Eosinophilic Panosteitis   An inflammatory bone disease found in fast-growing puppies, accompanied by increased eosinophils, a type of white blood cell.

Eye Abnormalities   The rottweiler is prone to abnormally growing eyelashes, abnormal development of the retina(s), and a rolling in or out of the eyelid(s).

Folliculitis   Inflammation of the hair follicle(s).

Heart Disease   The rottweiler is prone to a constriction of the valve between the heart and the aorta.

Hip Dysplasia   An abnormal development of the hip joint(s).

Immune-Mediated Hemolytic Anemia (IMHA)   Anemia resulting from an immune system–mediated destruction of the red blood cells.

Malabsorption   A condition in which the small intestine does not absorb nutrients properly.

Pigmentation Abnormality   A lack of color in the skin.

Progressive Retinal Atrophy (PRA)   A slow deterioration of the retina, leading to blindness.

Thrombocytopenia   An abnormal decrease in the number of blood platelets. Blood platelets play a role in blood clotting. Symptoms are tiny hemorrhages in the skin and mucous membranes.

Thyroid Disease   The rottweiler is prone to thyroiditis, lymphocytic thyroiditis, and hypothyroidism. Thyroiditis and lymphocytic thyroiditis are autoimmune diseases that lead to hypothyroidism, a common disease of thyroid hormone deficiency. The thyroid regulates your dog's metabolism. A large number of skin problems in dogs are caused by thyroid disease.

Von Willebrand's Disease   Abnormal blood-clotting defect involving both platelet and coagulation function (factor VIII).

Saint Bernard

Blood-Clotting Disorders   The Saint Bernard is prone to blood-clotting disorders due to coagulation factor I, VIII, or IX deficiency.

Bone Disease   The Saint Bernard is prone to diseases of the bone caused by a metabolic dysfunction.

Cancer   The Saint Bernard is prone to bone cancer.

Cataract   In elderly dogs the lens of the eye becomes cloudy, causing a partial or total loss of vision.

Dermoid Cyst   A skinlike growth, usually seen on the back.

Ehler's-Danlos Syndrome   A connective tissue disease in which the skin is very fragile and is easily cut or bruised.

Epilepsy   A brain disorder in which the dog experiences seizures (convulsions).

Eye Abnormalities   The Saint Bernard is prone to a rolling in or out of the eyelid(s), abnormally growing eyelashes, and protruding third eyelid(s).

Gastric Bloat and Torsion   Gastric bloat is a swelling of the stomach from excess gas and is usually followed by gastric torsion, a twisting of the stomach. Gastric torsion will result in death if not treated immediately.

Heart Disease   The Saint Bernard is prone to cardiomyopathy, or weakened heart muscles.

Hip Dysplasia   An abnormal development of the hip joint(s).

Hypothyroidism   A common disease of thyroid hormone deficiency. The thyroid regulates your dog's metabolism. A large number of skin problems in dogs are caused by thyroid disease.

Liver Abnormality   The Saint Bernard is prone to an abnormal formation of blood vessels in the liver.

Osteochondritis Dissecans   Inflammation of the cartilage in the joints. A form of arthritis.

Osteochondrosis   An abnormal development of joint cartilage. Most commonly found in the shoulder, knee, and elbow.

Pigmentation Abnormality   A lack of color in the skin.

Vaginal Hyperplasia   An increase in the number of cells in the tissues of the vagina, possibly indicating a precancerous condition.

Von Willebrand's Disease   Abnormal blood-clotting defect involving both platelet and coagulation function (factor VIII).

Scottish Deerhound

Cataract   In elderly dogs the lens of the eye becomes cloudy, causing a partial or total loss of vision.

Eosinophilic Panosteitis   An inflammatory bone disease found in fast-growing puppies, which is accompanied by increased eosinophils, a type of white blood cell.

Gastric Bloat and Torsion   Gastric bloat is a swelling of the stomach from excess gas and is usually followed by gastric torsion, a twisting of the stomach. Gastric torsion will result in death if not treated immediately.

Hypertrophic Osteodystrophy   A painful inflammation of the bones along with development of bony growths, found in fast-growing giant breeds.

Hypothyroidism   A common disease of thyroid hormone deficiency. The thyroid regulates your dog's metabolism. A large number of skin problems in dogs are caused by thyroid disease.

Osteochondritis Dissecans   Inflammation of the cartilage in the joints. A form of arthritis.

Osteochondrosis   An abnormal development of joint cartilage. Most commonly found in the shoulder, knee, and elbow.

Tibetan Mastiff

Elbow Dysplasia   An abnormal development of the elbow joint(s).

Hip Dysplasia   An abnormal development of the hip joint(s).

Hypertrophic Osteodystrophy   A painful inflammation of the bones along with development of bony growths, found in fast-growing giant breeds.

Osteochondritis Dissecans   Inflammation of the cartilage in the joints. A form of arthritis.

Thyroid Disease The Tibetan mastiff is prone to thyroiditis, lymphocytic thyroiditis, and hypothyroidism. Thyroiditis and lymphocytic thyroiditis are autoimmune diseases that lead to hypothyroidism, a common disease of thyroid hormone deficiency. The thyroid regulates your dog's metabolism. A large number of skin problems in dogs are caused by thyroid disease.

Von Willebrand's Disease Abnormal blood-clotting defect involving both platelet and coagulation function (factor VIII).

Purebred Large (50 to 100 Pounds)

Afghan Hound

Anesthetic Sensitivity A serious condition in which the dog is very sensitive to anesthesia. In many cases the dog is also sensitive to medications and flea control products that contain pesticides.

Blood-Clotting Disorder The Afghan hound is prone to a blood-clotting disorder due to coagulation factor VIII deficiency.

Cataract In elderly dogs the lens of the eye becomes cloudy, causing a partial or total loss of vision.

Corneal Dystrophy An inherited degenerative condition in which the cornea of the eye becomes cloudy or opaque.

Degenerative Myelopathy A progressive deterioration of the spinal cord.

Elbow Dysplasia An abnormal development of the elbow joint(s).

Eye Abnormalities The Afghan hound is prone to protruding third eyelid(s) and retinal dysplasia, an abnormal development of the retina(s).

Glaucoma   Pressure on the retina from excess fluid in the eyeball, which causes partial or total loss of vision.

Hip Dysplasia   An abnormal development of the hip joint(s).

Hypothyroidism   A common disease of thyroid hormone deficiency. The thyroid regulates your dog's metabolism. A large number of skin problems in dogs are caused by thyroid disease.

Narcolepsy   A neurological disorder in which the dog suddenly falls asleep.

Osteochondritis Dissecans   Inflammation of the cartilage in the joints. A form of arthritis.

Osteochondrosis   An abnormal development of joint cartilage. Most commonly found in the shoulder, knee, and elbow.

Pemphigus Erythematosus   An autoimmune skin disease.

Progressive Retinal Atrophy (PRA)   A slow deterioration of the retina, leading to blindness.

Vertebra Malformation   A condition in which only half the vertebra is formed.

Von Willebrand's Disease   Abnormal blood-clotting defect involving both platelet and coagulation function (factor VIII).

Airedale Terrier

Antibody (Type IgA) Deficiency   A deficiency of the production of type IgA antibody, causing a weakened immune system.

Blood-Clotting Disorder   The Airedale terrier is prone to a blood-clotting disorder due to coagulation factor IX deficiency.

Cerebellar Hypoplasia   Underdevelopment of a part of the brain called the cerebellum. The cerebellum gives your dog coordination, posture, and balance.

Corneal Dystrophy   An inherited degenerative condition in which the cornea of the eye becomes cloudy or opaque.

Eye Abnormalities   The Airedale terrier is prone to abnormally growing eyelashes, abnormal development of the retina(s), and a rolling in of the eyelid(s).

Growth Hormone–Responsive Dermatosis   Skin disorder caused by a deficiency of growth hormones.

Hip Dysplasia   An abnormal development of the hip joint(s).

Hot Spots   A bacterial skin infection that progresses into severe inflammation from excessive licking and chewing.

Hypothyroidism   A common disease of thyroid hormone deficiency. The thyroid regulates your dog's metabolism. A large number of skin problems in dogs are caused by thyroid disease.

Lick Granuloma (Acral Lick Dermatitis)   Inflammation or infection of the skin from excessive licking. Usually found on the leg or paw.

Narcolepsy   A neurological disorder in which the dog suddenly falls asleep.

Pannus   A progressive immune-mediated disease in which there is a growth of tissue over the cornea, causing inflammation and possible blindness.

Progressive Retinal Atrophy (PRA)   A slow deterioration of the retina, leading to blindness.

Umbilical Hernia   A tear in the muscle wall in the stomach where the umbilical cord was.

Von Willebrand's Disease   Abnormal blood-clotting defect involving both platelet and coagulation function (factor VIII).

Akita

Cataract   In elderly dogs the lens of the eye becomes cloudy, causing a partial or total loss of vision.

Corneal Dystrophy   An inherited degenerative condition in which the cornea of the eye becomes cloudy or opaque.

Cushing's Disease (Hyperadrenocorticism)   A condition in which the adrenal glands secrete too much cortisol. Cortisol is a steroid hormone that regulates carbohydrate, fat, and protein metabolism.

Eye Abnormalities   The Akita is prone to a rolling in of the eyelid(s) and protruding third eyelid(s).

Glaucoma   Pressure on the retina from excess fluid in the eyeball, which causes partial or total loss of vision.

Glycogen Storage Disease   An inability to store and use the complex carbohydrate glycogen, which is primarily stored in the liver and muscle.

Hip Dysplasia   An abnormal development of the hip joint(s).

Hot Spots   A bacterial skin infection that progresses into severe inflammation from excessive licking and chewing.

Immune-Mediated Hemolytic Anemia (IMHA)   Anemia resulting from an immune system–mediated destruction of the red blood cells.

Malabsorption   A condition in which the small intestine does not absorb nutrients properly.

Osteochondritis Dissecans   Inflammation of the cartilage in the joints. A form of arthritis.

Osteochondrosis   An abnormal development of joint cartilage. Most commonly found in the shoulder, knee, and elbow.

Pemphigus Foliaceous   An autoimmune skin disease.

Progressive Retinal Atrophy (PRA)   A slow deterioration of the retina, leading to blindness.

Thyroid Disease   The Akita is prone to thyroiditis, lymphocytic thyroiditis, and hypothyroidism. Thyroiditis and lymphocytic thyroiditis are autoimmune diseases that lead to hypothyroidism, a common disease of thyroid hormone deficiency. The thyroid regulates your dog's metabolism. A large number of skin problems in dogs are caused by thyroid disease.

Umbilical Hernia   A tear in the muscle wall in the stomach where the umbilical cord was.

Von Willebrand's Disease   Abnormal blood-clotting defect involving both platelet and coagulation function (factor VIII).

Alaskan Malamute

Anemia with Chondrodysplasia   An abnormal development of cartilage and red blood cells.

Blood-Clotting Disorders   The Alaskan malamute is prone to blood-clotting disorders due to coagulation factor VII, VIII, or IX deficiency.

Cataract   In elderly dogs the lens of the eye becomes cloudy, causing a partial or total loss of vision.

Corneal Dystrophy   An inherited degenerative condition in which the cornea of the eye becomes cloudy or opaque.

Corneal Ulcer   A deterioration of the cornea.

Diabetes Mellitus   A disease caused by an insufficient production or use of insulin.

Eye Abnormality   The Alaskan malamute is prone to abnormal development of the eye(s).

Glaucoma   Pressure on the retina from excess fluid in the eyeball, which causes partial or total loss of vision.

Hemeralopia   A disorder of the retina causing blindness during the day, with partial sight in dim light.

Hereditary Kidney Hypoplasia   A condition in which the dog is born with immature kidneys that never develop completely.

Hip Dysplasia   An abnormal development of the hip joint(s).

Hypothyroidism   A common disease of thyroid hormone deficiency. The thyroid regulates your dog's metabolism. A large number of skin problems in dogs are caused by thyroid disease.

Immune-Mediated Hemolytic Anemia (IMHA)   Anemia resulting from an immune system–mediated destruction of the red blood cells.

Narcolepsy   A neurological disorder in which the dog suddenly falls asleep.

Osteochondritis Dissecans   Inflammation of the cartilage in the joints. A form of arthritis.

Osteochondrosis   An abnormal development of joint cartilage. Most commonly found in the shoulder, knee, and elbow.

Progressive Retinal Atrophy (PRA)   A slow deterioration of the retina, leading to blindness.

Von Willebrand's Disease   Abnormal blood-clotting defect involving both platelet and coagulation function (factor VIII).

Zinc-Responsive Dermatosis   Skin disease caused by a zinc deficiency.

American Foxhound

Deafness   A partial or total loss of hearing.

Osteochondrosis (Spinal)   An abnormal development of the vertebrae.

Thrombocytopathy   The small blood cells that are needed to control bleeding are dysfunctional.

Bearded Collie

Addison's Disease   A disease in which the adrenal glands secrete an insufficient amount of cortisone, a steroid hormone.

Cataract   In elderly dogs the lens of the eye becomes cloudy, causing a partial or total loss of vision.

Corneal Dystrophy An inherited degenerative condition in which the cornea of the eye becomes cloudy or opaque.

Eye Abnormality The bearded collie is prone to abnormal development of the retina(s).

Hip Dysplasia An abnormal development of the hip joint(s).

Hypothyroidism A common disease of thyroid hormone deficiency. The thyroid regulates your dog's metabolism. A large number of skin problems in dogs are caused by thyroid disease.

Progressive Retinal Atrophy (PRA) A slow deterioration of the retina, leading to blindness.

Belgian Sheepdog

Cataract In elderly dogs the lens of the eye becomes cloudy, causing a partial or total loss of vision.

Epilepsy A brain disorder in which the dog experiences seizures (convulsions).

Eye Abnormality The Belgian sheepdog is prone to abnormal development of the retina(s).

Hip Dysplasia An abnormal development of the hip joint(s).

Hypothyroidism A common disease of thyroid hormone deficiency. The thyroid regulates your dog's metabolism. A large number of skin problems in dogs are caused by thyroid disease.

Muscular Dystrophy A progressive muscle disorder that causes a wasting of the muscles. It is an inherited disease, with symptoms of slow growth, difficulty eating and swallowing, and weakness.

Pannus A progressive immune-mediated disease in which there is a growth of tissue over the cornea, causing inflammation and possible blindness.

Progressive Retinal Atrophy (PRA) A slow deterioration of the retina, leading to blindness.

Belgian Tervuren

Cataract   In elderly dogs the lens of the eye becomes cloudy, causing a partial or total loss of vision.

Epilepsy   A brain disorder in which the dog experiences seizures (convulsions).

Hypothyroidism   A common disease of thyroid hormone deficiency. The thyroid regulates your dog's metabolism. A large number of skin problems in dogs are caused by thyroid disease.

Osteochondritis Dissecans   Inflammation of the cartilage in the joints. A form of arthritis.

Osteochondrosis   An abnormal development of joint cartilage. Most commonly found in the shoulder, knee, and elbow.

Pannus   A progressive immune-mediated disease in which there is a growth of tissue over the cornea, causing inflammation and possible blindness.

Progressive Retinal Atrophy (PRA)   A slow deterioration of the retina, leading to blindness.

Bernese Mountain Dog

Ataxia   A progressive loss of coordination.

Cataract   In elderly dogs the lens of the eye becomes cloudy, causing a partial or total loss of vision.

Cerebellar Degeneration/Malformation   A deterioration or malformation of a part of the brain.

Cleft Palate and/or Lip   Both are birth defects. With cleft palate, the roof of the mouth does not grow properly, leaving a hole from the roof of the mouth into the nose. With cleft lip, the skin below the nose does not grow together.

Eye Abnormalities The Bernese mountain dog is prone to a rolling in of the eyelid(s) and abnormal development of the retina(s).

Gastric Bloat and Torsion Gastric bloat is a swelling of the stomach from excess gas and is usually followed by gastric torsion, a twisting of the stomach. Gastric torsion will result in death if not treated immediately.

Hepatocerebellar Degeneration Progressive brain and liver disease of Bernese mountain dogs that are six to eight weeks old.

Hip Dysplasia An abnormal development of the hip joint(s).

Hypothyroidism A common disease of thyroid hormone deficiency. The thyroid regulates your dog's metabolism. A large number of skin problems in dogs are caused by thyroid disease.

Liver Abnormality The Bernese mountain dog is prone to an abnormal formation of blood vessels in the liver.

Osteochondritis Dissecans Inflammation of the cartilage in the joints. A form of arthritis.

Osteochondrosis An abnormal development of joint cartilage. Most commonly found in the shoulder, knee, and elbow.

Progressive Retinal Atrophy (PRA) A slow deterioration of the retina, leading to blindness.

Umbilical Hernia A tear in the muscle wall in the stomach where the umbilical cord was.

Black and Tan Coonhound

Blood-Clotting Disorder The coonhound (black and tan) is prone to a blood-clotting disorder due to coagulation factor IX deficiency.

Eye Abnormalities The coonhound (black and tan) is prone to a rolling in or rolling out of the eyelid(s).

Hip Dysplasia An abnormal development of the hip joint(s).

Osteochondritis Dissecans   Inflammation of the cartilage in the joints. A form of arthritis.

Osteochondrosis   An abnormal development of joint cartilage. Most commonly found in the shoulder, knee, and elbow.

Bloodhound

Eye Abnormalities   The bloodhound is prone to a rolling in or out of the eyelid(s), protruding third eyelid(s), and dry eye, a condition in which the eye(s) does not produce enough liquid.

Gastric Bloat and Torsion   Gastric bloat is a swelling of the stomach from excess gas and is usually followed by gastric torsion, a twisting of the stomach. This is the leading cause of death in bloodhounds.

Hip Dysplasia   An abnormal development of the hip joint(s).

Hypothyroidism   A common disease of thyroid hormone deficiency. The thyroid regulates your dog's metabolism. A large number of skin problems in dogs are caused by thyroid disease.

Osteochondritis Dissecans   Inflammation of the cartilage in the joints. A form of arthritis.

Osteochondrosis   An abnormal development of joint cartilage. Most commonly found in the shoulder, knee, and elbow.

Teeth Abnormalities   The number, placement, or development of the teeth is not normal.

Bluetick Coonhound

Globoid Cell Leukodystrophy   Degeneration of a type of brain cell.

Osteochondritis Dissecans   Inflammation of the cartilage in the joints. A form of arthritis.

Osteochondrosis   An abnormal development of joint cartilage. Most commonly found in the shoulder, knee, and elbow.

Bouvier des Flandres

Cataract   In elderly dogs the lens of the eye becomes cloudy, causing a partial or total loss of vision.

Cleft Palate   A birth defect in which the roof of the mouth does not grow properly, leaving a hole from the roof of the mouth into the nose.

Eye Abnormality   The Bouvier des Flandres is prone to a rolling in of the eyelid(s).

Gastric Bloat and Torsion   Gastric bloat is a swelling of the stomach from excess gas and is usually followed by gastric torsion, a twisting of the stomach. Gastric torsion will result in death if not treated immediately.

Glaucoma   Pressure on the retina from excess fluid in the eyeball, which causes partial or total loss of vision.

Hip Dysplasia   An abnormal development of the hip joint(s).

Hypothyroidism   A common disease of thyroid hormone deficiency. The thyroid regulates your dog's metabolism. A large number of skin problems in dogs are caused by thyroid disease.

Osteochondritis Dissecans   Inflammation of the cartilage in the joints. A form of arthritis.

Osteochondrosis   An abnormal development of joint cartilage. Most commonly found in the shoulder, knee, and elbow.

Reproductive Disorders   The Bouvier des Flandres is prone to ovarian cyst(s), experiencing complications giving birth, and endometritis, an inflammation of the uterus.

Umbilical Hernia   A tear in the muscle wall in the stomach where the umbilical cord was.

Von Willebrand's Disease   Abnormal blood-clotting defect involving both platelet and coagulation function (factor VIII).

Boxer

Acne   Pimples and blackheads on the chin and lips of young dogs.

Allergies   The boxer is prone to all types of allergies.

Blood-Clotting Disorders   The boxer is prone to blood-clotting disorders due to coagulation factor II or VIII deficiency.

Cancer   The boxer is prone to skin cancer and a rare form of cancer in which the mast cells become cancerous. The mast cell secretes histamine in response to allergens.

Cataract   In elderly dogs the lens of the eye becomes cloudy, causing a partial or total loss of vision.

Corneal Ulcer   A deterioration of the cornea.

Cushing's Disease (Hyperadrenocorticism)   A condition in which the adrenal glands secrete too much cortisol. Cortisol is a steroid hormone that regulates carbohydrate, fat, and protein metabolism.

Demodectic Mange   A skin disease in which canine mites are living in the skin, causing itching, loss of hair, and skin infections. Usually found on the face and front legs.

Dermoid Cyst   A skinlike growth, usually seen on the back.

Ehler's-Danlos Syndrome   A connective tissue disease in which the skin is very fragile and is easily cut or bruised.

Eye Abnormalities   The boxer is prone to a rolling in of the eyelid(s), abnormally growing eyelashes, and protruding third eyelid(s).

Fainting   A sudden, brief state of unconsciousness.

Gastric Bloat and Torsion Gastric bloat is a swelling of the stomach from excess gas and is usually followed by gastric torsion, a twisting of the stomach. Gastric torsion will result in death if not treated immediately.

Heart Disease The boxer is prone to cardiomyopathy, or weakened heart muscles, developmental abnormalities of the heart, and valve disease.

Histiocytoma A tumor that forms beneath the skin.

Incontinence Loss of control of urination and bowel movements.

Liver Abnormality The boxer is prone to an abnormal formation of blood vessels in the liver.

Osteochondritis Dissecans Inflammation of the cartilage in the joints. A form of arthritis.

Osteochondrosis An abnormal development of joint cartilage. Most commonly found in the shoulder, knee, and elbow.

Progressive Retinal Atrophy (PRA) A slow deterioration of the retina, leading to blindness.

Spondylosis A malformation of the vertebrae.

Teeth Abnormalities The number, placement, or development of the teeth is not normal.

Thyroid Disease The boxer is prone to thyroiditis, lymphocytic thyroiditis, and hypothyroidism. Thyroiditis and lymphocytic thyroiditis are autoimmune diseases that lead to hypothyroidism, a common disease of thyroid hormone deficiency. The thyroid regulates your dog's metabolism. A large number of skin problems in dogs are caused by thyroid disease.

Ulcerative Colitis A chronic inflammation of the colon that results in the formation of ulcers in the colon.

Urinary Stones A hard mass of magnesium-ammonium-phosphate stones or crystals in the urinary tract.

Vaginal Hyperplasia   An increase in the number of cells in the tissues of the vagina, possibly indicating a precancerous condition.

Von Willebrand's Disease   Abnormal blood-clotting defect involving both platelet and coagulation function (factor VIII).

Briard

Cancer   The briard is prone to cancer of the lymphatic system.

Cataract   In elderly dogs the lens of the eye becomes cloudy, causing a partial or total loss of vision.

Eosinophilic Panosteitis   An inflammatory bone disease found in fast-growing puppies, which is accompanied by increased eosinophils, a type of white blood cell.

Gastric Bloat and Torsion   Gastric bloat is a swelling of the stomach from excess gas and is usually followed by gastric torsion, a twisting of the stomach. Gastric torsion will result in death if not treated immediately.

Hip Dysplasia   An abnormal development of the hip joint(s).

Hypothyroidism   A common disease of thyroid hormone deficiency. The thyroid regulates your dog's metabolism. A large number of skin problems in dogs are caused by thyroid disease.

Progressive Retinal Atrophy (PRA)   A slow deterioration of the retina, leading to blindness.

Von Willebrand's Disease   Abnormal blood-clotting defect involving both platelet and coagulation function (factor VIII).

Bull Terrier

Acrodermatitis   A zinc deficiency caused by an inability to utilize and store zinc properly. Dogs with acrodermatitis do not respond to zinc supplementation.

Boils A deep infection of the skin.

Cancer The bull terrier is prone to skin cancer and a rare form of cancer in which the mast cells become cancerous. The mast cell secretes histamine in response to allergens.

Deafness A partial or total loss of hearing.

Eye Abnormalities The bull terrier is prone to a rolling in or out of the eyelid(s) and a condition in which the lens in the eye slips out of place.

Hernia A rupture of the wall of an internal organ in the groin area.

Osteochondritis Dissecans Inflammation of the cartilage in the joints. A form of arthritis.

Osteochondrosis An abnormal development of joint cartilage. Most commonly found in the shoulder, knee, and elbow.

Umbilical Hernia A tear in the muscle wall in the stomach where the umbilical cord was.

Chesapeake Bay Retriever

Blood-Clotting Disorder The Chesapeake Bay retriever is prone to a blood-clotting disorder due to coagulation factor IX deficiency.

Cataract In elderly dogs the lens of the eye becomes cloudy, causing a partial or total loss of vision.

Eye Abnormalities The Chesapeake Bay retriever is prone to abnormally growing eyelashes, a rolling in of the eyelid(s), protruding third eyelid(s), and an abnormal development of the retina(s).

Hip Dysplasia An abnormal development of the hip joint(s).

Osteochondritis Dissecans Inflammation of the cartilage in the joints. A form of arthritis.

Osteochondrosis An abnormal development of joint cartilage. Most commonly found in the shoulder, knee, and elbow.

Progressive Retinal Atrophy (PRA)   A slow deterioration of the retina, leading to blindness.

Von Willebrand's Disease   Abnormal blood-clotting defect involving both platelet and coagulation function (factor VIII).

Chow Chow

Behavioral Abnormalities   The chow chow is prone to a whole range of abnormal behavior patterns, such as aggression and panic disorders.

Cataract   In elderly dogs the lens of the eye becomes cloudy, causing a partial or total loss of vision.

Cerebellar Hypoplasia   Underdevelopment of a part of the brain called the cerebellum. The cerebellum gives your dog coordination, posture, and balance.

Cleft Palate   A birth defect in which the roof of the mouth does not grow properly, leaving a hole from the roof of the mouth into the nose.

Demodectic Mange   A skin disease in which canine mites are living in the skin, causing itching, loss of hair, and skin infections. Usually found on the face and front legs.

Elbow Dysplasia   An abnormal development of the elbow joint(s).

Epiphyseal Dysplasia   Abnormal development of the long bone.

Eye Abnormalities   The chow chow is prone to a rolling in or out of the eyelid(s) and abnormally growing eyelashes.

Gastric Bloat and Torsion   Gastric bloat is a swelling of the stomach from excess gas and is usually followed by gastric torsion, a twisting of the stomach. Gastric torsion will result in death if not treated immediately.

Glaucoma   Pressure on the retina from excess fluid in the eyeball, which causes partial or total loss of vision.

Growth Hormone–Responsive Dermatosis Skin disorder caused by a deficiency of growth hormones.

Hip Dysplasia An abnormal development of the hip joint(s).

Malabsorption A condition in which the small intestine does not absorb nutrients properly.

Muscular Dystrophy A progressive muscle disorder that causes a wasting of the muscles. It is an inherited disease, with symptoms of slow growth, difficulty eating and swallowing, and weakness.

Osteochondritis Dissecans Inflammation of the cartilage in the joints. A form of arthritis.

Osteochondrosis An abnormal development of joint cartilage. Most commonly found in the shoulder, knee, and elbow.

Pannus A progressive immune-mediated disease in which there is a growth of tissue over the cornea, causing inflammation and possible blindness.

Pemphigus Foliaceous An autoimmune skin disease.

Progressive Retinal Atrophy (PRA) A slow deterioration of the retina, leading to blindness.

Thyroid Disease The chow chow is prone to thyroiditis, lymphocytic thyroiditis, and hypothyroidism. Thyroiditis and lymphocytic thyroiditis are autoimmune diseases that lead to hypothyroidism, a common disease of thyroid hormone deficiency. The thyroid regulates your dog's metabolism. A large number of skin problems in dogs are caused by thyroid disease.

Clumber Spaniel

Eye Abnormality The clumber spaniel is prone to a rolling in or out of the eyelid(s).

Hip Dysplasia An abnormal development of the hip joint(s).

Jaw Abnormality   The lower jaw is longer than the upper jaw.

Teeth Abnormalities   The number, placement, or development of the teeth is not normal.

Collie

Blood-Clotting Disorder   The collie is prone to a blood-clotting disorder due to coagulation factor VIII deficiency.

Bullous Pemphigoid   An autoimmune disease in which painful blisters form just beneath the skin.

Cancer   The collie is prone to bladder cancer.

Cataract   In elderly dogs the lens of the eye becomes cloudy, causing a partial or total loss of vision.

Cerebellar Abiotrophy   Malformation of the neurons in the cerebellum. The cerebellum is the part of the brain that gives your dog coordination, posture, and balance.

Collie Eye Anomaly   An inherited disorder in which the narrow shape of the head causes the eyes to be malformed.

Corneal Dystrophy   An inherited degenerative condition in which the cornea of the eye becomes cloudy or opaque.

Cyclic Hematopoiesis   An inherited condition of gray collies in which periodically a type of white blood cell is not produced.

Deafness   A partial or total loss of hearing.

Demodectic Mange   A skin disease in which canine mites are living in the skin, causing itching, loss of hair, and skin infections. Usually found on the face and front legs.

Epilepsy   A brain disorder in which the dog experiences seizures (convulsions).

Eye Abnormalities   The collie is prone to a rolling in of the eyelid(s), abnormally growing eyelashes, malformed optic nerve(s), and abnormal development of the retina(s).

Hernia A rupture of the wall of an internal organ in the groin area.

Hip Dysplasia An abnormal development of the hip joint(s).

Histiocytoma A tumor that forms beneath the skin.

Hypothyroidism A common disease of thyroid hormone deficiency. The thyroid regulates your dog's metabolism. A large number of skin problems in dogs are caused by thyroid disease.

Keratitis Inflammation of the cornea.

Osteochondritis Dissecans Inflammation of the cartilage in the joints. A form of arthritis.

Osteochondrosis An abnormal development of joint cartilage. Most commonly found in the shoulder, knee, and elbow.

Progressive Retinal Atrophy (PRA) A slow deterioration of the retina, leading to blindness.

Skin Disorders The collie is prone to autoimmune skin disease, skin disease of the nose, and an inflammation of the skin and muscles.

Umbilical Hernia A tear in the muscle wall in the stomach where the umbilical cord was.

Von Willebrand's Disease Abnormal blood-clotting defect involving both platelet and coagulation function (factor VIII).

Curly-Coated Retriever

Cataract In elderly dogs the lens of the eye becomes cloudy, causing a partial or total loss of vision.

Ehler's-Danlos Syndrome A connective tissue disease in which the skin is very fragile and is easily cut or bruised.

Eye Abnormalities The curly-coated retriever is prone to a rolling in of the eyelid(s) and abnormally growing eyelashes.

Progressive Retinal Atrophy (PRA) A slow deterioration of the retina, leading to blindness.

Dalmatian

Allergies   The Dalmatian is prone to all types of allergies.

Blue Eyes   An adverse reaction to the adenovirus type 1 (hepatitis virus) vaccine, which causes a bluish discoloration to the cornea. In this case, use adenovirus type 2 vaccine.

Boils   A deep infection of the skin.

Cancer   The Dalmatian is prone to skin cancer.

Deafness   A partial or total loss of hearing.

Demodectic Mange   A skin disease in which canine mites are living in the skin, causing itching, loss of hair, and skin infections. Usually found on the face and front legs.

Eye Abnormalities   The Dalmatian is prone to a rolling in of the eyelid(s) and abnormally growing eyelashes.

Folliculitis   Inflammation of the hair follicle(s).

Glaucoma   Pressure on the retina from excess fluid in the eyeball, which causes partial or total loss of vision.

Globoid Cell Leukodystrophy   Degeneration of a type of brain cell.

Hip Dysplasia   An abnormal development of the hip joint(s).

Hypothyroidism   A common disease of thyroid hormone deficiency. The thyroid regulates your dog's metabolism. A large number of skin problems in dogs are caused by thyroid disease.

Osteochondritis Dissecans   Inflammation of the cartilage in the joints. A form of arthritis.

Osteochondrosis   An abnormal development of joint cartilage. Most commonly found in the shoulder, knee, and elbow.

Pannus   A progressive immune-mediated disease in which there is a growth of tissue over the cornea, causing inflammation and possible blindness.

Progressive Retinal Atrophy (PRA)   A slow deterioration of the retina, leading to blindness.

Uric Acid Excretion Abnormality   Dalmatians are prone to having an abnormally high amount of uric acid in their urine, which causes urinary stones.

Urinary Stones   A hard mass of magnesium-ammonium-phosphate stones or crystals in the urinary tract.

Doberman Pinscher

Acanthosis Nigricans   A rare skin disease characterized by dark skin, hair loss, and inflammation of the skin. Primarily found in the armpits.

Acne   Pimples and blackheads on the chin and lips of young dogs.

Antibody (Type IgM) Deficiency   A deficiency of antibody production during the initial response of the immune system to an antigen.

Behavioral Abnormalities   The Doberman pinscher is prone to a whole range of abnormal behavior patterns, such as aggression and panic disorders.

Blood-Clotting Disorders   The Doberman pinscher is prone to blood-clotting disorders due to coagulation factor VIII or IX deficiency.

Cancer   The Doberman pinscher is prone to hemangiosarcoma, which is a cancer of the blood vessels involving the liver, spleen, or skin, and bone cancer.

Cataract   In elderly dogs the lens of the eye becomes cloudy, causing a partial or total loss of vision.

Ciliary Dyskinesia   A condition in which the ciliated cells (hairlike cells lining the respiratory tract) are deformed and rigid. Causes pneumonia and other respiratory difficulties.

Copper Metabolism Abnormality   An inability to utilize and store copper properly. Results in liver disease if not treated.

Craniomandibular Osteopathy   Abnormally dense bones in the face and the jaw.

Demodectic Mange   A skin disease in which canine mites are living in the skin, causing itching, loss of hair, and skin infections. Usually found on the face and front legs.

Eosinophilic Panosteitis   An inflammatory bone disease found in fast-growing puppies, which is accompanied by increased eosinophils, a type of white blood cell.

Eye Abnormalities   The Doberman pinscher is prone to abnormal development of the eye(s) and a rolling in of the eye(s).

Fainting   A sudden, brief state of unconsciousness.

Folliculitis   Inflammation of the hair follicle(s).

Gastric Bloat and Torsion   Gastric bloat is a swelling of the stomach from excess gas and is usually followed by gastric torsion, a twisting of the stomach. Gastric torsion will result in death if not treated immediately.

Heart Disease   The Doberman pinscher is prone to cardiomyopathy, or weakened heart muscles, and a deterioration of the electrical system of the heart.

Hip Dysplasia   An abnormal development of the hip joint(s).

Immune-Mediated Hemolytic Anemia (IMHA)   Anemia resulting from an immune system–mediated destruction of the red blood cells.

Incontinence   Loss of control of urination and bowel movements.

Kidney Disease   The Doberman pinscher is prone to abnormally developed kidney(s).

Lick Granuloma (Acral Lick Dermatitis)   Inflammation or infection of the skin from excessive licking. Usually found on the leg or paw.

Narcolepsy   A neurological disorder in which the dog suddenly falls asleep.

Neck Vertebrae Malformation   An abnormal development of the vertebrae in the neck, causing nerve damage. Some dogs walk with a pronounced flexion of the knee, similar to a high-stepping horse.

Osteochondritis Dissecans   Inflammation of the cartilage in the joints. A form of arthritis.

Osteochondrosis   An abnormal development of joint cartilage. Most commonly found in the shoulder, knee, and elbow.

Pigmentation Abnormality   A lack of color in the skin.

Progressive Retinal Atrophy (PRA)   A slow deterioration of the retina, leading to blindness.

Teeth Abnormalities   The number, placement, or development of the teeth is not normal.

Thrombosis   The formation of a blood clot(s) in a blood vessel or the heart.

Thyroid Disease   The Doberman pinscher is prone to thyroiditis, lymphocytic thyroiditis, and hypothyroidism. Thyroiditis and lymphocytic thyroiditis are autoimmune diseases that lead to hypothyroidism, a common disease of thyroid hormone deficiency. The thyroid regulates your dog's metabolism. A large number of skin problems in dogs are caused by thyroid disease.

Ulcerative Colitis   A chronic inflammation of the colon that results in the formation of ulcers in the colon.

Von Willebrand's Disease   Abnormal blood-clotting defect involving both platelet and coagulation function (factor VIII).

Zinc-Responsive Dermatosis   Skin disease caused by a zinc deficiency.

English Bulldog

Acne   Pimples and blackheads on the chin and lips of young dogs.

Blood-Clotting Disorder   The English bulldog is prone to a blood-clotting disorder due to coagulation factor VII deficiency.

Cancer   The English bulldog is prone to cancer of the brain, spinal cord, and anus.

Cataract   In elderly dogs the lens of the eye becomes cloudy, causing a partial or total loss of vision.

Cleft Palate and/or Lip   Both are birth defects. With cleft palate, the roof of the mouth does not grow properly, leaving a hole from the roof of the mouth into the nose. With cleft lip, the skin below the nose does not grow together.

Dystocia   Complications giving birth.

Eye Abnormalities   The English bulldog is prone to abnormally growing eyelashes, a rolling in or out of the eyelid(s), and dry eye, a condition in which the eye(s) does not produce enough liquid.

Heart Disease   The English bulldog is prone to abnormal growth of the mitral valve(s) and malfunctioning valves.

Hip Dysplasia   An abnormal development of the hip joint(s).

Hydrocephalus   The accumulation of fluid in the brain.

Hypothyroidism   A common disease of thyroid hormone deficiency. The thyroid regulates your dog's metabolism. A large number of skin problems in dogs are caused by thyroid disease.

Pyloric Stenosis   A constriction of the opening of the lower end of the stomach.

Skin Disease   The English bulldog is prone to infections on the face and tail due to excessive skin folds, inflammation of the hair follicle(s), deep infections in the skin (boils), and demodectic mange. Demodectic mange is a skin disease in which canine mites are living in the skin, causing itching, loss of hair, and skin infections; it is usually found on the face and front legs.

Spina Bifida   A developmental abnormality in which the vertebrae fail to encircle the spinal cord.

Teeth Abnormalities   The number, placement, or development of the teeth is not normal.

Trachea Hypoplasia   Incomplete development of the trachea.

Vaginal Hyperplasia   An increase in the number of cells in the tissues of the vagina, possibly indicating a precancerous condition.

Vertebra Malformation   A condition in which only half the vertebra is formed.

Von Willebrand's Disease   Abnormal blood-clotting defect involving both platelet and coagulation function (factor VIII).

English Foxhound

Deafness   A partial or total loss of hearing.

Osteochondrosis (Spinal)   An abnormal development of the vertebrae.

English Setter

Blood-Clotting Disorder   The English setter is prone to a blood-clotting disorder due to coagulation factor VIII deficiency.

Cataract   In elderly dogs the lens of the eye becomes cloudy, causing a partial or total loss of vision.

Craniomandibular Osteopathy   Abnormally dense bones in the face and the jaw.

Deafness   A partial or total loss of hearing.

Eclampsia   Convulsions during or after whelping.

Eye Abnormalities   The English setter is prone to a rolling in or out of the eyelid(s) and dry eye, a condition in which the eye(s) does not produce enough liquid.

Gastric Bloat and Torsion   Gastric bloat is a swelling of the stomach from excess gas and is usually followed by gastric torsion, a twisting of the stomach. Gastric torsion will result in death if not treated immediately.

Hip Dysplasia   An abnormal development of the hip joint(s).

Hypoglycemia   A low level of glucose (blood sugar) in the blood.

Hypothyroidism   A common disease of thyroid hormone deficiency. The thyroid regulates your dog's metabolism. A large number of skin problems in dogs are caused by thyroid disease.

Lipidosis   An accumulation of lipids (fats) in the nerves.

Neuronal Ceroid-Lipofuscinosis   An accumulation of fatty pigments in the brain.

Osteochondritis Dissecans   Inflammation of the cartilage in the joints. A form of arthritis.

Osteochondrosis   An abnormal development of joint cartilage. Most commonly found in the shoulder, knee, and elbow.

Progressive Retinal Atrophy (PRA)   A slow deterioration of the retina, leading to blindness.

Von Willebrand's Disease   Abnormal blood-clotting defect involving both platelet and coagulation function (factor VIII).

Flat-Coated Retriever

Cataract   In elderly dogs the lens of the eye becomes cloudy, causing a partial or total loss of vision.

Eye Abnormalities   The flat-coated retriever is prone to a rolling in or out of the eyelid(s) and abnormally growing eyelashes.

Hip Dysplasia   An abnormal development of the hip joint(s).

Hypothyroidism   A common disease of thyroid hormone deficiency. The thyroid regulates your dog's metabolism. A large number of skin problems in dogs are caused by thyroid disease.

Progressive Retinal Atrophy (PRA)   A slow deterioration of the retina, leading to blindness.

German Shepherd

Allergies   The German shepherd is prone to all types of allergies.

Antibody (Type IgA) Deficiency   A deficiency of the production of type IgA antibody, causing a weakened immune system.

Behavioral Abnormalities   The German shepherd is prone to a whole range of abnormal behavior patterns, such as aggression and panic disorders.

Blood-Clotting Disorders   The German shepherd is prone to blood-clotting disorders due to coagulation factor VIII or IX deficiency.

Calcinosis   Hard lumps of calcium salt deposits in the skin.

Cancer   The German shepherd is prone to hemangiosarcoma, which is a cancer of the blood vessels involving the liver, spleen, or skin, and bone cancer.

Cataract   In elderly dogs the lens of the eye becomes cloudy, causing a partial or total loss of vision.

Cleft Palate and/or Lip   Both are birth defects. With cleft palate, the roof of the mouth does not grow properly, leaving a hole from the roof of the mouth into the nose. With cleft lip, the skin below the nose does not grow together.

Corneal Dystrophy   An inherited degenerative condition in which the cornea of the eye becomes cloudy or opaque.

Cutaneous Vasculopathy   A puppy disease characterized by swollen footpads that lose their color and lesions and crusting on the ear(s) and tail.

Degenerative Myelopathy   A progressive deterioration of the spinal cord.

Dermoid Cyst   A skinlike growth, usually seen on the back.

Ehler's-Danlos Syndrome   A connective tissue disease in which the skin is very fragile and is easily cut or bruised.

Elbow Dysplasia   An abnormal development of the elbow joint(s).

Eosinophilic Panosteitis   An inflammatory bone disease found in fast-growing puppies, which is accompanied by increased eosinophils, a type of white blood cell.

Epilepsy   A brain disorder in which the dog experiences seizures (convulsions).

Esophageal Disorder   Spasms of the muscles of the esophagus.

Eye Abnormalities   The German shepherd is prone to abnormal development of the eye(s), a rolling in of the eyelid(s), protruding third eyelid(s), and a disorder in which the lens of the eye(s) slips out of place.

Gastric Bloat and Torsion   Gastric bloat is a swelling of the stomach from excess gas and is usually followed by gastric torsion, a twisting of the stomach. Gastric torsion will result in death if not treated immediately.

Glycogen Storage Disease   An inability to store and use the complex carbohydrate glycogen, which is primarily stored in the liver and muscle.

Heart Disease   The German shepherd is prone to cardiomyopathy, or weakened heart muscles, and a malfunctioning valve(s).

Hereditary Kidney Hypoplasia   A condition in which the dog is born with immature kidneys that never develop completely.

Hip Dysplasia   An abnormal development of the hip joint(s).

Incontinence   Loss of control of urination and bowel movements.

Keratitis   Inflammation of the cornea.

Keratoacanthoma   Noncancerous skin tumor, usually found on the face.

Lymphedema   An accumulation of fluid in the tissues due to a disorder of the lymphatic system.

Malabsorption   A condition in which the small intestine does not absorb nutrients properly.

Myasthenia Gravis   An autoimmune disease characterized by progressive muscle fatigue and generalized weakness as the result of impaired transmission of nerve impulses.

Osteochondritis Dissecans   Inflammation of the cartilage in the joints. A form of arthritis.

Osteochondrosis   An abnormal development of joint cartilage. Most commonly found in the shoulder, knee, and elbow.

Pancreatic Insufficiency   A digestive enzyme deficiency.

Pannus   A progressive immune-mediated disease in which there is a growth of tissue over the cornea, causing inflammation and possible blindness.

Progressive Retinal Atrophy (PRA)   A slow deterioration of the retina, leading to blindness.

Silica Uroliths   Bladder stones formed primarily from silicone.

Skin Disease   The German shepherd is prone to deep infections in the skin (boils), autoimmune diseases of the skin, infections of the nose and ear(s), and seborrhea, which is characterized by scaly, crusty, greasy skin.

Systemic Lupus Erythematosus   An autoimmune disease characterized by skin infections, organ disorders, and blood abnormalities.

Thyroid Disease   The German shepherd is prone to thyroiditis, lymphocytic thyroiditis, and hypothyroidism. Thyroiditis and lymphocytic thyroiditis are autoimmune diseases that lead to hypothyroidism, a common disease of thyroid hormone deficiency. The thyroid regulates your dog's metabolism. A large number of skin problems in dogs are caused by thyroid disease.

Ulcerative Colitis   A chronic inflammation of the colon that results in the formation of ulcers in the colon.

Von Willebrand's Disease   Abnormal blood-clotting defect involving both platelet and coagulation function (factor VIII).

Zinc-Responsive Dermatosis   Skin disease caused by a zinc deficiency.

German Shorthaired Pointer

Acral Mutilation   Mutilation of the feet and legs from excessive licking. Seen in pointing breeds that are born without pain sensation.

Addison's Disease   A disease in which the adrenal glands secrete an insufficient amount of cortisone, a steroid hormone.

Cancer   The German shorthaired pointer is prone to cancer of the fibrous tissues and skin cancer.

Cataract   In elderly dogs the lens of the eye becomes cloudy, causing a partial or total loss of vision.

Corneal Dystrophy   An inherited degenerative condition in which the cornea of the eye becomes cloudy or opaque.

Eye Abnormalities   The German shorthaired pointer is prone to a rolling in of the eyelid(s) and protruding third eyelid(s).

Hip Dysplasia   An abnormal development of the hip joint(s).

Hypothyroidism   A common disease of thyroid hormone deficiency. The thyroid regulates your dog's metabolism. A large number of skin problems in dogs are caused by thyroid disease.

Lipidosis   An accumulation of lipids (fats) in the nerves.

Lymphedema   An accumulation of fluid in the tissues due to a disorder of the lymphatic system.

Neuronal Ceroid-Lipofuscinosis   An accumulation of fatty pigments in the brain.

Osteochondritis Dissecans   Inflammation of the cartilage in the joints. A form of arthritis.

Osteochondrosis   An abnormal development of joint cartilage. Most commonly found in the shoulder, knee, and elbow.

Pannus   A progressive immune-mediated disease in which there is a growth of tissue over the cornea, causing inflammation and possible blindness.

Progressive Retinal Atrophy (PRA)   A slow deterioration of the retina, leading to blindness.

Subaortic Stenosis   A constriction of the valve between the heart and the aorta.

Thrombocytopathy   The small blood cells that are needed to control bleeding are dysfunctional.

Von Willebrand's Disease   Abnormal blood-clotting defect involving both platelet and coagulation function (factor VIII).

Zinc-Responsive Dermatosis   Skin disease caused by a zinc deficiency.

German Wirehaired Pointer

Cataract   In elderly dogs the lens of the eye becomes cloudy, causing a partial or total loss of vision.

Eye Abnormalities   The German wirehaired pointer is prone to a rolling in of the eyelid(s) and abnormal development of the retina(s).

Hip Dysplasia   An abnormal development of the hip joint(s).

Osteochondritis Dissecans   Inflammation of the cartilage in the joints. A form of arthritis.

Osteochondrosis   An abnormal development of joint cartilage. Most commonly found in the shoulder, knee, and elbow.

Subcutaneous Cyst   A fluid-filled sac located just beneath the skin.

Von Willebrand's Disease   Abnormal blood-clotting defect involving both platelet and coagulation function (factor VIII).

Giant Schnauzer

Cataract   In elderly dogs the lens of the eye becomes cloudy, causing a partial or total loss of vision.

Eosinophilic Panosteitis   An inflammatory bone disease found in fast-growing puppies, which is accompanied by increased eosinophils, a type of white blood cell.

Eye Abnormality   The giant schnauzer is prone to abnormal development of the retina(s).

Glaucoma   Pressure on the retina from excess fluid in the eyeball, which causes partial or total loss of vision.

Hip Dysplasia   An abnormal development of the hip joint(s).

Hypertrophic Osteodystrophy   A painful inflammation of the bones along with development of bony growths, found in fast-growing giant and large breeds.

Immune-Mediated Hemolytic Anemia (IMHA)   Anemia resulting from an immune system–mediated destruction of the red blood cells.

Osteochondritis Dissecans   Inflammation of the cartilage in the joints. A form of arthritis.

Osteochondrosis   An abnormal development of joint cartilage. Most commonly found in the shoulder, knee, and elbow.

Progressive Retinal Atrophy (PRA)   A slow deterioration of the retina, leading to blindness.

Seborrhea   A skin disease characterized by raw, scaling skin and an excess of sebum (oil-like substance), which causes a rancid body odor.

Thrombocytopenia   An abnormal decrease in the number of blood platelets. Blood platelets play a role in blood clotting. Symptoms are tiny hemorrhages in the skin and mucous membranes.

Thyroid Disease   The giant schnauzer is prone to thyroiditis, lymphocytic thyroiditis, and hypothyroidism. Thyroiditis and lymphocytic thyroiditis are autoimmune diseases that lead to hypothyroidism, a common disease of thyroid hormone deficiency. The thyroid regulates your dog's metabolism. A large number of skin problems in dogs are caused by thyroid disease.

Vitamin B$_{12}$–Responsive Malabsorption A condition in which puppies have an inability to absorb vitamin B$_{12}$, which is characterized by chronic anemia, low white blood cell counts, and metabolites (methylmalonic acid) in the urine.

Golden Retriever

Allergies The golden retriever is prone to all types of allergies.

Blood-Clotting Disorders The golden retriever is prone to blood-clotting disorders due to coagulation factor VIII or IX deficiency.

Cancer The golden retriever is prone to cancer of the lymphatic system and hemangiosarcoma, which is a cancer of the blood vessels involving the liver, spleen, or skin.

Cataract In elderly dogs the lens of the eye becomes cloudy, causing a partial or total loss of vision.

Corneal Dystrophy An inherited degenerative condition in which the cornea of the eye becomes cloudy or opaque.

Elbow Dysplasia An abnormal development of the elbow joint(s).

Epilepsy A brain disorder in which the dog experiences seizures (convulsions).

Eye Abnormalities The golden retriever is prone to abnormally developing eye(s), a rolling in or out of the eyelid(s), malformation of the optic nerve, and abnormally growing eyelashes.

Heart Disease The golden retriever is prone to cardiomyopathy, or weakened heart muscles, and malfunctioning valve(s).

Hip Dysplasia An abnormal development of the hip joint(s).

Immune-Mediated Hemolytic Anemia (IMHA) Anemia resulting from an immune system–mediated destruction of the red blood cells.

Liver Abnormality The golden retriever is prone to an abnormal formation of blood vessels in the liver.

Muscular Dystrophy   A progressive muscle disorder that causes a wasting of the muscles. It is an inherited disease, with symptoms of slow growth, difficulty eating and swallowing, and weakness.

Myasthenia Gravis   An autoimmune disease characterized by progressive muscle fatigue and generalized weakness as the result of impaired transmission of nerve impulses.

Osteochondritis Dissecans   Inflammation of the cartilage in the joints. A form of arthritis.

Osteochondrosis   An abnormal development of joint cartilage. Most commonly found in the shoulder, knee, and elbow.

Pigmentation Abnormality   A lack of color in the skin.

Progressive Retinal Atrophy (PRA)   A slow deterioration of the retina, leading to blindness.

Skin Disease   The golden retriever is prone to inflammation of the hair follicle(s), deep infections of the skin (boils), bacterial skin infections that cause excessive licking and chewing and progress into severe inflammation (hot spots), and an inflammation or infection of the skin from excessive licking (lick granuloma).

Thyroid Disease   The golden retriever is prone to thyroiditis, lymphocytic thyroiditis, and hypothyroidism. Thyroiditis and lymphocytic thyroiditis are autoimmune diseases that lead to hypothyroidism, a common disease of thyroid hormone deficiency. The thyroid regulates your dog's metabolism. A large number of skin problems in dogs are caused by thyroid disease.

Von Willebrand's Disease   Abnormal blood-clotting defect involving both platelet and coagulation function (factor VIII).

Gordon Setter

Cataract   In elderly dogs the lens of the eye becomes cloudy, causing a partial or total loss of vision.

Cerebellar Abiotrophy   Malformation of the neurons in the cerebellum. The cerebellum is the part of the brain that gives your dog coordination, posture, and balance.

Eye Abnormalities   The Gordon setter is prone to dry eye, a condition in which the eye(s) does not produce enough liquid, a rolling in of the eyelid(s), and abnormal development of the retina(s).

Gastric Bloat and Torsion   Gastric bloat is a swelling of the stomach from excess gas and is usually followed by gastric torsion, a twisting of the stomach. Gastric torsion will result in death if not treated immediately.

Hip Dysplasia   An abnormal development of the hip joint(s).

Hypothyroidism   A common disease of thyroid hormone deficiency. The thyroid regulates your dog's metabolism. A large number of skin problems in dogs are caused by thyroid disease.

Osteochondritis Dissecans   Inflammation of the cartilage in the joints. A form of arthritis.

Osteochondrosis   An abnormal development of joint cartilage. Most commonly found in the shoulder, knee, and elbow.

Progressive Retinal Atrophy (PRA)   A slow deterioration of the retina, leading to blindness.

Greyhound

Anesthetic Sensitivity   A serious condition in which the dog is very sensitive to anesthesia. In many cases the dog is also sensitive to medications and flea control products that contain pesticides.

Blood-Clotting Disorder   The greyhound is prone to a blood-clotting disorder due to coagulation factor VIII deficiency.

Cancer   The greyhound is prone to bone cancer.

Cataract   In elderly dogs the lens of the eye becomes cloudy, causing a partial or total loss of vision.

Corneal Dystrophy   An inherited degenerative condition in which the cornea of the eye becomes cloudy or opaque.

Dystocia   Complications giving birth.

Ehler's-Danlos Syndrome   A connective tissue disease in which the skin is very fragile and is easily cut or bruised.

Epilepsy   A brain disorder in which the dog experiences seizures (convulsions).

Esophageal Disorder   Spasms of the muscles of the esophagus.

Eye Abnormalities   The greyhound is prone to abnormally growing eyelashes, the lens in the eye slipping out of place, and optic nerve malformation.

Gastric Bloat and Torsion   Gastric bloat is a swelling of the stomach from excess gas and is usually followed by gastric torsion, a twisting of the stomach. Gastric torsion will result in death if not treated immediately.

Hygroma   A thick-walled, fluid-filled sac, usually found on the elbows.

Hypothyroidism   A common disease of thyroid hormone deficiency. The thyroid regulates your dog's metabolism. A large number of skin problems in dogs are caused by thyroid disease.

Osteochondritis Dissecans   Inflammation of the cartilage in the joints. A form of arthritis.

Osteochondrosis   An abnormal development of joint cartilage. Most commonly found in the shoulder, knee, and elbow.

Pannus   A progressive immune-mediated disease in which there is a growth of tissue over the cornea, causing inflammation and possible blindness.

Progressive Retinal Atrophy (PRA)   A slow deterioration of the retina, leading to blindness.

Von Willebrand's Disease   Abnormal blood-clotting defect involving both platelet and coagulation function (factor VIII).

Irish Water Spaniel

Cataract In elderly dogs the lens of the eye becomes cloudy, causing a partial or total loss of vision.

Hip Dysplasia An abnormal development of the hip joint(s).

Hypothyroidism A common disease of thyroid hormone deficiency. The thyroid regulates your dog's metabolism. A large number of skin problems in dogs are caused by thyroid disease.

Hypotrichosis An abnormally small amount of hair growth.

Progressive Retinal Atrophy (PRA) A slow deterioration of the retina, leading to blindness.

Teeth Abnormalities The number, placement, or development of the teeth is not normal.

Von Willebrand's Disease Abnormal blood-clotting defect involving both platelet and coagulation function (factor VIII).

Keeshond

Cancer The keeshond is prone to skin cancer.

Cataract In elderly dogs the lens of the eye becomes cloudy, causing a partial or total loss of vision.

Cushing's Disease (Hyperadrenocorticism) A condition in which the adrenal glands secrete too much cortisol. Cortisol is a steroid hormone that regulates carbohydrate, fat, and protein metabolism.

Diabetes Mellitus A disease caused by an insufficient production or use of insulin.

Epilepsy A brain disorder in which the dog experiences seizures (convulsions).

Eye Abnormalities   The keeshond is prone to abnormally growing eyelashes and a rolling out of the eyelid(s).

Glaucoma   Pressure on the retina from excess fluid in the eyeball, which causes partial or total loss of vision.

Heart Disease   The keeshond is prone to abnormal development of the ventricle(s), valve(s), and aorta.

Hereditary Kidney Hypoplasia   A condition in which the dog is born with immature kidneys that never develop completely.

Hypothyroidism   A common disease of thyroid hormone deficiency. The thyroid regulates your dog's metabolism. A large number of skin problems in dogs are caused by thyroid disease.

Keratoacanthoma   Noncancerous skin tumor, usually found on the face.

Liver Abnormality   The keeshond is prone to an abnormal formation of blood vessels in the liver.

Progressive Retinal Atrophy (PRA)   A slow deterioration of the retina, leading to blindness.

Sebaceous Cyst   A fluid-filled sac in the sebaceous gland.

Skin Disease   The keeshond is prone to skin problems that clear up if the dog is neutered and a skin disease caused by a deficiency of growth hormones.

Von Willebrand's Disease   Abnormal blood-clotting defect involving both platelet and coagulation function (factor VIII).

Labrador Retriever

Addison's Disease   A disease in which the adrenal glands secrete an insufficient amount of cortisone, a steroid hormone.

Allergies   The Labrador retriever is prone to all types of allergies.

Blood-Clotting Disorders   The Labrador retriever is prone to blood-clotting disorders due to coagulation factor VIII or IX deficiency.

Cancer   The Labrador retriever is prone to skin cancer.

Cataract   In elderly dogs the lens of the eye becomes cloudy, causing a partial or total loss of vision.

Craniomandibular Osteopathy   Abnormally dense bones in the face and the jaw.

Deafness   A partial or total loss of hearing.

Diabetes Mellitus   A disease caused by an insufficient production or use of insulin.

Elbow Dysplasia   An abnormal development of the elbow joint(s).

Epilepsy   A brain disorder in which the dog experiences seizures (convulsions).

Eye Abnormalities   The Labrador retriever is prone to abnormally growing eyelashes, a rolling in or out of the eyelid(s), an abnormal development of the eye(s), and an abnormal development of the retina(s).

Gastric Bloat and Torsion   Gastric bloat is a swelling of the stomach from excess gas and is usually followed by gastric torsion, a twisting of the stomach. Gastric torsion will result in death if not treated immediately.

Hip Dysplasia   An abnormal development of the hip joint(s).

Hot Spots   A bacterial skin infection that progresses into severe inflammation from excessive licking and chewing.

Hypertrophic Osteodystrophy   A painful inflammation of the bones along with development of bony growths, found in fast-growing giant and large breeds.

Hypoglycemia   A low level of glucose (blood sugar) in the blood.

Hypothyroidism   A common disease of thyroid hormone deficiency. The thyroid regulates your dog's metabolism. A large number of skin problems in dogs are caused by thyroid disease.

Lick Granuloma (Acral Lick Dermatitis)   Inflammation or infection of the skin from excessive licking. Usually found on the leg or paw.

Liver Abnormality   The Labrador retriever is prone to an abnormal formation of blood vessels in the liver.

Muscle Fiber Deficiency   A deficiency in form and/or function of a specific type of muscle fiber.

Muscular Dystrophy   A progressive muscle disorder that causes a wasting of the muscles. It is an inherited disease, with symptoms of slow growth, difficulty eating and swallowing, and weakness.

Narcolepsy   A neurological disorder in which the dog suddenly falls asleep.

Osteochondritis Dissecans   Inflammation of the cartilage in the joints. A form of arthritis.

Osteochondrosis   An abnormal development of joint cartilage. Most commonly found in the shoulder, knee, and elbow.

Progressive Retinal Atrophy (PRA)   A slow deterioration of the retina, leading to blindness.

Prolapsed Rectum   The rectum slips outside the anus.

Prolapsed Uterus   The uterus slips into the vaginal canal or through the vaginal opening.

Seborrhea   A skin disease characterized by raw, scaling skin and an excess of sebum (oil-like substance), which causes a rancid body odor.

Shoulder Dysplasia   Abnormal development of the shoulder joint(s).

Teeth Abnormalities   The number, placement, or development of the teeth is not normal.

Von Willebrand's Disease   Abnormal blood-clotting defect involving both platelet and coagulation function (factor VIII).

Wrist Subluxation   The wrist bones are loose and become partially dislocated.

Zinc-Responsive Dermatosis   Skin disease caused by a zinc deficiency.

Old English Sheepdog

Addison's Disease   A disease in which the adrenal glands secrete an insufficient amount of cortisone, a steroid hormone.

Blood-Clotting Disorder   The Old English sheepdog is prone to a blood-clotting disorder due to coagulation factor IX deficiency.

Cataract   In elderly dogs the lens of the eye becomes cloudy, causing a partial or total loss of vision.

Demodectic Mange   A skin disease in which canine mites are living in the skin, causing itching, loss of hair, and skin infections. Usually found on the face and front legs.

Eye Abnormalities   The Old English sheepdog is prone to a rolling in of the eyelid(s), abnormal development of the retina(s), and abnormally growing eyelashes.

Folliculitis   Inflammation of the hair follicle(s).

Hip Dysplasia   An abnormal development of the hip joint(s).

Immune-Mediated Hemolytic Anemia (IMHA)   Anemia resulting from an immune system–mediated destruction of the red blood cells.

Incontinence   Loss of control of urination and bowel movements.

Malabsorption   A condition in which the small intestine does not absorb nutrients properly.

Osteochondritis Dissecans   Inflammation of the cartilage in the joints. A form of arthritis.

Osteochondrosis   An abnormal development of joint cartilage. Most commonly found in the shoulder, knee, and elbow.

Pigmentation Abnormality   A lack of color in the skin.

Progressive Retinal Atrophy (PRA)   A slow deterioration of the retina, leading to blindness.

Thrombocytopenia   An abnormal decrease in the number of blood platelets. Blood platelets play a role in blood clotting. Symptoms are tiny hemorrhages in the skin and mucous membranes.

Thyroid Disease   The Old English sheepdog is prone to thyroiditis, lymphocytic thyroiditis, and hypothyroidism. Thyroiditis and lymphocytic thyroiditis are autoimmune diseases that lead to hypothyroidism, a common disease of thyroid hormone deficiency. The thyroid regulates your dog's metabolism. A large number of skin problems in dogs are caused by thyroid disease.

Von Willebrand's Disease   Abnormal blood-clotting defect involving both platelet and coagulation function (factor VIII).

Otterhound

Blood-Clotting Disorder   The otterhound is prone to a blood-clotting disorder due to coagulation factor II deficiency.

Hip Dysplasia   An abnormal development of the hip joint(s).

Hypothyroidism   A common disease of thyroid hormone deficiency. The thyroid regulates your dog's metabolism. A large number of skin problems in dogs are caused by thyroid disease.

Osteochondritis Dissecans   Inflammation of the cartilage in the joints. A form of arthritis.

Osteochondrosis   An abnormal development of joint cartilage. Most commonly found in the shoulder, knee, and elbow.

Sebaceous Cyst   A fluid-filled sac in the sebaceous gland.

Thrombocytopathy   The small blood cells that are needed to control bleeding are dysfunctional.

Von Willebrand's Disease   Abnormal blood-clotting defect involving both platelet and coagulation function (factor VIII).

Pharaoh Hound

Allergies   The pharaoh hound is prone to all types of allergies.

Eye Abnormality   The pharaoh hound is prone to abnormal development of the optic nerve(s).

Hypothyroidism   A common disease of thyroid hormone deficiency. The thyroid regulates your dog's metabolism. A large number of skin problems in dogs are caused by thyroid disease.

Thrombocytopenia   An abnormal decrease in the number of blood platelets. Blood platelets play a role in blood clotting. Symptoms are tiny hemorrhages in the skin and mucous membranes.

Pointer

Acral Mutilation   Mutilation of the feet and legs from excessive licking. Seen in pointing breeds that are born without pain sensation.

Allergies   The pointer is prone to all types of allergies.

Calcinosis   Hard lumps of calcium salt deposits in the skin.

Cataract   In elderly dogs the lens of the eye becomes cloudy, causing a partial or total loss of vision.

Corneal Dystrophy   An inherited degenerative condition in which the cornea of the eye becomes cloudy or opaque.

Demodectic Mange   A skin disease in which canine mites are living in the skin, causing itching, loss of hair, and skin infections. Usually found on the face and front legs.

Eosinophilic Panosteitis   An inflammatory bone disease found in fast-growing puppies, which is accompanied by increased eosinophils, a type of white blood cell.

Epilepsy   A brain disorder in which the dog experiences seizures (convulsions).

Eye Abnormality   The pointer is prone to a rolling in of the eyelid(s).

Hip Dysplasia   An abnormal development of the hip joint(s).

Hypothyroidism   A common disease of thyroid hormone deficiency. The thyroid regulates your dog's metabolism. A large number of skin problems in dogs are caused by thyroid disease.

Nerve Disorder   The pointer is prone to a condition in which the nerves malfunction, causing a deterioration of the muscles and/or bone disease.

Pannus   A progressive immune-mediated disease in which there is a growth of tissue over the cornea, causing inflammation and possible blindness.

Pemphigus Foliaceous   An autoimmune skin disease.

Progressive Retinal Atrophy (PRA)   A slow deterioration of the retina, leading to blindness.

Umbilical Hernia   A tear in the muscle wall in the stomach where the umbilical cord was.

Von Willebrand's Disease   Abnormal blood-clotting defect involving both platelet and coagulation function (factor VIII).

Rhodesian Ridgeback

Cataract   In elderly dogs the lens of the eye becomes cloudy, causing a partial or total loss of vision.

Cerebellar Abiotrophy   Malformation of the neurons in the cerebellum. The cerebellum is the part of the brain that gives your dog coordination, posture, and balance.

Dermoid Cyst   A skinlike growth, usually seen on the back.

Eye Abnormality   The Rhodesian Ridgeback is prone to a rolling in of the eyelid(s).

Hip Dysplasia   An abnormal development of the hip joint(s).

Hypothyroidism   A common disease of thyroid hormone deficiency. The thyroid regulates your dog's metabolism. A large number of skin problems in dogs are caused by thyroid disease.

Neck Vertebrae Malformation   An abnormal development of the vertebrae in the neck, causing nerve damage. Some dogs walk with a pronounced flexion of the knee, similar to a high-stepping horse.

Osteochondritis Dissecans   Inflammation of the cartilage in the joints. A form of arthritis.

Osteochondrosis   An abnormal development of joint cartilage. Most commonly found in the shoulder, knee, and elbow.

Progressive Retinal Atrophy (PRA)   A slow deterioration of the retina, leading to blindness.

Samoyed

Blood-Clotting Disorder   The Samoyed is prone to a blood-clotting disorder due to coagulation factor VIII deficiency.

Cancer   The Samoyed is prone to cancer of the anus.

Cataract   In elderly dogs the lens of the eye becomes cloudy, causing a partial or total loss of vision.

Corneal Dystrophy   An inherited degenerative condition in which the cornea of the eye becomes cloudy or opaque.

Diabetes Mellitus   A disease caused by an insufficient production or use of insulin.

Eye Abnormalities   The Samoyed is prone to a rolling in of the eyelid(s), abnormal development of the retina(s), and abnormally growing eyelashes.

Glaucoma   Pressure on the retina from excess fluid in the eyeball, which causes partial or total loss of vision.

Heart Disease The Samoyed is prone to malfunctioning valves and a malformation of the dividing wall between two chambers of the heart.

Hip Dysplasia An abnormal development of the hip joint(s).

Hypothyroidism A common disease of thyroid hormone deficiency. The thyroid regulates your dog's metabolism. A large number of skin problems in dogs are caused by thyroid disease.

Liver Abnormality The Samoyed is prone to an abnormal formation of blood vessels in the liver.

Muscular Dystrophy A progressive muscle disorder that causes a wasting of the muscles. It is an inherited disease, with symptoms of slow growth, difficulty eating and swallowing, and weakness.

Osteochondritis Dissecans Inflammation of the cartilage in the joints. A form of arthritis.

Osteochondrosis An abnormal development of joint cartilage. Most commonly found in the shoulder, knee, and elbow.

Pigmentation Abnormality A lack of color in the skin.

Progressive Retinal Atrophy (PRA) A slow deterioration of the retina, leading to blindness.

Samoyed Hereditary Glomerulopathy A condition in male puppies in which the blood vessels of the kidneys become diseased, causing kidney failure. Females can be carriers, remaining healthy until they are older, when they also experience kidney failure from diseased blood vessels of the kidney.

Sebaceous Cyst A fluid-filled sac in the sebaceous gland.

Thrombocytopenia An abnormal decrease in the number of blood platelets. Blood platelets play a role in blood clotting. Symptoms are tiny hemorrhages in the skin and mucous membranes.

Von Willebrand's Disease Abnormal blood-clotting defect involving both platelet and coagulation function (factor VIII).

Siberian Husky

Allergies   The Siberian husky is prone to an allergic reaction (inflamed tissue) from an accumulation of eosinophils, a type of white blood cell that functions in an allergic reaction to parasites.

Blood-Clotting Disorder   The Siberian husky is prone to a blood-clotting disorder due to coagulation factor VIII deficiency.

Castration-Responsive Dermatosis   A skin condition, characterized by loss of hair, thickened skin, and inflammation, that responds to castration.

Cataract   In elderly dogs the lens of the eye becomes cloudy, causing a partial or total loss of vision.

Corneal Dystrophy   An inherited degenerative condition in which the cornea of the eye becomes cloudy or opaque.

Eye Abnormalities   The Siberian husky is prone to a rolling in of the eyelid(s), abnormal development of the retina(s), and a condition in which the eye(s) slips out of place.

Glaucoma   Pressure on the retina from excess fluid in the eyeball, which causes partial or total loss of vision.

Hip Dysplasia   An abnormal development of the hip joint(s).

Hypothyroidism   A common disease of thyroid hormone deficiency. The thyroid regulates your dog's metabolism. A large number of skin problems in dogs are caused by thyroid disease.

Osteochondritis Dissecans   Inflammation of the cartilage in the joints. A form of arthritis.

Osteochondrosis   An abnormal development of joint cartilage. Most commonly found in the shoulder, knee, and elbow.

Pannus   A progressive immune-mediated disease in which there is a growth of tissue over the cornea, causing inflammation and possible blindness.

Pigmentation Abnormality   A lack of color in the skin.

Progressive Retinal Atrophy (PRA)   A slow deterioration of the retina, leading to blindness.

Skin Disease   The Siberian husky is prone to autoimmune skin diseases and zinc-responsive dermatosis, a skin disease caused by a zinc deficiency.

Von Willebrand's Disease   Abnormal blood-clotting defect involving both platelet and coagulation function (factor VIII).

Spinone Italiano

Eclampsia   Convulsions during or after whelping.

Eye Abnormality   The spinone italiano is prone to a rolling in of the eyelid(s).

Vizsla

Blood-Clotting Disorder   The vizsla is prone to a blood-clotting disorder due to coagulation factor VIII deficiency.

Cancer   The vizsla is prone to hemangiosarcoma, which is a cancer of the blood vessels involving the liver, spleen, or skin, and cancer of the lymphatic system.

Cataract   In elderly dogs the lens of the eye becomes cloudy, causing a partial or total loss of vision.

Craniomandibular Osteopathy   Abnormally dense bones in the face and the jaw.

Demodectic Mange   A skin disease in which canine mites are living in the skin, causing itching, loss of hair, and skin infections. Usually found on the face and front legs.

Epilepsy   A brain disorder in which the dog experiences seizures (convulsions).

Eye Abnormality   The vizsla is prone to a rolling in of the eyelid(s).

Hip Dysplasia   An abnormal development of the hip joint(s).

Hypothyroidism   A common disease of thyroid hormone deficiency. The thyroid regulates your dog's metabolism. A large number of skin problems in dogs are caused by thyroid disease.

Jaw Abnormality   The lower jaw is longer than the upper jaw.

Osteochondritis Dissecans   Inflammation of the cartilage in the joints. A form of arthritis.

Osteochondrosis   An abnormal development of joint cartilage. Most commonly found in the shoulder, knee, and elbow.

Pigmentation Abnormality   A lack of color in the skin.

Progressive Retinal Atrophy (PRA)   A slow deterioration of the retina, leading to blindness.

Spinal Abnormality   Malformation of the spinal cord.

Sterile Pyogranuloma Syndrome   A noninfectious disease of the deep layers of the skin, characterized by inflammation and sores.

Umbilical Hernia   A tear in the muscle wall in the stomach where the umbilical cord was.

Weimaraner

Alopecia   Loss of hair.

Antibody (Type IgA) Deficiency   A deficiency of the production of type IgA antibody, causing a weakened immune system.

Antibody (Type IgG) Deficiency   A deficiency of circulating antibodies, causing a weakened immune system.

Antibody (Type IgM) Deficiency   A deficiency of antibody production during the initial response of the immune system to an antigen.

Blood-Clotting Disorder   The weimaraner is prone to a blood-clotting disorder due to coagulation factor VIII deficiency.

Cancer   The weimaraner is prone to mastocytoma, a rare form of cancer in which the mast cells become cancerous. The mast cell secretes histamine in response to allergens.

Corneal Dystrophy   An inherited degenerative condition in which the cornea of the eye becomes cloudy or opaque.

Eosinophilic Panosteitis   An inflammatory bone disease found in fast-growing puppies, which is accompanied by increased eosinophils, a type of white blood cell.

Eye Abnormalities   The weimaraner is prone to a rolling in of the eyelid(s), abnormally growing eyelashes, and protruding third eyelid(s)

Gastric Bloat and Torsion   Gastric bloat is a swelling of the stomach from excess gas and is usually followed by gastric torsion, a twisting of the stomach. Gastric torsion will result in death if not treated immediately.

Growth Hormone–Responsive Dermatosis   Skin disorder caused by a deficiency of growth hormones.

Hip Dysplasia   An abnormal development of the hip joint(s).

Hypertrophic Osteodystrophy   A painful inflammation of the bones along with development of bony growths, found in fast-growing giant and large breeds.

Hypothyroidism   A common disease of thyroid hormone deficiency. The thyroid regulates your dog's metabolism. A large number of skin problems in dogs are caused by thyroid disease.

Jaw Abnormality   The lower jaw is longer than the upper jaw.

Myasthenia Gravis   An autoimmune disease characterized by progressive muscle fatigue and generalized weakness as the result of impaired transmission of nerve impulses.

Progressive Retinal Atrophy (PRA)   A slow deterioration of the retina, leading to blindness.

Spinal Abnormality   Malformation of the spinal cord.

Sterile Pyogranuloma Syndrome   A noninfectious disease of the deep layers of the skin, characterized by inflammation and sores.

T-Cell Deficiency   A deficiency of a type of white blood cell, the T-lymphocyte cell, resulting in a weakened immune system.

Umbilical Hernia   A tear in the muscle wall in the stomach where the umbilical cord was.

Vaccination Reaction   Puppies are prone to an autoimmune reaction from modified live virus vaccines.

Wirehaired Pointing Griffon

Hip Dysplasia   An abnormal development of the hip joint(s).

Narcolepsy   A neurological disorder in which the dog suddenly falls asleep.

Otitis Externa   An inflammation of the external parts of the ear.

Purebred Medium (20 to 50 Pounds)

American Cocker Spaniel

Allergies   The American cocker spaniel is prone to all types of allergies.

Anasarca   Newborn puppies have an accumulation of fluids in various tissues and body cavities.

Behavioral Abnormalities   The American cocker spaniel is prone to a whole range of abnormal behavior patterns, such as aggression and panic disorders.

Blood-Clotting Disorders   The American cocker spaniel is prone to blood-clotting disorders due to coagulation factor VIII, IX, or X deficiency.

Cancer   The American cocker spaniel is prone to cancer of the anus, skin cancer, and cancer of the mammary glands.

Cataract   In elderly dogs the lens of the eye becomes cloudy, causing a partial or total loss of vision.

Cleft Palate and/or Lip   Both are birth defects. With cleft palate, the roof of the mouth does not grow properly, leaving a hole from the roof of the mouth into the nose. With cleft lip, the skin below the nose does not grow together.

Corneal Dystrophy   An inherited degenerative condition in which the cornea of the eye becomes cloudy or opaque.

Cyclic Hematopoiesis   An inherited condition in which, periodically, a type of white blood cell is not produced.

Ehler's-Danlos Syndrome   A connective tissue disease in which the skin is very fragile and is easily cut or bruised.

Elbow Dysplasia   An abnormal development of the elbow joint(s).

Epidermoid Cyst   A fluid-filled sac in the outermost layer of the skin.

Epilepsy   A brain disorder in which the dog experiences seizures (convulsions).

Eye Abnormalities   The American cocker spaniel is prone to a rolling in or out of the eyelid(s), abnormally growing eyelashes, a condition in which the eye slips out of place, abnormal development of the retina(s), and a condition called dry eye, in which the eye(s) does not produce enough liquid.

Glaucoma   Pressure on the retina from excess fluid in the eyeball, which causes partial or total loss of vision.

Heart Disease   The American cocker spaniel is prone to cardiomyopathy, or weakened heart muscles.

Hereditary Kidney Hypoplasia   A condition in which the dog is born with immature kidneys that never develop completely.

Hernia   A rupture of the wall of an internal organ in the groin area.

Hip Dysplasia   An abnormal development of the hip joint(s).

Hydrocephalus   The accumulation of fluid in the brain.

Hypothyroidism   A common disease of thyroid hormone deficiency. The thyroid regulates your dog's metabolism. A large number of skin problems in dogs are caused by thyroid disease.

Immune-Mediated Hemolytic Anemia (IMHA)   Anemia resulting from an immune system–mediated destruction of the red blood cells.

Intervertebral Disc Disease   Abnormal development of the discs between the vertebrae.

Jaw Abnormality   The American cocker spaniel is prone to have a lower jaw that is longer than the upper jaw or to have an overshot jaw, a condition in which the upper jaw is too long for the lower jaw.

Osteochondritis Dissecans   Inflammation of the cartilage in the joints. A form of arthritis.

Osteochondrosis   An abnormal development of joint cartilage. Most commonly found in the shoulder, knee, and elbow.

Otitis Externa   An infection of the external structures of the ear.

Patellar Luxation   The kneecap(s) slips out of place.

Progressive Retinal Atrophy (PRA)   A slow deterioration of the retina, leading to blindness.

Skin Disease   The American cocker spaniel is prone to all types of allergic, nutritional, hormonal, parasitic, and autoimmune skin disease.

Skin Tumor   The American cocker spaniel is prone to all types of skin tumors.

Umbilical Hernia   A tear in the muscle wall in the stomach where the umbilical cord was.

Von Willebrand's Disease   Abnormal blood-clotting defect involving both platelet and coagulation function (factor VIII).

American Eskimo

Allergy   Allergic reaction to flea bites.

Hip Dysplasia   An abnormal development of the hip joint(s).

Urolithiasis   Stones or crystals in the urinary tract.

Australian Cattle Dog (Blue Heeler)

Blood-Clotting Disorder   The Australian cattle dog is prone to a blood-clotting disorder due to coagulation factor VIII deficiency.

Cataract   In elderly dogs the lens of the eye becomes cloudy, causing a partial or total loss of vision.

Deafness   A partial or total loss of hearing.

Epilepsy   A brain disorder in which the dog experiences seizures (convulsions).

Eye Abnormalities   The Australian cattle dog is prone to a condition in which the lens in the eye slips out of place and an abnormal development of the retina(s).

Hernia   A rupture of the wall of an internal organ in the groin area.

Hip Dysplasia   An abnormal development of the hip joint(s).

Hypothyroidism   A common disease of thyroid hormone deficiency. The thyroid regulates your dog's metabolism. A large number of skin problems in dogs are caused by thyroid disease.

Jaw Abnormality   The Australian cattle dog is prone to have a lower jaw that is longer than the upper jaw or to have an overshot jaw, a condition in which the upper jaw is too long for the lower jaw.

Liver Abnormality   The Australian cattle dog is prone to an abnormal formation of blood vessels in the liver.

Neuronal Ceroid-Lipofuscinosis   An accumulation of fatty pigments in the brain.

Osteochondritis Dissecans   Inflammation of the cartilage in the joints. A form of arthritis.

Progressive Retinal Atrophy (PRA)   A slow deterioration of the retina, leading to blindness.

Teeth Abnormalities   The number, placement, or development of the teeth is not normal.

Umbilical Hernia   A tear in the muscle wall in the stomach where the umbilical cord was.

Australian Kelpie

Collie Eye Anomaly   An inherited disorder in which the narrow shape of the head causes the eyes to be malformed.

Progressive Retinal Atrophy (PRA)   A slow deterioration of the retina, leading to blindness.

Australian Shepherd

Cataract   In elderly dogs the lens of the eye becomes cloudy, causing a partial or total loss of vision.

Cleft Palate   A birth defect in which the roof of the mouth does not grow properly, leaving a hole from the roof of the mouth into the nose.

Deafness   A partial or total loss of hearing.

Eye Abnormalities   The Australian shepherd is prone to abnormal development of the retina(s) and collie eye anomaly, which is an inherited disorder in which the narrow shape of the head causes the eyes to be malformed.

Hip Dysplasia   An abnormal development of the hip joint(s).

Hypothyroidism A common disease of thyroid hormone deficiency. The thyroid regulates your dog's metabolism. A large number of skin problems in dogs are caused by thyroid disease.

Osteochondritis Dissecans Inflammation of the cartilage in the joints. A form of arthritis.

Osteochondrosis An abnormal development of joint cartilage. Most commonly found in the shoulder, knee, and elbow.

Pigmentation Abnormality A lack of color in the skin.

Progressive Retinal Atrophy (PRA) A slow deterioration of the retina, leading to blindness.

Spina Bifida A developmental abnormality in which the vertebrae fail to encircle the spinal cord.

Umbilical Hernia A tear in the muscle wall in the stomach where the umbilical cord was.

Von Willebrand's Disease Abnormal blood-clotting defect involving both platelet and coagulation function (factor VIII).

Basenji

Blood-Clotting Disorder The basenji is prone to a blood-clotting disorder due to coagulation factor XII deficiency.

Coliform Enteritis Inflammation of the small intestine caused by bacteria.

Eye Abnormalities The basenji is prone to an abnormal development of the eye(s) or an abnormal development of the retina(s).

Hernia A rupture of the wall of an internal organ in the groin area.

Hypothyroidism A common disease of thyroid hormone deficiency. The thyroid regulates your dog's metabolism. A large number of skin problems in dogs are caused by thyroid disease.

Immune-Mediated Hemolytic Anemia (IMHA)   Anemia resulting from an immune system–mediated destruction of the red blood cells.

Malabsorption   A condition in which the small intestine does not absorb nutrients properly.

Progressive Retinal Atrophy (PRA)   A slow deterioration of the retina, leading to blindness.

Pyruvate Kinase Deficiency   A symptom of immune-mediated hemolytic anemia in basenjis. Pyruvate kinase is an essential red blood cell enzyme.

Renal Tubular Dysfunction   A condition in which the kidneys do not filter waste properly. In basenjis renal tubular dysfunction often leads to glycosuria (excess sugar in the urine).

Umbilical Hernia   A tear in the muscle wall in the stomach where the umbilical cord was.

Basset Hound

Addison's Disease   A disease in which the adrenal glands secrete an insufficient amount of cortisone, a steroid hormone.

Antibody (Type IgA) Deficiency   A deficiency of the production of type IgA antibody, causing a weakened immune system.

Antibody (Type IgG) Deficiency   A deficiency of circulating antibodies, causing a weakened immune system.

Antibody (Type IgM) Deficiency   A deficiency of antibody production during the initial response of the immune system to an antigen.

Behavioral Abnormalities   The basset hound is prone to a whole range of abnormal behavior patterns, such as aggression and panic disorders.

Blood-Clotting Disorders   The basset hound is prone to blood-clotting disorders due to coagulation factor VII or VIII deficiency.

Bone Disease   The basset hound is prone to developmental abnormalities of the bones.

Cryptorchidism   A developmental condition in which one or both testicles fail to descend into the scrotum.

Eosinophilic Panosteitis   An inflammatory bone disease found in fast-growing puppies, which is accompanied by increased eosinophils, a type of white blood cell.

Epilepsy   A brain disorder in which the dog experiences seizures (convulsions).

Eye Abnormalities   The basset hound is prone to a rolling in or out of the eyelid(s), protruding third eyelid(s), and a condition in which the lens in the eye slips out of place.

Gastric Bloat and Torsion   Gastric bloat is a swelling of the stomach from excess gas and is usually followed by gastric torsion, a twisting of the stomach. Gastric torsion will result in death if not treated immediately.

Glaucoma   Pressure on the retina from excess fluid in the eyeball, which causes partial or total loss of vision.

Globoid Cell Leukodystrophy   Degeneration of a type of brain cell.

Hernia   A rupture of the wall of an internal organ in the groin area.

Hot Spots   A bacterial skin infection that progresses into severe inflammation from excessive licking and chewing.

Hypothyroidism   A common disease of thyroid hormone deficiency. The thyroid regulates your dog's metabolism. A large number of skin problems in dogs are caused by thyroid disease.

Immune-Mediated Hemolytic Anemia (IMHA)   Anemia resulting from an immune system–mediated destruction of the red blood cells.

Intussusception   A section of the intestinal tract slips into an adjoining section.

Lung Torsion   A twisting of the lung upon itself.

Osteochondritis Dissecans   Inflammation of the cartilage in the joints. A form of arthritis.

Osteochondrosis   An abnormal development of joint cartilage. Most commonly found in the shoulder, knee, and elbow.

Patellar Luxation   The kneecap(s) slips out of place.

Platelet Dysfunction   Platelets, which are small blood cells needed to control bleeding, do not function properly.

Progressive Retinal Atrophy (PRA)   A slow deterioration of the retina, leading to blindness.

Sebaceous Cyst   A fluid-filled sac in the sebaceous gland.

Splenic Torsion   A twisting of the spleen upon itself.

T-Cell Deficiency   A deficiency of a type of white blood cell, the T-lymphocyte cell, resulting in a weakened immune system.

Thrombocytopathy   The small blood cells that are needed to control bleeding are dysfunctional.

Umbilical Hernia   A tear in the muscle wall in the stomach where the umbilical cord was.

Vertebra Abnormality   Malformation of the third cervical vertebra, which is one of the neck bones in the spinal column.

Von Willebrand's Disease   Abnormal blood-clotting defect involving both platelet and coagulation function (factor VIII).

Wobbler's Syndrome   The neck vertebrae are malformed, causing them to slip out of place, leading to incoordination of the rear legs.

Beagle

Allergies   The beagle is prone to all types of allergies.

Amyloidosis   Degeneration of the tissues from a buildup of hard, waxy deposits made of protein and polysaccharides (amyloid).

Antibody (Type IgA) Deficiency   A deficiency of the production of type IgA antibody, causing a weakened immune system.

Atopic Dermatitis   Skin disease from inhalant allergies.

Blood-Clotting Disorders   The beagle is prone to blood-clotting disorders due to coagulation factor VII, VIII, or IX deficiency.

Cancer   The beagle is prone to bladder cancer and cancer of the anus.

Cataract   In elderly dogs the lens of the eye becomes cloudy, causing a partial or total loss of vision.

Cleft Palate and/or Lip   Both are birth defects. With cleft palate, the roof of the mouth does not grow properly, leaving a hole from the roof of the mouth into the nose. With cleft lip, the skin below the nose does not grow together.

Corneal Dystrophy   An inherited degenerative condition in which the cornea of the eye becomes cloudy or opaque.

Demodectic Mange   A skin disease in which canine mites are living in the skin, causing itching, loss of hair, and skin infections. Usually found on the face and front legs.

Ear Infection   The beagle is prone to ear infections from dying cells in the ear and surrounding tissue.

Ehler's-Danlos Syndrome   A connective tissue disease in which the skin is very fragile and is easily cut or bruised.

Epilepsy   A brain disorder in which the dog experiences seizures (convulsions).

Epiphyseal Dysplasia   Abnormal development of the long bone.

Eye Abnormalities   The beagle is prone to abnormally growing eyelashes, protruding third eyelid(s), abnormal development of the retina(s), and malformation of the optic nerve.

Glaucoma   Pressure on the retina from excess fluid in the eyeball, which causes partial or total loss of vision.

Globoid Cell Leukodystrophy   Degeneration of a type of brain cell.

Heart Disease   The beagle is prone to malfunctioning valve(s) and abnormal development of the heart.

Immune-Mediated Hemolytic Anemia (IMHA)   Anemia resulting from an immune system–mediated destruction of the red blood cells.

Intervertebral Disc Disease   Abnormal development of the discs between the vertebrae.

Kidney Disease   The beagle is prone to abnormal development of the kidney(s) and a condition where there is only one kidney.

Lipidosis   An accumulation of lipids (fats) in the nerves.

Progressive Retinal Atrophy (PRA)   A slow deterioration of the retina, leading to blindness.

Sebaceous Gland Tumor   A skin tumor.

Thyroid Disease   The beagle is prone to thyroiditis, lymphocytic thyroiditis, and hypothyroidism. Thyroiditis and lymphocytic thyroiditis are autoimmune diseases that lead to hypothyroidism, a common disease of thyroid hormone deficiency. The thyroid regulates your dog's metabolism. A large number of skin problems in dogs are caused by thyroid disease.

Von Willebrand's Disease   Abnormal blood-clotting defect involving both platelet and coagulation function (factor VIII).

Belgian Malinois

Epilepsy   A brain disorder in which the dog experiences seizures (convulsions).

Hip Dysplasia   An abnormal development of the hip joint(s).

Hypothyroidism   A common disease of thyroid hormone deficiency. The thyroid regulates your dog's metabolism. A large number of skin problems in dogs are caused by thyroid disease.

Progressive Retinal Atrophy (PRA)   A slow deterioration of the retina, leading to blindness.

Border Collie

Corneal Dystrophy   An inherited degenerative condition in which the cornea of the eye becomes cloudy or opaque.

Epilepsy   A brain disorder in which the dog experiences seizures (convulsions).

Eye Abnormality   The Border collie is prone to a condition in which the lens in the eye slips out of place.

Hip Dysplasia   An abnormal development of the hip joint(s).

Neuronal Ceroid-Lipofuscinosis   An accumulation of fatty pigments in the brain.

Osteochondritis Dissecans   Inflammation of the cartilage in the joints. A form of arthritis.

Osteochondrosis   An abnormal development of joint cartilage. Most commonly found in the shoulder, knee, and elbow.

Progressive Retinal Atrophy (PRA)   A slow deterioration of the retina, leading to blindness.

Brittany Spaniel

Blood-Clotting Disorder   The Brittany spaniel is prone to a blood-clotting disorder due to coagulation factor VIII deficiency.

Cataract   In elderly dogs the lens of the eye becomes cloudy, causing a partial or total loss of vision.

Cleft Palate   A birth defect in which the roof of the mouth does not grow properly, leaving a hole from the roof of the mouth into the nose.

Eye Abnormalities   The Brittany spaniel is prone to abnormally growing eyelashes, a condition in which the lens in the eye slips out of place, and abnormal development of the retina(s).

Hereditary Glomerulopathy   A condition in male puppies in which the blood vessels of the kidneys become diseased, causing kidney failure. Females can be carriers, remaining healthy until they are older, when they also experience kidney failure from diseased blood vessels of the kidney.

Osteochondritis Dissecans   Inflammation of the cartilage in the joints. A form of arthritis.

Osteochondrosis   An abnormal development of joint cartilage. Most commonly found in the shoulder, knee, and elbow.

Progressive Retinal Atrophy (PRA)   A slow deterioration of the retina, leading to blindness.

Canaan Dog

Hip Dysplasia   An abnormal development of the hip joint(s).

Thyroid Disease   The Canaan dog is prone to thyroiditis, lymphocytic thyroiditis, and hypothyroidism. Thyroiditis and lymphocytic thyroiditis are autoimmune diseases that lead to hypothyroidism, a common disease of thyroid hormone deficiency. The thyroid regulates your dog's metabolism. A large number of skin problems in dogs are caused by thyroid disease.

Cardigan Welsh Corgi

Antibody (Type IgA) Deficiency   A deficiency of the production of type IgA antibody, causing a weakened immune system.

Antibody (Type IgG) Deficiency   A deficiency of circulating antibodies, causing a weakened immune system.

Antibody (Type IgM) Deficiency   A deficiency of antibody production during the initial response of the immune system to an antigen.

Dystocia   Complications giving birth.

Eye Abnormalities   The Cardigan Welsh corgi is prone to a rolling in of the eyelid(s), abnormal development of the retina(s), and a condition in which the lens in the eye slips out of place.

Glaucoma   Pressure on the retina from excess fluid in the eyeball, which causes partial or total loss of vision.

Intervertebral Disc Disease   Abnormal development of the discs between the vertebrae.

Progressive Retinal Atrophy (PRA)   A slow deterioration of the retina, leading to blindness.

T-Cell Deficiency   A deficiency of a type of white blood cell, the T-lymphocyte cell, resulting in a weakened immune system.

Chinese Shar-Pei

Allergies   The Chinese shar-pei is prone to all types of allergies.

Antibody (Type IgA) Deficiency   A deficiency of the production of type IgA antibody, causing a weakened immune system.

Carpal Laxity   Weak carpal (wrist) ligaments.

Demodectic Mange   A skin disease in which canine mites are living in the skin, causing itching, loss of hair, and skin infections. Usually found on the face and front legs.

Dermatitis   An inflammation in the skin folds.

Eye Abnormalities   The Chinese shar-pei is prone to a rolling in or out of the eyelid(s), tight muscles around the eyes causing repetitive blinking, abnormal development of the retina(s), and a condition in which the lens in the eye slips out of place.

Folliculitis   Inflammation of the hair follicle(s).

Gastric Bloat and Torsion   Gastric bloat is a swelling of the stomach from excess gas and is usually followed by gastric torsion, a twisting of the stomach. Gastric torsion will result in death if not treated immediately.

Glaucoma   Pressure on the retina from excess fluid in the eyeball, which causes partial or total loss of vision.

Hip Dysplasia   An abnormal development of the hip joint(s).

Hypothyroidism   A common disease of thyroid hormone deficiency. The thyroid regulates your dog's metabolism. A large number of skin problems in dogs are caused by thyroid disease.

Jaw Abnormality   The lower jaw is longer than the upper jaw.

Malabsorption   A condition in which the small intestine does not absorb nutrients properly.

Osteochondritis Dissecans   Inflammation of the cartilage in the joints. A form of arthritis.

Osteochondrosis   An abnormal development of joint cartilage. Most commonly found in the shoulder, knee, and elbow.

Otitis Externa   An infection of the external structures of the ear.

Patellar Luxation   The kneecap(s) slips out of place.

Progressive Retinal Atrophy (PRA)   A slow deterioration of the retina, leading to blindness.

Seborrhea   A skin disease characterized by raw, scaling skin and an excess of sebum (oil-like substance), which causes a rancid body odor.

Stenotic Nares   A condition in which excess flesh causes the openings of the nose (nares) to be too small to breathe with ease.

Tight Lip Syndrome   A condition in which the lower lip is too big and covers the lower teeth.

English Cocker Spaniel

Blood-Clotting Disorders   The English cocker spaniel is prone to blood-clotting disorders due to coagulation factor II or VIII deficiency.

Cataract   In elderly dogs the lens of the eye becomes cloudy, causing a partial or total loss of vision.

Cryptorchidism   A developmental condition in which one or both testicles fail to descend into the scrotum.

Eye Abnormalities   The English cocker spaniel is prone to a rolling in or out of the eyelid(s), abnormally growing eyelashes, abnormal development of the retina(s), and a condition in which the lens in the eye slips out of place.

Glaucoma   Pressure on the retina from excess fluid in the eyeball, which causes partial or total loss of vision.

Hypothyroidism   A common disease of thyroid hormone deficiency. The thyroid regulates your dog's metabolism. A large number of skin problems in dogs are caused by thyroid disease.

Neuronal Ceroid-Lipofuscinosis   An accumulation of fatty pigments in the brain.

Osteochondritis Dissecans   Inflammation of the cartilage in the joints. A form of arthritis.

Osteochondrosis   An abnormal development of joint cartilage. Most commonly found in the shoulder, knee, and elbow.

Progressive Retinal Atrophy (PRA)   A slow deterioration of the retina, leading to blindness.

Skin Disease   The English cocker spaniel is prone to allergic, nutritional, hormonal, parasitic, and autoimmune skin disease.

Swimmer Puppies   A developmental condition caused by a weakness of the muscles puppies use to pull their legs together. Newborns are unable to put their feet under them to walk.

Von Willebrand's Disease   Abnormal blood-clotting defect involving both platelet and coagulation function (factor VIII).

English Springer Spaniel

Addison's Disease   A disease in which the adrenal glands secrete an insufficient amount of cortisone, a steroid hormone.

Allergies   The English springer spaniel is prone to all types of allergies.

Anasarca   Newborn puppies have an accumulation of fluids in various tissues and body cavities.

Behavioral Abnormalities   The English springer spaniel is prone to a whole range of abnormal behavior patterns, such as aggression, panic disorders, and sudden attacks of rage.

Blood-Clotting Disorders   The English springer spaniel is prone to blood-clotting disorders due to coagulation factor VIII, IX, X, or XI deficiency.

Cancer   The English springer spaniel is prone to skin cancer, cancer of the anus, and cancer of the mammary glands.

Cataract   In elderly dogs the lens of the eye becomes cloudy, causing a partial or total loss of vision.

Cleft Palate and/or Lip   Both are birth defects. With cleft palate, the roof of the mouth does not grow properly, leaving a hole from the roof of the mouth into the nose. With cleft lip, the skin below the nose does not grow together.

Corneal Dystrophy   An inherited degenerative condition in which the cornea of the eye becomes cloudy or opaque.

Ehler's-Danlos Syndrome   A connective tissue disease in which the skin is very fragile and is easily cut or bruised.

Elbow Dysplasia   An abnormal development of the elbow joint(s).

Epidermoid Cyst   A fluid-filled sac in the outermost layer of the skin.

Epilepsy   A brain disorder in which the dog experiences seizures (convulsions).

Eye Abnormalities   The English springer spaniel is prone to abnormal development of the eye(s), a rolling in or out of the eyelid(s), abnormally growing eyelashes, and abnormal development of the retina(s).

Glaucoma   Pressure on the retina from excess fluid in the eyeball, which causes partial or total loss of vision.

Hereditary Kidney Hypoplasia   A condition in which the dog is born with immature kidneys that never develop completely.

Hernia   A rupture of the wall of an internal organ in the groin area.

Hip Dysplasia   An abnormal development of the hip joint(s).

Hydrocephalus   The accumulation of fluid in the brain.

Hypothyroidism   A common disease of thyroid hormone deficiency. The thyroid regulates your dog's metabolism. A large number of skin problems in dogs are caused by thyroid disease.

Immune-Mediated Hemolytic Anemia (IMHA)   Anemia resulting from an immune system–mediated destruction of the red blood cells.

Intervertebral Disc Disease   Abnormal development of the discs between the vertebrae.

Jaw Abnormality   The English springer spaniel is prone to have a lower jaw longer than the upper jaw or to have an overshot jaw, a condition in which the upper jaw is too long for the lower jaw.

Narcolepsy   A neurological disorder in which the dog suddenly falls asleep.

Osteochondritis Dissecans   Inflammation of the cartilage in the joints. A form of arthritis.

Osteochondrosis   An abnormal development of joint cartilage. Most commonly found in the shoulder, knee, and elbow.

Otitis Externa   An infection of the external structures of the ear.

Patellar Luxation   The kneecap(s) slips out of place.

Phosphofructokinase Deficiency   A deficiency of a specific red blood cell enzyme.

Progressive Retinal Atrophy (PRA)   A slow deterioration of the retina, leading to blindness.

Seborrhea   A skin disease characterized by raw, scaling skin and an excess of sebum (oil-like substance), which causes a rancid body odor.

Skin Tumors   The English springer spaniel is prone to all types of skin tumors.

Umbilical Hernia   A tear in the muscle wall in the stomach where the umbilical cord was.

Von Willebrand's Disease   Abnormal blood-clotting defect involving both platelet and coagulation function (factor VIII).

Field Spaniel

Anesthetic Sensitivity   A serious condition in which the dog is very sensitive to anesthesia. In many cases the dog is also sensitive to medications and flea control products that contain pesticides.

Cataract   In elderly dogs the lens of the eye becomes cloudy, causing a partial or total loss of vision.

Eye Abnormality   The field spaniel is prone to abnormal development of the retina(s).

Hypothyroidism   A common disease of thyroid hormone deficiency. The thyroid regulates your dog's metabolism. A large number of skin problems in dogs are caused by thyroid disease.

Progressive Retinal Atrophy (PRA)   A slow deterioration of the retina, leading to blindness.

Finnish Spitz

Diabetes Mellitus   A disease caused by an insufficient production or use of insulin.

French Bulldog

Blood-Clotting Disorders   The French bulldog is prone to blood-clotting disorders due to coagulation factor II, VIII, or IX deficiency.

Cataract   In elderly dogs the lens of the eye becomes cloudy, causing a partial or total loss of vision.

Cleft Palate and/or Lip   Both are birth defects. With cleft palate, the roof of the mouth does not grow properly, leaving a hole from the roof of the mouth into the nose. With cleft lip, the skin below the nose does not grow together.

Eye Abnormalities   The French bulldog is prone to abnormally growing eyelashes and a rolling in of the eyelid(s).

Vertebra Malformation   A condition in which only half the vertebra is formed.

Von Willebrand's Disease   Abnormal blood-clotting defect involving both platelet and coagulation function (factor VIII).

Harrier

Epilepsy   A brain disorder in which the dog experiences seizures (convulsions).

Hip Dysplasia   An abnormal development of the hip joint(s).

Hungarian Puli

Behavioral Abnormalities   The Hungarian puli is prone to a whole range of abnormal behavior patterns, such as aggression and panic disorders.

Cataract   In elderly dogs the lens of the eye becomes cloudy, causing a partial or total loss of vision.

Eye Abnormality   The Hungarian puli is prone to abnormal development of the retina(s).

Hip Dysplasia   An abnormal development of the hip joint(s).

Progressive Retinal Atrophy (PRA)   A slow deterioration of the retina, leading to blindness.

Ibizan Hound

Allergies   The Ibizan hound is prone to all types of allergies.

Anesthetic Sensitivity   A serious condition in which the dog is very sensitive to anesthesia. In many cases the dog is also sensitive to medications and flea control products that contain pesticides.

Cataract   In elderly dogs the lens of the eye becomes cloudy, causing a partial or total loss of vision.

Cryptorchidism   A developmental condition in which one or both testicles fail to descend into the scrotum.

Eye Abnormality   The Ibizan hound is prone to abnormal development of the retina(s).

Hypothyroidism   A common disease of thyroid hormone deficiency. The thyroid regulates your dog's metabolism. A large number of skin problems in dogs are caused by thyroid disease.

Thrombocytopenia   An abnormal decrease in the number of blood platelets. Blood platelets play a role in blood clotting. Symptoms are tiny hemorrhages in the skin and mucous membranes.

Irish Setter

Allergies   The Irish setter is prone to all types of allergies.

Blood-Clotting Disorder   The Irish setter is prone to a blood-clotting disorder due to coagulation factor VIII deficiency.

Bone Disease   The Irish setter is prone to diseases of the bone caused by a metabolic dysfunction.

Cataract   In elderly dogs the lens of the eye becomes cloudy, causing a partial or total loss of vision.

Corneal Dystrophy   An inherited degenerative condition in which the cornea of the eye becomes cloudy or opaque.

Elbow Dysplasia   An abnormal development of the elbow joint(s).

Epilepsy   A brain disorder in which the dog experiences seizures (convulsions).

Eye Abnormalities   The Irish setter is prone to a rolling in of the eyelid(s), abnormal development of the optic nerve, abnormally growing eyelashes, and a condition in which the lens in the eye slips out of place.

Folliculitis   Inflammation of the hair follicle(s).

Gastric Bloat and Torsion   Gastric bloat is a swelling of the stomach from excess gas and is usually followed by gastric torsion, a twisting of the stomach. Gastric torsion will result in death if not treated immediately.

Generalized Myopathy   A muscle disorder that affects all muscles.

Hip Dysplasia   An abnormal development of the hip joint(s).

Hypothyroidism   A common disease of thyroid hormone deficiency. The thyroid regulates your dog's metabolism. A large number of skin problems in dogs are caused by thyroid disease.

Immune-Mediated Hemolytic Anemia (IMHA)   Anemia resulting from an immune system–mediated destruction of the red blood cells.

Lick Granuloma (Acral Lick Dermatitis)   Inflammation or infection of the skin from excessive licking. Usually found on the leg or paw.

Lymphedema   An accumulation of fluid in the tissues due to a disorder of the lymphatic system.

Narcolepsy   A neurological disorder in which the dog suddenly falls asleep.

Osteochondritis Dissecans   Inflammation of the cartilage in the joints. A form of arthritis.

Osteochondrosis   An abnormal development of joint cartilage. Most commonly found in the shoulder, knee, and elbow.

Pigmentation Abnormality   A lack of color in the skin.

Progressive Retinal Atrophy (PRA)   A slow deterioration of the retina, leading to blindness.

Skin Disease   The Irish setter is prone to deep infections of the skin (boils), infections from allergies, and seborrhea, which is a skin disease characterized by raw, scaling skin and an excess of sebum (oil-like substance), causing a rancid body odor.

Thrombocytopenia   An abnormal decrease in the number of blood platelets. Blood platelets play a role in blood clotting. Symptoms are tiny hemorrhages in the skin and mucous membranes.

Wrist Subluxation   The wrist bones are loose and become partially dislocated.

Irish Terrier

Hyperkeratosis   An enlargement and thickening of the footpads, causing them to become cracked and infected if not treated.

Muscular Dystrophy   A progressive muscle disorder that causes a wasting of the muscles. It is an inherited disease, with symptoms of slow growth, difficulty eating and swallowing, and weakness.

Progressive Retinal Atrophy (PRA)   A slow deterioration of the retina, leading to blindness.

Kerry Blue Terrier

Blood-Clotting Disorder   The Kerry blue terrier is prone to a blood-clotting disorder due to coagulation factor XI deficiency.

Cataract   In elderly dogs the lens of the eye becomes cloudy, causing a partial or total loss of vision.

Elbow Dysplasia   An abnormal development of the elbow joint(s).

Eye Abnormalities   The Kerry blue terrier is prone to abnormally growing eyelashes, a rolling in of the eyelid(s), too small an opening between the upper and lower eyelids, and dry eye, a condition in which the eye(s) does not produce enough liquid.

Hair Follicle Tumors   Abnormal growths of the hair follicles.

Hypothyroidism   A common disease of thyroid hormone deficiency. The thyroid regulates your dog's metabolism. A large number of skin problems in dogs are caused by thyroid disease.

Neuron Malfunction   The neurons in the cerebellum (brain) and spinal cord are malformed.

Progressive Retinal Atrophy (PRA)   A slow deterioration of the retina, leading to blindness.

Thrombocytopenia   An abnormal decrease in the number of blood platelets. Blood platelets play a role in blood clotting. Symptoms are tiny hemorrhages in the skin and mucous membranes.

Von Willebrand's Disease   Abnormal blood-clotting defect involving both platelet and coagulation function (factor VIII).

Miniature Bull Terrier

Eye Abnormalities   The miniature bull terrier is prone to a rolling in of the eyelid(s) and a condition in which the lens in the eye slips out of place

Hypothyroidism   A common disease of thyroid hormone deficiency. The thyroid regulates your dog's metabolism. A large number of skin problems in dogs are caused by thyroid disease.

Miniature Poodle

Allergies   The miniature poodle is prone to all types of allergies.

Behavioral Abnormalities   The miniature poodle is prone to a whole range of abnormal behavior patterns, such as aggression and panic disorders.

Blood-Clotting Disorder   The miniature poodle is prone to a blood-clotting disorder due to coagulation factor VIII deficiency.

Bone Disease   The miniature poodle is prone to abnormal mineralization of the bones, leading to a weak bone structure.

Cancer   The miniature poodle is prone to skin cancer and cancer of the toe.

Cataract   In elderly dogs the lens of the eye becomes cloudy, causing a partial or total loss of vision.

Cushing's Disease (Hyperadrenocorticism)   A condition in which the adrenal glands secrete too much cortisol. Cortisol is a steroid hormone that regulates carbohydrate, fat, and protein metabolism.

Deafness   A partial or total loss of hearing.

Epilepsy   A brain disorder in which the dog experiences seizures (convulsions).

Epiphyseal Dysplasia   Abnormal development of the long bone.

Eye Abnormalities   The miniature poodle is prone to a rolling in of the eyelid(s) and abnormal development of the eyelashes, tear ducts, optic nerve, and retina(s).

Glaucoma   Pressure on the retina from excess fluid in the eyeball, which causes partial or total loss of vision.

Globoid Cell Leukodystrophy   Degeneration of a type of brain cell.

Heart Disease   The miniature poodle is prone to abnormal development of the heart.

Hemeralopia   A disorder of the retina causing blindness during the day, with partial sight in dim light.

Hypothyroidism   A common disease of thyroid hormone deficiency. The thyroid regulates your dog's metabolism. A large number of skin problems in dogs are caused by thyroid disease.

Immune-Mediated Hemolytic Anemia (IMHA)   Anemia resulting from an immune system–mediated destruction of the red blood cells.

Intervertebral Disc Disease   Abnormal development of the discs between the vertebrae.

Iris Atrophy   A deterioration of the iris.

Myasthenia Gravis   An autoimmune disease characterized by progressive muscle fatigue and generalized weakness as the result of impaired transmission of nerve impulses.

Osteochondritis Dissecans   Inflammation of the cartilage in the joints. A form of arthritis.

Osteochondrosis   An abnormal development of joint cartilage. Most commonly found in the shoulder, knee, and elbow.

Otitis Externa   An infection of the external structures of the ear.

Pannus   A progressive immune-mediated disease in which there is a growth of tissue over the cornea, causing inflammation and possible blindness.

Patellar Luxation   The kneecap(s) slips out of place.

Progressive Retinal Atrophy (PRA)   A slow deterioration of the retina, leading to blindness.

Sebaceous Gland Tumor   A skin tumor.

Skin Disease   The miniature poodle is prone to skin disease from allergies and from a deficiency of growth hormones.

Urolithiasis   Stones or crystals in the urinary tract.

Von Willebrand's Disease   Abnormal blood-clotting defect involving both platelet and coagulation function (factor VIII).

Norwegian Dunker Hound

Deafness   A partial or total loss of hearing.

Norwegian Elkhound

Cataract   In elderly dogs the lens of the eye becomes cloudy, causing a partial or total loss of vision.

Eye Abnormalities   The Norwegian elkhound is prone to a rolling in of the eyelid(s), abnormally growing eyelashes, and a condition in which the lens in the eye slips out of place.

Glaucoma   Pressure on the retina from excess fluid in the eyeball, which causes partial or total loss of vision.

Hereditary Kidney Hypoplasia   A condition in which the dog is born with immature kidneys that never develop completely.

Hip Dysplasia   An abnormal development of the hip joint(s).

Hypothyroidism   A common disease of thyroid hormone deficiency. The thyroid regulates your dog's metabolism. A large number of skin problems in dogs are caused by thyroid disease.

Keratoacanthoma   Noncancerous skin tumor, usually found on the face.

Progressive Retinal Atrophy (PRA)   A slow deterioration of the retina, leading to blindness.

Sebaceous Gland Tumor   A skin tumor.

Seborrhea   A skin disease characterized by raw, scaling skin and an excess of sebum (oil-like substance), which causes a rancid body odor.

Subcutaneous Cysts   A fluid-filled sac located just beneath the skin.

Nova Scotia Duck Tolling Retriever

Addison's Disease   A disease in which the adrenal glands secrete an insufficient amount of cortisone, a steroid hormone.

Cataract   In elderly dogs the lens of the eye becomes cloudy, causing a partial or total loss of vision.

Hypothyroidism   A common disease of thyroid hormone deficiency. The thyroid regulates your dog's metabolism. A large number of skin problems in dogs are caused by thyroid disease.

Progressive Retinal Atrophy (PRA)   A slow deterioration of the retina, leading to blindness.

Pembroke Welsh Corgi

Blood-Clotting Disorder   The Pembroke Welsh corgi is prone to a blood-clotting disorder due to coagulation factor IX deficiency.

Cataract   In elderly dogs the lens of the eye becomes cloudy, causing a partial or total loss of vision.

Cervical Spondylosis   A degenerative disease of the neck vertebrae.

Corneal Dystrophy   An inherited degenerative condition in which the cornea of the eye becomes cloudy or opaque.

Dystocia Complications giving birth.

Ehler's-Danlos Syndrome A connective tissue disease in which the skin is very fragile and is easily cut or bruised.

Epilepsy A brain disorder in which the dog experiences seizures (convulsions).

Eye Abnormalities The Pembroke Welsh corgi is prone to abnormal development of the retina(s) and a condition in which the lens in the eye slips out of place.

Hypothyroidism A common disease of thyroid hormone deficiency. The thyroid regulates your dog's metabolism. A large number of skin problems in dogs are caused by thyroid disease.

Progressive Retinal Atrophy (PRA) A slow deterioration of the retina, leading to blindness.

Von Willebrand's Disease Abnormal blood-clotting defect involving both platelet and coagulation function (factor VIII).

Petit Basset Griffon Vendeen

Allergies The petit basset griffon vendeen is prone to all types of allergies.

Cryptorchidism A developmental condition in which one or both testicles fail to descend into the scrotum.

Epilepsy A brain disorder in which the dog experiences seizures (convulsions).

Eye Abnormalities The petit basset griffon vendeen is prone to abnormal development of the retina(s), a condition in which the lens slips out of place, and an overproduction of tears.

Glaucoma Pressure on the retina from excess fluid in the eyeball, which causes partial or total loss of vision.

Hip Dysplasia An abnormal development of the hip joint(s).

Patellar Luxation　　The kneecap(s) slips out of place.

Thyroid Disease　　The petit basset griffon vendeen is prone to thyroiditis, lymphocytic thyroiditis, and hypothyroidism. Thyroiditis and lymphocytic thyroiditis are autoimmune diseases that lead to hypothyroidism, a common disease of thyroid hormone deficiency. The thyroid regulates your dog's metabolism. A large number of skin problems in dogs are caused by thyroid disease.

Portuguese Water Dog

Addison's Disease　　A disease in which the adrenal glands secrete an insufficient amount of cortisone, a steroid hormone.

Cataract　　In elderly dogs the lens of the eye becomes cloudy, causing a partial or total loss of vision.

Eye Abnormality　　The Portuguese water dog is prone to abnormally growing eyelashes.

Hypothyroidism　　A common disease of thyroid hormone deficiency. The thyroid regulates your dog's metabolism. A large number of skin problems in dogs are caused by thyroid disease.

Lipidosis　　An accumulation of lipids (fats) in the nerves.

Progressive Retinal Atrophy (PRA)　　A slow deterioration of the retina, leading to blindness.

Saluki

Anesthetic Sensitivity　　A serious condition in which the dog is very sensitive to anesthesia. In many cases the dog is also sensitive to medications and flea control products that contain pesticides.

Behavioral Abnormalities　　The saluki is prone to a whole range of abnormal behavior patterns, such as aggression and panic disorders.

Cataract   In elderly dogs the lens of the eye becomes cloudy, causing a partial or total loss of vision.

Corneal Dystrophy   An inherited degenerative condition in which the cornea of the eye becomes cloudy or opaque.

Eye Abnormalities   The saluki is prone to a rolling in of the eyelid and abnormal development of the retina(s).

Hypothyroidism   A common disease of thyroid hormone deficiency. The thyroid regulates your dog's metabolism. A large number of skin problems in dogs are caused by thyroid disease.

Immune-Mediated Hemolytic Anemia (IMHA)   Anemia resulting from an immune system–mediated destruction of the red blood cells.

Neuronal Ceroid-Lipofuscinosis   An accumulation of fatty pigments in the brain.

Progressive Retinal Atrophy (PRA)   A slow deterioration of the retina, leading to blindness.

Thrombocytopenia   An abnormal decrease in the number of blood platelets. Blood platelets play a role in blood clotting. Symptoms are tiny hemorrhages in the skin and mucous membranes.

Von Willebrand's Disease   Abnormal blood-clotting defect involving both platelet and coagulation function (factor VIII).

Skye Terrier

Behavioral Abnormalities   The Skye terrier is prone to a whole range of abnormal behavior patterns, such as aggression and panic disorders.

Epiphyseal Dysplasia   Abnormal development of the long bone.

Eye Abnormalities   The Skye terrier is prone to abnormally growing eyelashes and a condition in which the lens in the eye slips out of place.

Hypoplasia of Larynx   Abnormal development of the larynx.

Myasthenia Gravis   An autoimmune disease characterized by progressive muscle fatigue and generalized weakness as the result of impaired transmission of nerve impulses.

Thyroid Disease   The Skye terrier is prone to thyroiditis, lymphocytic thyroiditis, and hypothyroidism. Thyroiditis and lymphocytic thyroiditis are autoimmune diseases that lead to hypothyroidism, a common disease of thyroid hormone deficiency. The thyroid regulates your dog's metabolism. A large number of skin problems in dogs are caused by thyroid disease.

Ulcerative Colitis   A chronic inflammation of the colon that results in the formation of ulcers in the colon.

Von Willebrand's Disease   Abnormal blood-clotting defect involving both platelet and coagulation function (factor VIII).

Soft-Coated Wheaten Terrier

Addison's Disease   A disease in which the adrenal glands secrete an insufficient amount of cortisone, a steroid hormone.

Allergies   The soft-coated wheaten terrier is prone to all types of allergies.

Cataract   In elderly dogs the lens of the eye becomes cloudy, causing a partial or total loss of vision.

Eye Abnormalities   The soft-coated wheaten terrier is prone to abnormal development of the optic nerve and abnormal development of the retina(s).

Hypothyroidism   A common disease of thyroid hormone deficiency. The thyroid regulates your dog's metabolism. A large number of skin problems in dogs are caused by thyroid disease.

Malabsorption   A condition in which the small intestine does not absorb nutrients properly.

Renal Dysplasia   Abnormal development of the kidney(s).

Von Willebrand's Disease   Abnormal blood-clotting defect involving both platelet and coagulation function (factor VIII).

Staffordshire Bull Terrier

Cataract   In elderly dogs the lens of the eye becomes cloudy, causing a partial or total loss of vision.

Cleft Palate and/or Lip   Both are birth defects. With cleft palate, the roof of the mouth does not grow properly, leaving a hole from the roof of the mouth into the nose. With cleft lip, the skin below the nose does not grow together.

Eye Abnormalities   The Staffordshire bull terrier is prone to a rolling in of the eyelid(s) and abnormally growing eyelashes.

Hypothyroidism   A common disease of thyroid hormone deficiency. The thyroid regulates your dog's metabolism. A large number of skin problems in dogs are caused by thyroid disease.

Muscular Dystrophy   A progressive muscle disorder that causes a wasting of the muscles. It is an inherited disease, with symptoms of slow growth, difficulty eating and swallowing, and weakness.

Osteochondritis Dissecans   Inflammation of the cartilage in the joints. A form of arthritis.

Osteochondrosis   An abnormal development of joint cartilage. Most commonly found in the shoulder, knee, and elbow.

Progressive Retinal Atrophy (PRA)   A slow deterioration of the retina, leading to blindness.

Standard Poodle

Addison's Disease   A disease in which the adrenal glands secrete an insufficient amount of cortisone, a steroid hormone.

Allergies   The standard poodle is prone to all types of allergies.

Behavioral Abnormalities   The standard poodle is prone to a whole range of abnormal behavior patterns, such as aggression and panic disorders.

Blood-Clotting Disorders   The standard poodle is prone to blood-clotting disorders due to coagulation factor VIII or XII deficiency.

Bone Disease   The standard poodle is prone to abnormal mineralization of the bones, leading to a weak bone structure.

Cancer   The standard poodle is prone to cancer of the toe.

Cataract   In elderly dogs the lens of the eye becomes cloudy, causing a partial or total loss of vision.

Epilepsy   A brain disorder in which the dog experiences seizures (convulsions).

Epiphora   An overproduction of tears.

Eye Abnormalities   The standard poodle is prone to a rolling in of the eyelid(s), a condition in which the lens in the eye slips out of place, and abnormal development of the eyelashes, tear ducts, retina(s), and optic nerve.

Gastric Bloat and Torsion   Gastric bloat is a swelling of the stomach from excess gas and is usually followed by gastric torsion, a twisting of the stomach. Gastric torsion will result in death if not treated immediately.

Glaucoma   Pressure on the retina from excess fluid in the eyeball, which causes partial or total loss of vision.

Hemeralopia   A disorder of the retina causing blindness during the day, with partial sight in dim light.

Hip Dysplasia   An abnormal development of the hip joint(s).

Hypothyroidism   A common disease of thyroid hormone deficiency. The thyroid regulates your dog's metabolism. A large number of skin problems in dogs are caused by thyroid disease.

Immune-Mediated Hemolytic Anemia (IMHA) Anemia resulting from an immune system–mediated destruction of the red blood cells.

Iris Atrophy A deterioration of the iris.

Osteochondritis Dissecans Inflammation of the cartilage in the joints. A form of arthritis.

Osteochondrosis An abnormal development of joint cartilage. Most commonly found in the shoulder, knee, and elbow.

Pannus A progressive immune-mediated disease in which there is a growth of tissue over the cornea, causing inflammation and possible blindness.

Progressive Retinal Atrophy (PRA) A slow deterioration of the retina, leading to blindness.

Thrombocytopenia An abnormal decrease in the number of blood platelets. Blood platelets play a role in blood clotting. Symptoms are tiny hemorrhages in the skin and mucous membranes.

Urolithiasis Stones or crystals in the urinary tract.

Von Willebrand's Disease Abnormal blood-clotting defect involving both platelet and coagulation function (factor VIII).

Standard Schnauzer

Blood-Clotting Disorder The standard schnauzer is prone to a blood-clotting disorder due to coagulation factor VIII deficiency.

Cancer The standard schnauzer is prone to cancer of the anus.

Cataract In elderly dogs the lens of the eye becomes cloudy, causing a partial or total loss of vision.

Conjunctivitis Inflammation of the eye.

Eye Abnormality The standard schnauzer is prone to abnormal development of the retina(s).

Heart Disease   The standard schnauzer is prone to malfunctioning valve(s).

Hypothyroidism   A common disease of thyroid hormone deficiency. The thyroid regulates your dog's metabolism. A large number of skin problems in dogs are caused by thyroid disease.

Osteochondritis Dissecans   Inflammation of the cartilage in the joints. A form of arthritis.

Osteochondrosis   An abnormal development of joint cartilage. Most commonly found in the shoulder, knee, and elbow.

Von Willebrand's Disease   Abnormal blood-clotting defect involving both platelet and coagulation function (factor VIII).

Sussex Spaniel

Cataract   In elderly dogs the lens of the eye becomes cloudy, causing a partial or total loss of vision.

Eye Abnormalities   The Sussex spaniel is prone to abnormally growing eyelashes, a rolling in of the eyelid(s), and abnormal development of the retina(s).

Heart Disease   The Sussex spaniel is prone to cardiomyopathy, or weakened heart muscles.

Tibetan Terrier

Anesthetic Sensitivity   A serious condition in which the dog is very sensitive to anesthesia. In many cases the dog is also sensitive to medications and flea control products that contain pesticides.

Cataract   In elderly dogs the lens of the eye becomes cloudy, causing a partial or total loss of vision.

Eye Abnormalities   The Tibetan terrier is prone to a rolling in of the eyelid(s), abnormal development of the retina(s), and a condition in which the lens in the eye slips out of place.

Neuronal Ceroid-Lipofuscinosis   An accumulation of fatty pigments in the brain.

Progressive Retinal Atrophy (PRA)   A slow deterioration of the retina, leading to blindness.

Water Spaniel

Cataract   In elderly dogs the lens of the eye becomes cloudy, causing a partial or total loss of vision.

Eye Abnormality   The water spaniel is prone to abnormal development of the retina(s).

Welsh Springer Spaniel

Cataract   In elderly dogs the lens of the eye becomes cloudy, causing a partial or total loss of vision.

Glaucoma   Pressure on the retina from excess fluid in the eyeball, which causes partial or total loss of vision.

Hip Dysplasia   An abnormal development of the hip joint(s).

Progressive Retinal Atrophy (PRA)   A slow deterioration of the retina, leading to blindness.

Purebred Small (Up to 20 Pounds)

Affenpinscher

Anasarca   Newborn puppies have an accumulation of fluids in various tissues and body cavities.

Cleft Palate   A birth defect in which the roof of the mouth does not grow properly, leaving a hole from the roof of the mouth into the nose.

Patellar Luxation   The kneecap(s) slips out of place.

Teeth Abnormalities   The number, placement, or development of the teeth is not normal.

Von Willebrand's Disease   Abnormal blood-clotting defect involving both platelet and coagulation function (factor VIII).

Australian Terrier

Diabetes Mellitus   A disease caused by an insufficient production or use of insulin.

Eye Abnormality   The Australian terrier is prone to abnormal development of the retina(s).

Legg-Perthes Disease   The blood vessels feeding the thigh bone deteriorate, leading to a deterioration of the femoral head, a part of the hip.

Progressive Retinal Atrophy (PRA)   A slow deterioration of the retina, leading to blindness.

Bedlington Terrier

Bone Disease   The Bedlington terrier is prone to abnormal mineralization of the bones, leading to a weak bone structure.

Cataract   In elderly dogs the lens of the eye becomes cloudy, causing a partial or total loss of vision.

Copper Metabolism Abnormality   An inability to utilize and store copper properly. Results in liver disease if not treated.

Eye Abnormalities   The Bedlington terrier is prone to a rolling out of the eyelid(s) and abnormal development of the tear ducts, eyelashes, and retina(s).

Hereditary Kidney Hypoplasia   A condition in which the dog is born with immature kidneys that never develop completely.

Progressive Retinal Atrophy (PRA)   A slow deterioration of the retina, leading to blindness.

Bichon Frise

Blood-Clotting Disorder   The bichon frise is prone to a blood-clotting disorder due to coagulation factor IX deficiency.

Cataract   In elderly dogs the lens of the eye becomes cloudy, causing a partial or total loss of vision.

Ciliary Dyskinesia   A condition in which the ciliated cells (hairlike cells lining the respiratory tract) are deformed and rigid. Causes pneumonia and other respiratory difficulties.

Corneal Dystrophy   An inherited degenerative condition in which the cornea of the eye becomes cloudy or opaque.

Epilepsy   A brain disorder in which the dog experiences seizures (convulsions).

Eye Abnormalities   The bichon frise is prone to a rolling in of the eyelid(s).

Patellar Luxation   The kneecap(s) slips out of place.

Skin Allergy   Allergic reaction that causes inflammation and itching of the skin.

White Dog Shaker Syndrome   A condition, brought on by stress or overexcitement, in which the dog has rapid eye movements, tremors, and incoordination.

Border Terrier

Cancer   The Border terrier is prone to cancer of the neck, aorta, spine, brain, pituitary gland, and mast cells. The mast cell secretes histamine in response to allergens.

Cataract   In elderly dogs the lens of the eye becomes cloudy, causing a partial or total loss of vision.

Collie Eye Anomaly   A inherited disorder in which the narrow shape of the head causes the eyes to be malformed.

Craniomandibular Osteopathy   Abnormally dense bones in the face and the jaw.

Cryptorchidism   A developmental condition in which one or both testicles fail to descend into the scrotum.

Eye Abnormalities   The Border terrier is prone to abnormal development of the retina(s) and a condition in which the lens in the eye slips out of place.

Heart Disease   The Border terrier is prone to abnormal development of the heart.

Histiocytoma   A tumor that forms beneath the skin.

Patellar Luxation   The kneecap(s) slips out of place.

Progressive Retinal Atrophy (PRA) A slow deterioration of the retina, leading to blindness.

Vertebra Malformation A condition in which only half the vertebra is formed.

Boston Terrier

Allergies The Boston terrier is prone to all types of allergies.

Anasarca Newborn puppies have an accumulation of fluids in various tissues and body cavities.

Cancer The Boston terrier is prone to cancer of the neck, aorta, pituitary gland, and mast cells. The mast cell secretes histamine in response to allergens.

Cataract In elderly dogs the lens of the eye becomes cloudy, causing a partial or total loss of vision.

Cleft Palate and/or Lip Both are birth defects. With cleft palate, the roof of the mouth does not grow properly, leaving a hole from the roof of the mouth into the nose. With cleft lip, the skin below the nose does not grow together.

Corneal Dystrophy An inherited degenerative condition in which the cornea of the eye becomes cloudy or opaque.

Corneal Ulcer A deterioration of the cornea.

Craniomandibular Osteopathy Abnormally dense bones in the face and the jaw.

Cushing's Disease (Hyperadrenocorticism) A condition in which the adrenal glands secrete too much cortisol. Cortisol is a steroid hormone that regulates carbohydrate, fat, and protein metabolism.

Deafness A partial or total loss of hearing.

Demodectic Mange A skin disease in which canine mites are living in the skin, causing itching, loss of hair, and skin infections. Usually found on the face and front legs.

Dermatitis An inflammation in the skin folds of the tail.

Dystocia Complications giving birth.

Esophageal Disorder Spasms of the muscles of the esophagus.

Eye Abnormalities The Boston terrier is prone to a rolling in of the eyelid(s), abnormally growing eyelashes, abnormal growth of the gland of the third eyelid(s), protruding third eyelid(s), and dry eye, a condition in which the eye(s) does not produce enough liquid.

Glaucoma Pressure on the retina from excess fluid in the eyeball, which causes partial or total loss of vision.

Hernia A rupture of the wall of an internal organ in the groin area.

Hydrocephalus The accumulation of fluid in the brain.

Hypothyroidism A common disease of thyroid hormone deficiency. The thyroid regulates your dog's metabolism. A large number of skin problems in dogs are caused by thyroid disease.

Intussusception A section of the intestinal tract slips into an adjoining section.

Patellar Luxation The kneecap(s) slips out of place.

Progressive Retinal Atrophy (PRA) A slow deterioration of the retina, leading to blindness.

Pyometra The uterus fills with pus, usually from a severe bacterial infection.

Sebaceous Gland Tumor A skin tumor.

Stenotic Nares A condition in which excess flesh causes the openings of the nose (nares) to be too small to breathe with ease.

Swimmer Puppies   A developmental condition caused by a weakness of the muscles puppies use to pull their legs together. Newborns are unable to put their feet under them to walk.

Vertebra Malformation   A condition in which only half the vertebra is formed.

Brussels Griffon

Cataract   In elderly dogs the lens of the eye becomes cloudy, causing a partial or total loss of vision.

Eye Abnormality   The Brussels griffon is prone to abnormally growing eyelashes.

Progressive Retinal Atrophy (PRA)   A slow deterioration of the retina, leading to blindness.

Shoulder Abnormality   Disorders of the shoulder joint from malformation or dislocation.

Cairn Terrier

Blood-Clotting Disorders   The cairn terrier is prone to blood-clotting disorders due to coagulation factor VIII or IX deficiency.

Cataract   In elderly dogs the lens of the eye becomes cloudy, causing a partial or total loss of vision.

Cerebellar Hypoplasia   Underdevelopment of a part of the brain called the cerebellum. The cerebellum gives your dog coordination, posture, and balance.

Craniomandibular Osteopathy   Abnormally dense bones in the face and the jaw.

Eye Abnormalities   The cairn terrier is prone to abnormally growing eyelashes, abnormal development of the retina(s), and a condition in which the lens in the eye slips out of place.

Glaucoma   Pressure on the retina from excess fluid in the eyeball, which causes partial or total loss of vision.

Globoid Cell Leukodystrophy   Degeneration of a type of brain cell.

Hernia   A rupture of the wall of an internal organ in the groin area.

Hypothyroidism   A common disease of thyroid hormone deficiency. The thyroid regulates your dog's metabolism. A large number of skin problems in dogs are caused by thyroid disease.

Liver Abnormality   The cairn terrier is prone to an abnormal formation of blood vessels in the liver.

Progressive Retinal Atrophy (PRA)   A slow deterioration of the retina, leading to blindness.

Urolithiasis   Stones or crystals in the urinary tract.

Von Willebrand's Disease   Abnormal blood-clotting defect involving both platelet and coagulation function (factor VIII).

Cavalier King Charles Spaniel

Cataract   In elderly dogs the lens of the eye becomes cloudy, causing a partial or total loss of vision.

Corneal Dystrophy   An inherited degenerative condition in which the cornea of the eye becomes cloudy or opaque.

Diabetes Mellitus   A disease caused by an insufficient production or use of insulin.

Eye Abnormalities   The cavalier King Charles spaniel is prone to abnormally growing eyelashes, abnormal development of the retina(s), a rolling in of the eyelid(s), and dry eye, a condition in which the eye(s) does not produce enough liquid.

Heart Disease   The cavalier King Charles spaniel is prone to deterioration of the heart valves.

Hypothyroidism   A common disease of thyroid hormone deficiency. The thyroid regulates your dog's metabolism. A large number of skin problems in dogs are caused by thyroid disease.

Patellar Luxation   The kneecap(s) slips out of place.

Progressive Retinal Atrophy (PRA)   A slow deterioration of the retina, leading to blindness.

Thrombocytopenia   An abnormal decrease in the number of blood platelets. Blood platelets play a role in blood clotting. Symptoms are tiny hemorrhages in the skin and mucous membranes.

Chihuahua

Blood-Clotting Disorder   The Chihuahua is prone to a blood-clotting disorder due to coagulation factor VIII deficiency.

Cleft Palate   A birth defect in which the roof of the mouth does not grow properly, leaving a hole from the roof of the mouth into the nose.

Collapsed Trachea   Malformation of the trachea, causing it to collapse easily.

Corneal Dystrophy   An inherited degenerative condition in which the cornea of the eye becomes cloudy or opaque.

Eye Abnormalities   The Chihuahua is prone to a rolling in of the eyelid(s), a condition in which the lens in the eye slips out of place, and dry eye, a condition in which the eye(s) does not produce enough liquid.

Glaucoma   Pressure on the retina from excess fluid in the eyeball, which causes partial or total loss of vision.

Heart Disease   The Chihuahua is prone to abnormal growth of the mitral valve and malfunctioning valves.

Hydrocephalus   The accumulation of fluid in the brain.

Hypoglycemia   A low level of glucose (blood sugar) in the blood.

Hypothyroidism   A common disease of thyroid hormone deficiency. The thyroid regulates your dog's metabolism. A large number of skin problems in dogs are caused by thyroid disease.

Iris Atrophy   A deterioration of the iris.

Liver Abnormality   The Chihuahua is prone to an abnormal formation of blood vessels in the liver.

Neuronal Ceroid-Lipofuscinosis   An accumulation of fatty pigments in the brain.

Osteochondritis Dissecans   Inflammation of the cartilage in the joints. A form of arthritis.

Osteochondrosis   An abnormal development of joint cartilage. Most commonly found in the shoulder, knee, and elbow.

Patellar Luxation   The kneecap(s) slips out of place.

Progressive Retinal Atrophy (PRA)   A slow deterioration of the retina, leading to blindness.

Shoulder Dislocation   The shoulder joint slips out of place.

Vertebra Malformation   An abnormal development of the second vertebra, causing unsteadiness.

Chinese Crested

Acne   Pimples and blackheads on the hairless dogs.

Cancer   The Chinese crested is prone to skin cancer.

Patellar Luxation   The kneecap(s) slips out of place.

Dachshund

Elbow Dysplasia   An abnormal development of the elbow joint(s).

Epilepsy   A brain disorder in which the dog experiences seizures (convulsions).

Keratitis   Inflammation of the cornea.

Urolithiasis   Stones or crystals in the urinary tract.

Dandie Dinmont Terrier

Cataract   In elderly dogs the lens of the eye becomes cloudy, causing a partial or total loss of vision.

Corneal Ulcer   A deterioration of the cornea.

Elbow Dislocation   The elbow joint slips out of place.

Eye Abnormality   The Dandie Dinmont terrier is prone to a rolling in of the eyelid(s).

Glaucoma   Pressure on the retina from excess fluid in the eyeball, which causes partial or total loss of vision.

Hip Dysplasia   An abnormal development of the hip joint(s).

Hypothyroidism   A common disease of thyroid hormone deficiency. The thyroid regulates your dog's metabolism. A large number of skin problems in dogs are caused by thyroid disease.

Intervertebral Disc Disease   Abnormal development of the discs between the vertebrae.

Patellar Luxation   The kneecap(s) slips out of place.

Shoulder Abnormality   Disorders of the shoulder joint from malformation or dislocation.

Teeth Abnormalities   The number, placement, or development of the teeth is not normal.

English Toy Spaniel

Cataract   In elderly dogs the lens of the eye becomes cloudy, causing a partial or total loss of vision.

Cleft Palate   A birth defect in which the roof of the mouth does not grow properly, leaving a hole from the roof of the mouth into the nose.

Corneal Dystrophy   An inherited degenerative condition in which the cornea of the eye becomes cloudy or opaque.

Diabetes Mellitus   A disease caused by an insufficient production or use of insulin.

Eye Abnormalities   The English toy spaniel is prone to a rolling in of the eyelid(s) and abnormal development of the retina(s).

Patellar Luxation   The kneecap(s) slips out of place.

Umbilical Hernia   A tear in the muscle wall in the stomach where the umbilical cord was.

Havanese

Cataract   In elderly dogs the lens of the eye becomes cloudy, causing a partial or total loss of vision.

Eye Abnormality   The Havanese is prone to abnormal development of the retina(s).

Progressive Retinal Atrophy (PRA)   A slow deterioration of the retina, leading to blindness.

Italian Greyhound

Anesthetic Sensitivity   A serious condition in which the dog is very sensitive to anesthesia. In many cases the dog is also sensitive to medications and flea control products that contain pesticides.

Cataract   In elderly dogs the lens of the eye becomes cloudy, causing a partial or total loss of vision.

Corneal Dystrophy   An inherited degenerative condition in which the cornea of the eye becomes cloudy or opaque.

Cryptorchidism   A developmental condition in which one or both testicles fail to descend into the scrotum.

Epilepsy   A brain disorder in which the dog experiences seizures (convulsions).

Eye Abnormality   The Italian greyhound is prone to abnormal development of the optic nerve.

Glaucoma   Pressure on the retina from excess fluid in the eyeball, which causes partial or total loss of vision.

Progressive Retinal Atrophy (PRA)   A slow deterioration of the retina, leading to blindness.

Thrombocytopenia   An abnormal decrease in the number of blood platelets. Blood platelets play a role in blood clotting. Symptoms are tiny hemorrhages in the skin and mucous membranes.

Jack Russell Terrier

Ataxia   A progressive loss of coordination.

Blood-Clotting Disorder   The Jack Russell terrier is prone to a blood-clotting disorder due to coagulation factor X deficiency.

Eye Abnormality   The Jack Russell terrier is prone to a condition in which the lens in the eye slips out of place.

Myasthenia Gravis   An autoimmune disease characterized by progressive muscle fatigue and generalized weakness as the result of impaired transmission of nerve impulses.

Von Willebrand's Disease   Abnormal blood-clotting defect involving both platelet and coagulation function (factor VIII).

Japanese Spaniel (Japanese Chin)

Cataract   In elderly dogs the lens of the eye becomes cloudy, causing a partial or total loss of vision.

Cryptorchidism   A developmental condition in which one or both testicles fail to descend into the scrotum.

Eye Abnormalities   The Japanese spaniel is prone to abnormally growing eyelashes and a rolling in of the eyelid(s).

Glycogen Storage Disease   An inability to store and use the complex carbohydrate glycogen, which is primarily stored in the liver and muscle.

Progressive Retinal Atrophy (PRA)   A slow deterioration of the retina, leading to blindness.

Lakeland Terrier

Cataract   In elderly dogs the lens of the eye becomes cloudy, causing a partial or total loss of vision.

Cryptorchidism   A developmental condition in which one or both testicles fail to descend into the scrotum.

Elbow Dysplasia   An abnormal development of the elbow joint(s).

Eye Abnormalities   The Lakeland terrier is prone to abnormally growing eyelashes and a condition in which the lens in the eye slips out of place.

Hypothyroidism   A common disease of thyroid hormone deficiency. The thyroid regulates your dog's metabolism. A large number of skin problems in dogs are caused by thyroid disease.

Jaw Abnormality   The lower jaw is longer than the upper jaw.

Von Willebrand's Disease   Abnormal blood-clotting defect involving both platelet and coagulation function (factor VIII).

Lhasa Apso

Allergies   The Lhasa apso is prone to all types of allergies.

Cataract   In elderly dogs the lens of the eye becomes cloudy, causing a partial or total loss of vision.

Corneal Dystrophy   An inherited degenerative condition in which the cornea of the eye becomes cloudy or opaque.

Eye Abnormalities   The Lhasa apso is prone to abnormally growing eyelashes, a rolling in or out of the eyelid(s), and dry eye, a condition in which the eye(s) does not produce enough liquid.

Hereditary Kidney Hypoplasia   A condition in which the dog is born with immature kidneys that never develop completely.

Hernia   A rupture of the wall of an internal organ in the groin area.

Hypothyroidism   A common disease of thyroid hormone deficiency. The thyroid regulates your dog's metabolism. A large number of skin problems in dogs are caused by thyroid disease.

Patellar Luxation   The kneecap(s) slips out of place.

Progressive Retinal Atrophy (PRA)   A slow deterioration of the retina, leading to blindness.

Von Willebrand's Disease   Abnormal blood-clotting defect involving both platelet and coagulation function (factor VIII).

Maltese

Blindness   The Maltese is prone to an inability to see from a wide variety of eye diseases.

Cryptorchidism   A developmental condition in which one or both testicles fail to descend into the scrotum.

Deafness   A partial or total loss of hearing.

Epiphora   An overproduction of tears.

Eye Abnormalities   The Maltese is prone to abnormally growing eyelashes and abnormal development of the retina(s).

Glaucoma   Pressure on the retina from excess fluid in the eyeball, which causes partial or total loss of vision.

Hip Dysplasia   An abnormal development of the hip joint(s).

Hypoglycemia   A low level of glucose (blood sugar) in the blood.

Liver Abnormality   The Maltese is prone to an abnormal formation of blood vessels in the liver.

Patellar Luxation   The kneecap(s) slips out of place.

Progressive Retinal Atrophy (PRA)   A slow deterioration of the retina, leading to blindness.

Thyroid Disease   The Maltese is prone to thyroiditis, lymphocytic thyroiditis, and hypothyroidism. Thyroiditis and lymphocytic thyroiditis are autoimmune diseases that lead to hypothyroidism, a common disease of thyroid hormone deficiency. The thyroid regulates your dog's metabolism. A large number of skin problems in dogs are caused by thyroid disease.

Von Willebrand's Disease   Abnormal blood-clotting defect involving both platelet and coagulation function (factor VIII).

White Dog Shaker Syndrome   A condition, brought on by stress or overexcitement, in which the dog has rapid eye movements, tremors, and incoordination.

Mexican Hairless

Acne   Pimples and blackheads on the hairless dogs.

Cancer   The Mexican hairless is prone to skin cancer.

Patellar Luxation   The kneecap(s) slips out of place.

Miniature Dachshund

Acanthosis Nigricans   A rare skin disease characterized by dark skin, hair loss, and inflammation of the skin. Primarily found in the armpits.

Baldness   Loss of hair.

Cataract   In elderly dogs the lens of the eye becomes cloudy, causing a partial or total loss of vision.

Cleft Palate and/or Lip   Both are birth defects. With cleft palate, the roof of the mouth does not grow properly, leaving a hole from the roof of the mouth into the nose. With cleft lip, the skin below the nose does not grow together.

Corneal Dystrophy   An inherited degenerative condition in which the cornea of the eye becomes cloudy or opaque.

Cushing's Disease (Hyperadrenocorticism)   A condition in which the adrenal glands secrete too much cortisol. Cortisol is a steroid hormone that regulates carbohydrate, fat, and protein metabolism.

Deafness   A partial or total loss of hearing.

Demodectic Mange   A skin disease in which canine mites are living in the skin, causing itching, loss of hair, and skin infections. Usually found on the face and front legs.

Diabetes Mellitus   A disease caused by an insufficient production or use of insulin.

Ehler's-Danlos Syndrome   A connective tissue disease in which the skin is very fragile and is easily cut or bruised.

Folliculitis   Inflammation of the hair follicle(s).

Hypothyroidism   A common disease of thyroid hormone deficiency. The thyroid regulates your dog's metabolism. A large number of skin problems in dogs are caused by thyroid disease.

Immune-Mediated Hemolytic Anemia (IMHA)   Anemia resulting from an immune system–mediated destruction of the red blood cells.

Intervertebral Disc Disease   Abnormal development of the discs between the vertebrae.

Narcolepsy   A neurological disorder in which the dog suddenly falls asleep.

Neuronal Ceroid-Lipofuscinosis   An accumulation of fatty pigments in the brain.

Osteopetrosis   The bones are abnormally thick and hard.

Overshot Jaw   A condition in which the upper jaw is too long for the lower jaw.

Pannus   A progressive immune-mediated disease in which there is a growth of tissue over the cornea, causing inflammation and possible blindness.

Pemphigus Foliaceous   An autoimmune skin disease.

Pigmentation Abnormality   A lack of color in the skin.

Progressive Retinal Atrophy (PRA)   A slow deterioration of the retina, leading to blindness.

Renal Hypoplasia   A condition in which the kidney(s) does not develop completely.

Sebaceous Gland Tumor   A skin tumor.

Sterile Pyogranuloma Syndrome   A noninfectious disease of the deep layers of the skin, characterized by inflammation and sores.

T-Cell Deficiency   A deficiency of a type of white blood cell, the T-lymphocyte cell, resulting in a weakened immune system.

Von Willebrand's Disease   Abnormal blood-clotting defect involving both platelet and coagulation function (factor VIII).

Miniature Pinscher

Cataract   In elderly dogs the lens of the eye becomes cloudy, causing a partial or total loss of vision.

Corneal Dystrophy An inherited degenerative condition in which the cornea of the eye becomes cloudy or opaque.

Eye Abnormalities The miniature pinscher is prone to a rolling in of the eyelid(s) and dry eye, a condition in which the eye(s) does not produce enough liquid.

Hernia A rupture of the wall of an internal organ in the groin area.

Legg-Perthes Disease The blood vessels feeding the thigh bone deteriorate, leading to a deterioration of the femoral head, a part of the hip.

Pannus A progressive immune-mediated disease in which there is a growth of tissue over the cornea, causing inflammation and possible blindness.

Progressive Retinal Atrophy (PRA) A slow deterioration of the retina, leading to blindness.

Shoulder Dislocation The shoulder joint slips out of place.

Miniature Schnauzer

Allergies The miniature schnauzer is prone to all types of allergies.

Blood-Clotting Disorders The miniature schnauzer is prone to blood-clotting disorders due to coagulation factor XIII or IX deficiency.

Cataract In elderly dogs the lens of the eye becomes cloudy, causing a partial or total loss of vision.

Cryptorchidism A developmental condition in which one or both testicles fail to descend into the scrotum.

Cystitis Infection of the bladder.

Dermatitis Inflammation between the layers of the skin.

Esophageal Disorder Spasms of the muscles of the esophagus.

Eye Abnormalities The miniature schnauzer is prone to abnormally growing eyelashes and a rolling in of the eyelid(s).

Fainting   A sudden, brief state of unconsciousness.

Heart Disease   The miniature schnauzer is prone to malfunction of the valve(s).

Hepatic Lipidosis   A degenerative disease in which the liver is unable to excrete fat.

Hypothyroidism   A common disease of thyroid hormone deficiency. The thyroid regulates your dog's metabolism. A large number of skin problems in dogs are caused by thyroid disease.

Immune-Mediated Hemolytic Anemia (IMHA)   Anemia resulting from an immune system–mediated destruction of the red blood cells.

Legg-Perthes Disease   The blood vessels feeding the thigh bone deteriorate, leading to a deterioration of the femoral head, a part of the hip.

Liver Abnormality   The miniature schnauzer is prone to an abnormal formation of blood vessels in the liver.

Osteochondritis Dissecans   Inflammation of the cartilage in the joints. A form of arthritis.

Osteochondrosis   An abnormal development of joint cartilage. Most commonly found in the shoulder, knee, and elbow.

Renal Dysplasia   Abnormal development of the kidney(s).

Schnauzer Comedo Syndrome   Blackheads from abnormal development of the hair follicles.

Stomach Hemorrhage   A serious disorder of the stomach and intestine that comes on suddenly and is characterized by bloody diarrhea.

Thrombocytopenia   An abnormal decrease in the number of blood platelets. Blood platelets play a role in blood clotting. Symptoms are tiny hemorrhages in the skin and mucous membranes.

Urolithiasis   Stones or crystals in the urinary tract.

Von Willebrand's Disease   Abnormal blood-clotting defect involving both platelet and coagulation function (factor VIII).

Norfolk Terrier

Epilepsy   A brain disorder in which the dog experiences seizures (convulsions).

Patellar Luxation   The kneecap(s) slips out of place.

Skin Allergy   Allergic reaction that causes inflammation and itching of the skin.

Norwich Terrier

Corneal Dystrophy   An inherited degenerative condition in which the cornea of the eye becomes cloudy or opaque.

Epilepsy   A brain disorder in which the dog experiences seizures (convulsions).

Eye Abnormality   The Norwich terrier is prone to a condition in which the lens in the eye slips out of place.

Hypothyroidism   A common disease of thyroid hormone deficiency. The thyroid regulates your dog's metabolism. A large number of skin problems in dogs are caused by thyroid disease.

Patellar Luxation   The kneecap(s) slips out of place.

Skin Allergy   Allergic reaction that causes inflammation and itching of the skin.

Von Willebrand's Disease   Abnormal blood-clotting defect involving both platelet and coagulation function (factor VIII).

Papillon

Anasarca   Newborn puppies have an accumulation of fluids in various tissues and body cavities.

Cataract   In elderly dogs the lens of the eye becomes cloudy, causing a partial or total loss of vision.

Corneal Dystrophy   An inherited degenerative condition in which the cornea of the eye becomes cloudy or opaque.

Eye Abnormality   The papillon is prone to a rolling in of the eyelid(s).

Hypothyroidism   A common disease of thyroid hormone deficiency. The thyroid regulates your dog's metabolism. A large number of skin problems in dogs are caused by thyroid disease.

Patellar Luxation   The kneecap(s) slips out of place.

Von Willebrand's Disease   Abnormal blood-clotting defect involving both platelet and coagulation function (factor VIII).

Pekingese

Cataract   In elderly dogs the lens of the eye becomes cloudy, causing a partial or total loss of vision.

Dermatitis   An inflammation in the skin folds in the face.

Eye Abnormalities   The Pekingese is prone to abnormally growing eyelashes, a rolling in of the eyelid(s), abnormally developed tear ducts, a condition in which the lens in the eye slips out of place, and dry eye, a condition in which the eye(s) does not produce enough liquid.

Hernia   A rupture of the wall of an internal organ in the groin area.

Hypothyroidism   A common disease of thyroid hormone deficiency. The thyroid regulates your dog's metabolism. A large number of skin problems in dogs are caused by thyroid disease.

Immune-Mediated Hemolytic Anemia (IMHA)   Anemia resulting from an immune system–mediated destruction of the red blood cells.

Intervertebral Disc Disease   Abnormal development of the discs between the vertebrae.

Keratitis   Inflammation of the cornea.

Pannus   A progressive immune-mediated disease in which there is a growth of tissue over the cornea, causing inflammation and possible blindness.

Progressive Retinal Atrophy (PRA)   A slow deterioration of the retina, leading to blindness.

Swimmer Puppies   A developmental condition caused by a weakness of the muscles puppies use to pull their legs together. Newborns are unable to put their feet under them to walk.

Thrombocytopenia   An abnormal decrease in the number of blood platelets. Blood platelets play a role in blood clotting. Symptoms are tiny hemorrhages in the skin and mucous membranes.

Umbilical Hernia   A tear in the muscle wall in the stomach where the umbilical cord was.

Vertebra Malformation   An abnormal development of the second vertebra, causing unsteadiness.

Pomeranian

Cataract   In elderly dogs the lens of the eye becomes cloudy, causing a partial or total loss of vision.

Collapsed Trachea   Malformation of the trachea, causing it to collapse easily.

Cryptorchidism   A developmental condition in which one or both testicles fail to descend into the scrotum.

Cyclic Hematopoiesis   An inherited condition in which periodically a type of white blood cell is not produced.

Eye Abnormalities   The Pomeranian is prone to a rolling in of the eyelid(s), abnormally growing eyelashes, an overproduction of tears, abnormal development of the tear duct(s), and a condition in which the lens in the eye slips out of place.

Globoid Cell Leukodystrophy   Degeneration of a type of brain cell.

Glycogen Storage Disease   An inability to store and use the complex carbohydrate glycogen, which is primarily stored in the liver and muscle.

Growth Hormone–Responsive Dermatosis   Skin disorder caused by a deficiency of growth hormones.

Hypothyroidism   A common disease of thyroid hormone deficiency. The thyroid regulates your dog's metabolism. A large number of skin problems in dogs are caused by thyroid disease.

Liver Abnormality   The Pomeranian is prone to an abnormal formation of blood vessels in the liver.

Patellar Luxation   The kneecap(s) slips out of place.

Progressive Retinal Atrophy (PRA)   A slow deterioration of the retina, leading to blindness.

Shoulder Dislocation   The shoulder joint slips out of place.

Vertebra Malformation   An abnormal development of the second vertebra, causing unsteadiness.

Pug

Allergies   The pug is prone to all types of allergies.

Cancer   The pug is prone to cancer of the mast cells. The mast cell secretes histamine in response to allergens.

Cervical Spondylosis   A degenerative disease of the neck vertebrae.

Cleft Lip   A birth defect in which the skin below the nose does not grow together.

Collapsed Trachea   Malformation of the trachea, causing it to collapse easily.

Corneal Dystrophy   An inherited degenerative condition in which the cornea of the eye becomes cloudy or opaque.

Corneal Ulcer   A deterioration of the cornea.

Cystitis   Infection of the bladder.

Demodectic Mange   A skin disease in which canine mites are living in the skin, causing itching, loss of hair, and skin infections. Usually found on the face and front legs.

Dermatitis   An inflammation of the skin folds in the face and the tail.

Dystocia   Complications giving birth.

Encephalitis   Inflammation of the brain. Sometimes a cause of epilepsy.

Epilepsy   A brain disorder in which the dog experiences seizures (convulsions).

Eye Abnormalities   The pug is prone to a rolling in of the eyelid(s) and dry eye, a condition in which the eye(s) does not produce enough liquid.

Fainting   A sudden, brief state of unconsciousness.

Hip Dysplasia   An abnormal development of the hip joint(s).

Hypothyroidism   A common disease of thyroid hormone deficiency. The thyroid regulates your dog's metabolism. A large number of skin problems in dogs are caused by thyroid disease.

Intervertebral Disc Disease   Abnormal development of the discs between the vertebrae.

Keratitis   Inflammation of the cornea.

Legg-Perthes Disease   The blood vessels feeding the thigh bone deteriorate, leading to a deterioration of the femoral head, a part of the hip.

Liver Abnormality   The pug is prone to an abnormal formation of blood vessels in the liver.

Pannus   A progressive immune-mediated disease in which there is a growth of tissue over the cornea, causing inflammation and possible blindness.

Patellar Luxation   The kneecap(s) slips out of place.

Progressive Retinal Atrophy (PRA)   A slow deterioration of the retina, leading to blindness.

Spondylosis   A malformation of the vertebrae.

Stenotic Nares   A condition in which excess flesh causes the openings of the nose (nares) to be too small to breathe with ease.

Teeth Abnormalities   The number, placement, or development of the teeth is not normal.

Urolithiasis   Stones or crystals in the urinary tract.

Schipperke

Cataract   In elderly dogs the lens of the eye becomes cloudy, causing a partial or total loss of vision.

Diabetes Mellitus   A disease caused by an insufficient production or use of insulin.

Eye Abnormalities   The schipperke is prone to abnormally growing eyelashes, a rolling in of the eyelid(s), and an abnormal development of the upper and lower eyelids.

Hypothyroidism   A common disease of thyroid hormone deficiency. The thyroid regulates your dog's metabolism. A large number of skin problems in dogs are caused by thyroid disease.

Legg-Perthes Disease   The blood vessels feeding the thigh bone deteriorate, leading to a deterioration of the femoral head, a part of the hip.

Pemphigus Foliaceous   An autoimmune skin disease.

Progressive Retinal Atrophy (PRA)   A slow deterioration of the retina, leading to blindness.

Scottish Terrier

Allergies   The Scottish terrier is prone to all types of allergies.

Blood-Clotting Disorder   The Scottish terrier is prone to a blood-clotting disorder due to coagulation factor IX deficiency.

Cancer   The Scottish terrier is prone to bladder cancer, skin cancer, and cancer of the lymphatic system.

Cataract   In elderly dogs the lens of the eye becomes cloudy, causing a partial or total loss of vision.

Craniomandibular Osteopathy   Abnormally dense bones in the face and the jaw.

Deafness   A partial or total loss of hearing.

Eye Abnormality   The Scottish terrier is prone to a condition in which the lens in the eye slips out of place.

Folliculitis   Inflammation of the hair follicle(s).

Hypothyroidism   A common disease of thyroid hormone deficiency. The thyroid regulates your dog's metabolism. A large number of skin problems in dogs are caused by thyroid disease.

Immune-Mediated Hemolytic Anemia (IMHA)   Anemia resulting from an immune system–mediated destruction of the red blood cells.

Progressive Retinal Atrophy (PRA)   A slow deterioration of the retina, leading to blindness.

Scotty Cramp   Periodic involuntary muscle contractions.

Von Willebrand's Disease   Abnormal blood-clotting defect involving both platelet and coagulation function (factor VIII).

Sealyham Terrier

Allergies   The Sealyham terrier is prone to inhalant allergies.

Cataract   In elderly dogs the lens of the eye becomes cloudy, causing a partial or total loss of vision.

Eye Abnormalities   The Sealyham terrier is prone to abnormal development of the retina(s) and a condition in which the lens in the eye slips out of place.

Glaucoma   Pressure on the retina from excess fluid in the eyeball, which causes partial or total loss of vision.

Hypothyroidism   A common disease of thyroid hormone deficiency. The thyroid regulates your dog's metabolism. A large number of skin problems in dogs are caused by thyroid disease.

Progressive Retinal Atrophy (PRA)   A slow deterioration of the retina, leading to blindness.

Skin Allergy   Allergic reaction that causes inflammation and itching of the skin.

Shetland Sheepdog

Blood-Clotting Disorders   The Shetland sheepdog is prone to blood-clotting disorders due to coagulation factor VIII or IX deficiency.

Cataract   In elderly dogs the lens of the eye becomes cloudy, causing a partial or total loss of vision.

Corneal Dystrophy   An inherited degenerative condition in which the cornea of the eye becomes cloudy or opaque.

Dermatomyositis   An inflammation of the skin and muscles.

Discoid Lupus Erythematosus   A form of autoimmune disease affecting the skin.

Eye Abnormalities   The Shetland sheepdog is prone to an abnormal development of the eye(s), retina(s), eyelashes, and optic nerve(s).

Folliculitis   Inflammation of the hair follicle(s).

Hepatic Lipidosis   A degenerative disease in which the liver is unable to excrete fat.

Hip Dysplasia   An abnormal development of the hip joint(s).

Pigmentation Abnormality   A lack of color in the skin.

Progressive Retinal Atrophy (PRA)   A slow deterioration of the retina, leading to blindness.

Systemic Lupus Erythematosus   An autoimmune disease characterized by skin infections, organ disorders, and blood abnormalities.

Thyroid Disease   The Shetland sheepdog is prone to thyroiditis, lymphocytic thyroiditis, and hypothyroidism. Thyroiditis and lymphocytic thyroiditis are autoimmune diseases that lead to hypothyroidism, a common disease of thyroid hormone deficiency. The thyroid regulates your dog's metabolism. A large number of skin problems in dogs are caused by thyroid disease.

Von Willebrand's Disease   Abnormal blood-clotting defect involving both platelet and coagulation function (factor VIII).

Shiba Inu

Hip Dysplasia   An abnormal development of the hip joint(s).

Patellar Luxation   The kneecap(s) slips out of place.

Progressive Retinal Atrophy (PRA)   A slow deterioration of the retina, leading to blindness.

Shih Tzu

Cataract   In elderly dogs the lens of the eye becomes cloudy, causing a partial or total loss of vision.

Cleft Palate and/or Lip   Both are birth defects. With cleft palate, the roof of the mouth does not grow properly, leaving a hole from the roof of the mouth into the nose. With cleft lip, the skin below the nose does not grow together.

Dermoid Cyst   A skinlike growth, usually seen on the back.

Eye Abnormalities   The shih tzu is prone to a rolling in or out of the eyelid(s), abnormally growing eyelashes, and abnormal development of the retina(s).

Hereditary Kidney Hypoplasia   A condition in which the dog is born with immature kidneys that never develop completely.

Hypothyroidism   A common disease of thyroid hormone deficiency. The thyroid regulates your dog's metabolism. A large number of skin problems in dogs are caused by thyroid disease.

Immune-Mediated Hemolytic Anemia (IMHA)   Anemia resulting from an immune system–mediated destruction of the red blood cells.

Keratitis   Inflammation of the cornea.

Kidney Disease   Abnormal development of a kidney.

Liver Abnormality   The shih tzu is prone to an abnormal formation of blood vessels in the liver.

Progressive Retinal Atrophy (PRA)   A slow deterioration of the retina, leading to blindness.

Thrombocytopenia   An abnormal decrease in the number of blood platelets. Blood platelets play a role in blood clotting. Symptoms are tiny hemorrhages in the skin and mucous membranes.

Von Willebrand's Disease   Abnormal blood-clotting defect involving both platelet and coagulation function (factor VIII).

Silky Terrier

Cataract   In elderly dogs the lens of the eye becomes cloudy, causing a partial or total loss of vision.

Collapsed Trachea   Malformation of the trachea, causing it to collapse easily.

Cryptorchidism   A developmental condition in which one or both testicles fail to descend into the scrotum.

Diabetes Mellitus   A disease caused by an insufficient production or use of insulin.

Hydrocephalus   The accumulation of fluid in the brain.

Legg-Perthes Disease   The blood vessels feeding the thigh bone deteriorate, leading to a deterioration of the femoral head, a part of the hip.

Lipidosis   An accumulation of lipids (fats) in the nerves.

Patellar Luxation   The kneecap(s) slips out of place.

Progressive Retinal Atrophy (PRA)   A slow deterioration of the retina, leading to blindness.

Thrombocytopenia   An abnormal decrease in the number of blood platelets. Blood platelets play a role in blood clotting. Symptoms are tiny hemorrhages in the skin and mucous membranes.

Smooth Fox Terrier

Allergies   The smooth fox terrier is prone to all types of allergies.

Cataract   In elderly dogs the lens of the eye becomes cloudy, causing a partial or total loss of vision.

Deafness   A partial or total loss of hearing.

Esophageal Disorder   Spasms of the muscles of the esophagus.

Eye Abnormalities   The smooth fox terrier is prone to abnormally growing eyelashes and a condition in which the lens in the eye slips out of place.

Glaucoma   Pressure on the retina from excess fluid in the eyeball, which causes partial or total loss of vision.

Heart Disease   The smooth fox terrier is prone to malfunctioning valve(s).

Hypothyroidism   A common disease of thyroid hormone deficiency. The thyroid regulates your dog's metabolism. A large number of skin problems in dogs are caused by thyroid disease.

Legg-Perthes Disease   The blood vessels feeding the thigh bone deteriorate, leading to a deterioration of the femoral head, a part of the hip.

Osteochondritis Dissecans   Inflammation of the cartilage in the joints. A form of arthritis.

Osteochondrosis   An abnormal development of joint cartilage. Most commonly found in the shoulder, knee, and elbow.

Shoulder Dislocation   The shoulder joint slips out of place.

Skin Allergy   Allergic reaction that causes inflammation and itching of the skin.

Teeth Abnormalities   The number, placement, or development of the teeth is not normal.

Von Willebrand's Disease   Abnormal blood-clotting defect involving both platelet and coagulation function (factor VIII).

Standard Dachshund

Acanthosis Nigricans   A rare skin disease characterized by dark skin, hair loss, and inflammation of the skin. Primarily found in the armpits.

Baldness   Loss of hair.

Cataract   In elderly dogs the lens of the eye becomes cloudy, causing a partial or total loss of vision.

Cleft Palate and/or Lip   Both are birth defects. With cleft palate, the roof of the mouth does not grow properly, leaving a hole from the roof of the mouth into the nose. With cleft lip, the skin below the nose does not grow together.

Corneal Dystrophy   An inherited degenerative condition in which the cornea of the eye becomes cloudy or opaque.

Cushing's Disease (Hyperadrenocorticism)   A condition in which the adrenal glands secrete too much cortisol. Cortisol is a steroid hormone that regulates carbohydrate, fat, and protein metabolism.

Deafness   A partial or total loss of hearing.

Demodectic Mange   A skin disease in which canine mites are living in the skin, causing itching, loss of hair, and skin infections. Usually found on the face and front legs.

Dermoid Cyst   A skinlike growth, usually seen on the back.

Diabetes Mellitus   A disease caused by an insufficient production or use of insulin.

Ehler's-Danlos Syndrome   A connective tissue disease in which the skin is very fragile and is easily cut or bruised.

Eye Abnormalities   The standard dachshund is prone to abnormally growing eyelashes, a rolling in of the eyelid(s), abnormal development of the optic nerve, and dry eye, a condition in which the eye(s) does not produce enough liquid.

Folliculitis   Inflammation of the hair follicle(s).

Glaucoma   Pressure on the retina from excess fluid in the eyeball, which causes partial or total loss of vision.

Hypothyroidism   A common disease of thyroid hormone deficiency. The thyroid regulates your dog's metabolism. A large number of skin problems in dogs are caused by thyroid disease.

Intervertebral Disc Disease   Abnormal development of the discs between the vertebrae.

Neuronal Ceroid-Lipofuscinosis   An accumulation of fatty pigments in the brain.

Osteopetrosis   The bones are abnormally thick and hard.

Overshot Jaw   A condition in which the upper jaw is too long for the lower jaw.

Pannus   A progressive immune-mediated disease in which there is a growth of tissue over the cornea, causing inflammation and possible blindness.

Pemphigus Foliaceous   An autoimmune skin disease.

Pigmentation Abnormality   A lack of color in the skin.

Progressive Retinal Atrophy (PRA)   A slow deterioration of the retina, leading to blindness.

Renal Dysplasia   Abnormal development of the kidney(s).

Sebaceous Gland Tumor   A skin tumor.

Sterile Pyogranuloma Syndrome   A noninfectious disease of the deep layers of the skin, characterized by inflammation and sores.

Von Willebrand's Disease   Abnormal blood-clotting defect involving both platelet and coagulation function (factor VIII).

Standard Manchester Terrier

Cataract   In elderly dogs the lens of the eye becomes cloudy, causing a partial or total loss of vision.

Ehler's-Danlos Syndrome   A connective tissue disease in which the skin is very fragile and is easily cut or bruised.

Epilepsy   A brain disorder in which the dog experiences seizures (convulsions).

Eye Abnormality   The standard Manchester terrier is prone to a condition in which the lens in the eye slips out of place.

Glaucoma   Pressure on the retina from excess fluid in the eyeball, which causes partial or total loss of vision.

Hypothyroidism   A common disease of thyroid hormone deficiency. The thyroid regulates your dog's metabolism. A large number of skin problems in dogs are caused by thyroid disease.

Legg-Perthes Disease   The blood vessels feeding the thigh bone deteriorate, leading to a deterioration of the femoral head, a part of the hip.

Progressive Retinal Atrophy (PRA)   A slow deterioration of the retina, leading to blindness.

Von Willebrand's Disease   Abnormal blood-clotting defect involving both platelet and coagulation function (factor VIII).

Tibetan Spaniel

Anesthetic Sensitivity   A serious condition in which the dog is very sensitive to anesthesia. In many cases the dog is also sensitive to medications and flea control products that contain pesticides.

Progressive Retinal Atrophy (PRA)   A slow deterioration of the retina, leading to blindness.

Toy Manchester Terrier

Cataract   In elderly dogs the lens of the eye becomes cloudy, causing a partial or total loss of vision.

Eye Abnormality   The toy Manchester terrier is prone to a condition in which the lens in the eye slips out of place.

Hypothyroidism   A common disease of thyroid hormone deficiency. The thyroid regulates your dog's metabolism. A large number of skin problems in dogs are caused by thyroid disease.

Progressive Retinal Atrophy (PRA)   A slow deterioration of the retina, leading to blindness.

Von Willebrand's Disease   Abnormal blood-clotting defect involving both platelet and coagulation function (factor VIII).

Toy Poodle

Allergies   The toy poodle is prone to all types of allergies.

Behavioral Abnormalities   The toy poodle is prone to a whole range of abnormal behavior patterns, such as aggression and panic disorders.

Blood-Clotting Disorders   The toy poodle is prone to blood-clotting disorders due to coagulation factor VIII or XII deficiency.

Bone Disease   The toy poodle is prone to abnormal mineralization of the bones, leading to a weak bone structure.

Cancer   The toy poodle is prone to skin cancer and cancer of the toe.

Cataract   In elderly dogs the lens of the eye becomes cloudy, causing a partial or total loss of vision.

Cushing's Disease (Hyperadrenocorticism)   A condition in which the adrenal glands secrete too much cortisol. Cortisol is a steroid hormone that regulates carbohydrate, fat, and protein metabolism.

Deafness   A partial or total loss of hearing.

Epilepsy   A brain disorder in which the dog experiences seizures (convulsions).

Epiphyseal Dysplasia   Abnormal development of the long bone.

Eye Abnormalities   The toy poodle is prone to a rolling in of the eyelid(s), abnormally growing eyelashes, an overproduction of tears, an abnormal development of the tear duct(s), and an abnormal development of the retina(s).

Glaucoma   Pressure on the retina from excess fluid in the eyeball, which causes partial or total loss of vision.

Globoid Cell Leukodystrophy   Degeneration of a type of brain cell.

Growth Hormone–Responsive Dermatosis   Skin disorder caused by a deficiency of growth hormones.

Heart Disease   The toy poodle is prone to abnormal development of the heart.

Hemeralopia   A disorder of the retina causing blindness during the day, with partial sight in dim light.

Hypothyroidism   A common disease of thyroid hormone deficiency. The thyroid regulates your dog's metabolism. A large number of skin problems in dogs are caused by thyroid disease.

Immune-Mediated Hemolytic Anemia (IMHA)   Anemia resulting from an immune system–mediated destruction of the red blood cells.

Intervertebral Disc Disease   Abnormal development of the discs between the vertebrae.

Iris Atrophy   A deterioration of the iris.

Liver Abnormality   The toy poodle is prone to an abnormal formation of blood vessels in the liver.

Osteochondritis Dissecans   Inflammation of the cartilage in the joints. A form of arthritis.

Osteochondrosis   An abnormal development of joint cartilage. Most commonly found in the shoulder, knee, and elbow.

Otitis Externa   An infection of the external structures of the ear.

Pannus   A progressive immune-mediated disease in which there is a growth of tissue over the cornea, causing inflammation and possible blindness.

Patellar Luxation   The kneecap(s) slips out of place.

Progressive Retinal Atrophy (PRA)   A slow deterioration of the retina, leading to blindness.

Sebaceous Gland Tumor   A skin tumor.

Skin Allergy   Allergic reaction that causes inflammation and itching of the skin.

Urolithiasis   Stones or crystals in the urinary tract.

Von Willebrand's Disease   Abnormal blood-clotting defect involving both platelet and coagulation function (factor VIII).

Welsh Terrier

Cataract   In elderly dogs the lens of the eye becomes cloudy, causing a partial or total loss of vision.

Eye Abnormality   The Welsh terrier is prone to a condition in which the lens in the eye slips out of place.

Glaucoma   Pressure on the retina from excess fluid in the eyeball, which causes partial or total loss of vision.

Hypothyroidism   A common disease of thyroid hormone deficiency. The thyroid regulates your dog's metabolism. A large number of skin problems in dogs are caused by thyroid disease.

Von Willebrand's Disease   Abnormal blood-clotting defect involving both platelet and coagulation function (factor VIII).

West Highland White Terrier

Acanthosis Nigricans   A rare skin disease characterized by dark skin, hair loss, and inflammation of the skin. Primarily found in the armpits.

Addison's Disease   A disease in which the adrenal glands secrete an insufficient amount of cortisone, a steroid hormone.

Allergies   The West Highland white terrier is highly prone to all types of allergies.

Cataract   In elderly dogs the lens of the eye becomes cloudy, causing a partial or total loss of vision.

Copper Metabolism Abnormality   An inability to utilize and store copper properly. Results in liver disease if not treated.

Craniomandibular Osteopathy   Abnormally dense bones in the face and the jaw.

Cushing's Disease (Hyperadrenocorticism)   A condition in which the adrenal glands secrete too much cortisol. Cortisol is a steroid hormone that regulates carbohydrate, fat, and protein metabolism.

Epidermal Dysplasia   Abnormal development of the outer layer of the skin.

Eye Abnormalities   The West Highland white terrier is prone to a condition in which the lens in the eye slips out of place, abnormal development of the retina(s), and dry eye, a condition in which the eye(s) does not produce enough liquid.

Globoid Cell Leukodystrophy   Degeneration of a type of brain cell.

Hernia   A rupture of the wall of an internal organ in the groin area.

Immune-Mediated Hemolytic Anemia (IMHA)   Anemia resulting from an immune system–mediated destruction of the red blood cells.

Legg-Perthes Disease   The blood vessels feeding the thigh bone deteriorate, leading to a deterioration of the femoral head, a part of the hip.

Seborrhea   A skin disease characterized by raw, scaling skin and an excess of sebum (oil-like substance), which causes a rancid body odor.

Skin Allergy   Allergic reaction that causes inflammation and itching of the skin.

White Dog Shaker Syndrome   A condition, brought on by stress or overexcitement, in which the dog has rapid eye movements, tremors, and incoordination.

Whippet

Baldness   Loss of hair.

Cancer   The whippet is prone to hemangiosarcoma, which is a cancer of the blood vessels involving the liver, spleen, or skin.

Cataract   In elderly dogs the lens of the eye becomes cloudy, causing a partial or total loss of vision.

Cryptorchidism   A developmental condition in which one or both testicles fail to descend into the scrotum.

Demodectic Mange   A skin disease in which canine mites are living in the skin, causing itching, loss of hair, and skin infections. Usually found on the face and front legs.

Eye Abnormalities   The whippet is prone to a rolling in of the eyelid(s) and a condition in which the lens in the eye slips out of place.

Hypothyroidism   A common disease of thyroid hormone deficiency. The thyroid regulates your dog's metabolism. A large number of skin problems in dogs are caused by thyroid disease.

Osteochondritis Dissecans   Inflammation of the cartilage in the joints. A form of arthritis.

Osteochondrosis   An abnormal development of joint cartilage. Most commonly found in the shoulder, knee, and elbow.

Progressive Retinal Atrophy (PRA)   A slow deterioration of the retina, leading to blindness.

Von Willebrand's Disease   Abnormal blood-clotting defect involving both platelet and coagulation function (factor VIII).

Wirehaired Fox Terrier

Allergies   The wirehaired fox terrier is prone to inhalant allergies.

Ataxia   A progressive loss of coordination from a spinal cord abnormality.

Cataract   In elderly dogs the lens of the eye becomes cloudy, causing a partial or total loss of vision.

Deafness   A partial or total loss of hearing.

Esophageal Disorder   Spasms of the muscles of the esophagus.

Eye Abnormalities   The wirehaired fox terrier is prone to a rolling in of the eyelid(s), abnormally growing eyelashes, and a condition in which the lens in the eye slips out of place.

Glaucoma   Pressure on the retina from excess fluid in the eyeball, which causes partial or total loss of vision.

Heart Disease   The wirehaired fox terrier is prone to malfunction of the valve(s) and abnormal development of the heart.

Legg-Perthes Disease   The blood vessels feeding the thigh bone deteriorate, leading to a deterioration of the femoral head, a part of the hip.

Progressive Retinal Atrophy (PRA)   A slow deterioration of the retina, leading to blindness.

Shoulder Dislocation   The shoulder joint slips out of place.

Teeth Abnormalities   The number, placement, or development of the teeth is not normal.

Thyroid Disease   Inflammation of the thyroid.

Von Willebrand's Disease   Abnormal blood-clotting defect involving both platelet and coagulation function (factor VIII).

Yorkshire Terrier

Cataract   In elderly dogs the lens of the eye becomes cloudy, causing a partial or total loss of vision.

Demodectic Mange   A skin disease in which canine mites are living in the skin, causing itching, loss of hair, and skin infections. Usually found on the face and front legs.

Eye Abnormalities   The Yorkshire terrier is prone to abnormally growing eyelashes, abnormal development of the retina(s), a rolling in of the eyelid(s), and dry eye, a condition in which the eye(s) does not produce enough liquid.

Hydrocephalus   The accumulation of fluid in the brain.

Hypothyroidism   A common disease of thyroid hormone deficiency. The thyroid regulates your dog's metabolism. A large number of skin problems in dogs are caused by thyroid disease.

Legg-Perthes Disease   The blood vessels feeding the thigh bone deteriorate, leading to a deterioration of the femoral head, a part of the hip.

Liver Abnormality   The Yorkshire terrier is prone to an abnormal formation of blood vessels in the liver.

Patellar Luxation   The kneecap(s) slips out of place.

Progressive Retinal Atrophy (PRA)   A slow deterioration of the retina, leading to blindness.

Seborrhea   A skin disease characterized by raw, scaling skin and an excess of sebum (oil-like substance), which causes a rancid body odor.

Vertebra Malformation   An abnormal development of the second vertebra, causing unsteadiness.

Von Willebrand's Disease   Abnormal blood-clotting defect involving both platelet and coagulation function (factor VIII).

Recommended Reading

Dr. Earl Mindell's "What You Should Know About" books are easy to read and pack a lot of information in a small book. They are available at GNC (General Nutrition Center) stores.

Belfield, Wendell O., D.V.M, and Martin Zucker. *How to Have a Healthier Dog.* San Jose, CA: Orthomolecular Specialties, 1981. (408) 227-9334.

Mindell, Earl, R.Ph., Ph.D. *Earl Mindell's Food As Medicine.* New York: Fireside, 1994.

Mindell, Earl, R.Ph., Ph.D., and Virginia L. Hopkins. *Dr. Earl Mindell's What You Should Know About the Super Antioxidant Miracle.* New Canaan, CT: Keats Publishing, Inc., 1996.

Mindell, Earl, R.Ph., Ph.D., and Virginia L. Hopkins. *Dr. Earl Mindell's What You Should Know About 22 Ways to a Healthier Heart.* New Canaan, CT: Keats Publishing, Inc., 1996.

Mindell, Earl, R.Ph., Ph.D., and Virginia L. Hopkins. *Dr. Earl Mindell's What You Should Know About Creating Your Personal Vitamin Plan.* New Canaan, CT: Keats Publishing, Inc., 1996.

Mindell, Earl, R.Ph., Ph.D., and Virginia L. Hopkins. *Dr. Earl Mindell's What You Should Know About Trace Minerals.* New Canaan, CT: Keats Publishing, Inc., 1997.

Pitcairn, Richard H., D.V.M., Ph.D., and Susan Hubble Pitcairn. *Dr. Pitcairn's Complete Guide to Natural Health for Dogs and Cats.* Emmaus, PA: Rodale Press, Inc., 1995.

Volhard, Wendy, and Kerry Brown, D.V.M. *The Holistic Guide for a Healthy Dog.* New York: Howell Book House, 1995.

If you enjoyed this book, you will enjoy *The Dog Love Letter.* Editor Elizabeth Renaghan and holistic veterinarian Beverly Cappel-King, D.V.M., give you the latest information to naturally care for your dog.

The Dog Love Letter
    P.O. Box 1855
    North Falmouth, MA 02556-2322
    (800) 580-3644 or (508) 563-7162; fax: (508) 563-7162
    e-mail: doglove44@aol.com

One-year, twelve issues, $36. Make check payable to *The Dog Love Letter.*

Resources

Dog Food

Abady

Dry and canned dog food, supplements

    201 Smith Street

    Poughkeepsie, NY 12601

    (914) 473-1900

Flint River Ranch

Organic dry dog food

    1243 Columbia Avenue, B6

    Riverside, CA 92507

    (909) 682-5048; fax: (909) 682-5057

    www.flintriverranch.com

Solid Gold

Organic dry dog food, supplements

    1483 North Cuyamaca

    El Cajon, CA 92020

    (619) 258-1914; fax: (619) 258-3907

    e-mail: dane@electric.com

    www.solid-gold-inc.com

Wysong

Organic dry and canned dog food, supplements

    1880 North Eastman

    Midland, MI 48640

    (800) 748-0233 or (517) 631-0009

Flea Control

Fleabusters
House and yard flea control using sodium polyborate powder
>   6555 N.W. 9th Avenue, Suite 412
>   Ft. Lauderdale, FL 33309
>   (800) 666-3532 or (954) 351-9244; fax: (954) 351-9266
>   www.fleabusters.com

Hop-Off
Nutritional supplement
>   P.O. Box 567
>   Marston Mills, MA 02648
>   (800) 393-6666 or (508) 428-1478; fax: (508) 420-5757
>   e-mail: hopoffinc@aol.com
>   www.hopoff.com

Fleas Flee
Nutritional supplement
>   811 South Main Street
>   Chestnut Ridge, NY 10977
>   (914) 356-3838; fax: (914) 356-4307

Labs That Do Antibody Titer Tests

Have your veterinarian call for shipping information.

Hemopet
>   (310) 828-4804

Antech Diagnostics
>   (800) 872-1001 for the lab nearest you

Cornell Diagnostic Lab
>   (607) 253-3900

Mail Order for High-Quality Pet Products

Waggin Tails Pet Essentials
> 480 Pleasant Street
> Lee, MA 01238
> (800) 946-8245; fax: (888) 946-8245
> www.waggintails.com

The Vet at the Barn
> 811 South Main Street
> Chestnut Ridge, NY 10977
> (914) 356-4104

Water Filters

Clean Water Revival
> 100 Carney Street
> Glen Cove, NY 11542
> (800) 444-3563; fax: (516) 674-3788

Homeopathic Remedies for Small Animals

EarthRider Laboratories
Formulas for pets and a homeopathic kit for animals and people
> P.O. Box 3805
> Boulder, CO 80307-3805
> (303) 543-9888; fax: (303) 543-9777
> e-mail: psyched@diac.com

Holistic Veterinarian Phone Consultation

Dr. Beverly Cappel-King
> (914) 356-3838

Holistic Veterinary Medicine

For more information on holistic veterinary medicine or for the name of a holistic veterinarian in your area, call:

The American Holistic Veterinary Medical Association
> 2214 Old Emmorton Road
> Bel Air, MD 21015
> (410) 569-0795; fax: (410) 569-2346
> e-mail: 74253.2560@compuserve.com

References by Chapter

PART 1: CREATING OPTIMUM NUTRITION FOR YOUR DOG

Chapter 1: Feeding Your Dog for Naturally Great Health

Case, Linda, M.S., Daniel Carey, D.V.M., and Diane Hirakawa, Ph.D. *Canine and Feline Nutrition.* St. Louis, MO: Mosby-Year Book, Inc., 1995.

Coffman, Howard. *The Dry Dog Food Reference.* Nashua, NH: Pig Dog Press, 1995.

Everett, Susann. *What Many Dog Food Manufacturers Don't Want You to Know.* Unpalatable Dog Food Facts, http://www.albany.net/~sterling/foodfax.htm.

Franklin, Deborah. "Is My Kitchen Faucet Poisoning Me with Lead?" *Health Magazine,* March/April 1993:21.

Hallman, J. E., et al. "Cellulose, Beet Pulp, and Pectin/Gum Arabic Effects on Canine Colonic Microstructure and Histopathology." *Veterinary Clinical Nutrition,* 1995; vol. 2, no. 4:137–142.

Health Effects of Lead in Drinking Water. Pure Water Solutions, http://www.cris.com/~compaid/lead.htm.

Hickman, Sandra. "Focus on Food." *Canine Health Naturally,* 1996; vol. 1, issue 1.

Keller, Kathryn. "Water Works Wonders." *Redbook,* May 1990; vol. 175.D.

Lemonick, Michael, et al., "Toxins on Tap*," Time Magazine,* 11/15/93; vol. 142, no. 20.

"News from Down Under: Dogs on Pet Food Risk Early Death." *The London Sunday Telegraph,* October 1, 1995.

Pitcairn, Richard, D.V.M., Ph.D., and Susan Hubble Pitcairn. *Dr. Pitcairn's Complete Guide to Natural Health for Dogs and Cats.* Emmaus, PA: Rodale Press, Inc., 1995.

Pittman, David. "Health Trends." *Share-Net News,* November 15, 1993; vol. 1, no. 1.

Pollack, William, D.V.M. "The Effects of a Natural vs. Commercial Pet Food Diet on the Wellness of Common Companion Animals—A Holistic Perspective." *Journal of the American Holistic Veterinary Medical Association,* 1996–1997; vol. 15, no. 4:21–25.

Rowe, John. "Canine Clinic." *The American Field,* 1995.

Santillo, Humbart, B.S., M.H. *Food Enzymes: The Missing Link to Radiant Health.* Prescott, AZ: Hohm Press, 1993.

Schachter, Michael, M.D., P.A. "The Dangers of Fluoride and Fluoridation." *Nutritional Medicine,* 1996, http://205.180.229.2/library/articles/schacter/fluoride.n.htm.

Volhard, Wendy, and Kerry Brown, D.V.M. *The Holistic Guide for a Healthy Dog.* New York: Howell Book House, 1995.

Wampler, Sharon. *Prevent Disease and Extend Your Life.* Scottsdale, AZ: Health Watchers System, 1995.

Whitney, George, D.V.M. *The Complete Book of Dog Care.* New York: Doubleday, 1985.

Williams, David. "Water Quality Alert." *Alternatives for the Health Conscious Individual* (Mountain Home Publishing), June 1997; vol. 6, no. 24:185–192.

Chapter 3: Vitamins for Your Dog

Belfield, Wendell, D.V.M., and Martin Zucker. *How to Have a Healthier Dog.* San Jose, CA: Orthomolecular Specialties, 1981.

Case, Linda, M.S., Daniel Carey, D.V.M., and Diane Hirakawa, Ph.D. *Canine and Feline Nutrition.* St. Louis, MO: Mosby-Year Book, Inc., 1995.

Goldy, G. "Effects of Measured Doses of Vitamin A Fed to Healthy Beagle Dogs for 26 Weeks." *Veterinary Clinical Nutrition,* 1996; vol. 3, no. 2:45–49.

Hannigan, B. "Diet and Immune Function." *M. British Journal of Biomedical Sciences,* 1994; no. 51:252–259.

Hazewinkel, H. A. W., et al. "Influence of Protein, Minerals, and Vitamin D on Skeletal Development of Dogs." *Veterinary Clinical Nutrition,* 1995; vol. 2, no. 3:93–99.

Kirk, R. W. "Nutrition and the Integument." *Journal of Small Animal Practice,* 1991; no. 32:283–288.

Lazarus, Pat. *Keep Your Pet Healthy the Natural Way.* New Canaan, CT: Keats Publishing, 1986.

Mazzotta, M., Ph.D. "Nutrition and Wound Healing." *Journal of the American Podiatric Medical Association,* 1994; no. 84(9):456–462.

Miller, W., Jr., V.M.D. "Nutritional Considerations in Small Animal Dermatology." *Small Animal Practice,* 1989; vol. 19, no. 3:497–511.

Plechner, Alfred, D.V.M., and Martin Zucker. *Pet Allergies: Remedies for an Epidemic.* Inglewood, CA: Dr. Goodpet Laboratories Very Healthy Enterprises, Inc., 1986.

Robertson, J. M., et al. "A Possible Role for Vitamins C and E in Cataract Prevention." *American Journal of Clinical Nutrition,* 1991; no. 53:346S–351S.

Sheffy, B. E., et al. "Nutrition and the Immune Response." *Cornell Veterinarian,* 1978; no. 68:48–61.

Sheffy, B. E., et al. "Influence of Vitamin E and Selenium on Immune Response Mechanisms." *Federation Proceedings,* 1979; vol. 38, no. 7:2139–2143.

Veterinary Product News Staff Report. "Antioxidants May Improve Pet Health." *Veterinary Product News,* 1994; vol. 6, no. 3.

Volhard, Wendy, and Kerry Brown, D.V.M. *The Holistic Guide for a Healthy Dog.* New York: Howell Book House, 1995.

Chapter 4: Minerals for Your Dog

Belfield, Wendell, D.V.M., and Martin Zucker. *How to Have a Healthier Dog.* San Jose, CA: Orthomolecular Specialties, 1981.

Case, Linda, M.S., Daniel Carey, D.V.M., and Diane Hirakawa, Ph.D. *Canine and Feline Nutrition.* St. Louis, MO: Mosby-Year Book, Inc., 1995.

Falck, Geir. "High Magnesium Improves the Post Ischemic Recovery of Cardiac Function." *Cardiovascular Research,* 1995; no. 29:439.

Hazewinkel, H. A. W., et al. "Influence of Protein, Minerals, and Vitamin D on Skeletal Development of Dogs." *Veterinary Clinical Nutrition,* 1995; vol. 2, no. 3:93–99.

Kirk, R. W. "Nutrition and the Integument." *Journal of Small Animal Practice,* 1991; no. 32:283–288.

Krook, L. "Overnutrition and Skeletal Disease in the Dog." *Overnutrition and Skeletal Disease in the Dog,* Department of Pathology, New York State Veterinary College, 1974; 87–89

Miller, William, Jr., V.M.D. "Nutritional Considerations in Small Animal Dermatology." *Small Animal Practice,* 1989; vol. 19, no. 3:497–511.

Sheffy, B. E., et al. "Influence of Vitamin E and Selenium on Immune Response Mechanisms." *Federation Proceedings,* 1979; vol. 38, no. 7:2139–2143.

Volhard, Wendy, and Kerry Brown, D.V.M. *The Holistic Guide for a Healthy Dog.* New York: Howell Book House, 1995.

Chapter 5: Special Nutritional Needs

Belfield, Wendell, D.V.M., and Martin Zucker. *How to Have a Healthier Dog.* San Jose, CA: Orthomolecular Specialties, 1981.

Carlson, Delbert, and James Giffin. *Dog Owners Home Veterinary Handbook.* New York: Howell Book House, 1992.

Case, Linda, M.S., Daniel Carey, D.V.M., and Diane Hirakawa, Ph.D. *Canine and Feline Nutrition.* St. Louis, MO: Mosby-Year Book, Inc., 1995.

Faculty and Staff, School of Veterinary Medicine University of California, Davis. *UCDAVIS School of Veterinary Medicine Book of Dogs.* New York: HarperCollins, 1995.

Mazzotta, M., Ph.D. "Nutrition and Wound Healing." *Journal of the American Podiatric Medical Association,* 1994; no. 84(9):456–462.

Mizelle, H. L., et al. "Abnormal Cardiovascular Responses to Exercise During the Development of Obesity in Dogs." *American Journal of Hypertension,* 1994; vol. 7:374–378.

Morley, J., M.B., "Nutritional Modulation of Behavior and Immunocompetence." *Nutrition Reviews,* 1994; no. 52(8):S6–S8.

Sheffy, B. E., et al. "Nutrition and Metabolism of the Geriatric Dog." *Cornell Veterinarian,* 1985; no. 75:324–347.

Teare, J. A., et al. "Rapid Growth and Skeletal Disease in Dogs." *Rapid Growth and Skeletal Disease in Dogs.* Ithaca, NY: Cornell University, 1980; 126–130.

PART 2: KEEPING YOUR DOG'S IMMUNE SYSTEM STRONG

Chapter 6: The Importance of a Strong Immune System

"Are We Vaccinating Too Much?" *Journal of the American Veterinary Medical Association,* 1995; vol. 207, no. 4:421–425.

Bogdon, J., Ph.D. "Micronutrient Nutrition and Immunity." *Nutrition Report,* February 1995; no. 13(2):1.

Brennan, Mary, D.V.M., and Norma Eckroate. *The Natural Dog.* New York: Penguin Group, 1994.

"Carpet Chemicals May Pose Serious Health Risk, EPA and Carpet Industry Under Fire." *Public Citizen Health Research Group Health Letter,* March 1993; no. 9(3):1–3, 11.

Case, Linda, M.S., Daniel Carey, D.V.M., and Diane Hirakawa, Ph.D. *Canine and Feline Nutrition.* St. Louis, MO: Mosby-Year Book, Inc., 1995.

"CSPI Proposes Modest Increase in Pesticide Tax." *Nutrition Week,* 1995; no. 25(19):4, 5.

Diegelman, Nathan. *Poison in the Grass: The Hazards and Consequences of Lawn Pesticides.* The S.T.A.T.E. Foundation, b1891@FreeNet.Buffalo.EDU.

Faculty and Staff, School of Veterinary Medicine University of California, Davis. *UCDAVIS School of Veterinary Medicine Book of Dogs.* New York: HarperCollins, 1995.

Hadden, J. "The Treatment of Zinc Deficiency Is an Immunotherapy." *International Journal of Immunopharmacology,* 1995; no. 17(9):697–701.

Hickman, Sandra. "Focus on Food." *Canine Health Naturally,* 1996; vol. 1, issue 1.

Lewis, R. G., et al. "Evaluations of Methods for Monitoring the Potential Exposure of Small Children to Pesticides in the Residential Environment." *Environment Contamination Toxicology,* 1994; vol. 26:37–46.

Lowengart, R. A., et al. "Childhood Leukemia and Parents Occupational and Home Exposures." *Journal of the National Cancer Institute,* 1987, no. 79:37–46.

McCluggage, David, D.V.M. "Vaccinations in Veterinary Medicine—A New Perspective." *Journal of the American Veterinary Medical Association,* 1995; vol. 14, no. 2.

Mockett, A., et al. "Comparing How Puppies with Passive Immunity Respond to Three Canine Parvovirus Vaccines." *Veterinary Medicine,* 1995; 430–438.

"Pesticide Usage." *Nutrition Week,* 1995; no. 25(20):7.

Pet Immunizations, Townsend Letter for Doctors and Patients, June 1996.

Pike, J., et al. "Effect of Vitamin and Trace Element Supplementation on Immune Indices in Healthy Elderly." *International Journal of Vitamin and Nutrition Research,* 1995; no. 65:117–120.

Pitcairn, Richard, D.V.M., Ph.D., and Susan Hubble Pitcairn. *Dr. Pitcairn's Complete Guide to Natural Health for Dogs and Cats.* Emmaus, PA: Rodale Press, Inc., 1995.

Plechner, Alfred, D.V.M., and Martin Zucker. *Pet Allergies: Remedies for an Epidemic.* Inglewood, CA: Dr. Goodpet Laboratories Very Healthy Enterprises, Inc., 1986.

"Pollution—Our Breath-Taking Air." *U.S. News and World Report,* May 20, 1996; 15.

Schoen, Allen M., and Susan G. Wynn, editors. *Complimentary and Alternative Veterinary Medicine, Principles and Practice.* St. Louis, MO: Mosby, Inc., 1998.

Schueler, Tom. "Urban Pesticides: From the Lawn to the Stream." *Watershed Protection Techniques,* 1995; vol. 2, no. 1.

Sheffy, B. E. "Nutrition, Infection and Immunity." *Compendium on Continuing Education for the Practicing Veterinarian,* 1985; vol. 7, no. 12:990–997.

Sheffy, B. E., et al. "Influence of Vitamin E and Selenium on Immune Response Mechanisms." *Federation Proceedings,* 1979; vol. 38, no. 7:2139–2143.

Steinman, David, and Michael Wisner. *Living Healthy in a Toxic World.* Berkeley, CA: Berkeley Publishing Company, 1996.

Taylor, E. "Selenium and Cellular Immunity; Evidence That Selenoproteins May Be Encoded in the +1 Reading Frame Overlapping the Human CD4, CD8, and HLA-DR Genes." *Biological Trace Element Research,* 1995; no. 49:85–95.

"Veterinary Alternatives Can Help Your Pet." *Alternative Medicine Digest,* 1997; issue 19:94–99.

Veterinary Product News Staff Report. "Antioxidants May Improve Pet Health." *Veterinary Product News,* 1994; vol. 6, no. 3.

Volhard, Wendy, and Kerry Brown, D.V.M. *The Holistic Guide for a Healthy Dog.* New York: Howell Book House, 1995.

Williams, B., Ph.D. "Latex Allergen in Respirable Particulate Air Pollution," *Journal of Allergy and Clinical Immunology,* 1995; no. 95(1/Part I):88–95.

Wynn, Susan, D.V.M. *Vaccination Decisions,* http://www.altvetmed.com/vaccine.html.

PART 3: A FLEA-FREE HOUSEHOLD NATURALLY

Chapter 7: Natural Flea Control for Your Dog

Attia, A. M., et al. "Carbaryl-Induced Changes in Indoleamine Synthesis in the Pineal Gland and Its Effects on Nighttime Serum Melatonin Concentration." *Journal of Toxicology,* 1991; vol. 65:305–314.

Dog Watch. Cornell University College of Veterinary Medicine, Torstar Publications, 1997; vol. 1, no. 2.

Lazarus, Pat. *Keep Your Pet Healthy the Natural Way.* New Canaan, CT: Keats Publishing, 1986.

Pant, N., et al. "Effects of Carbaryl on the Rat's Male Reproductive System." *Journal of Vet Hum Toxicology,* 1995; vol. 37:421–425.

Pant, N., et al. "Spermatotoxic Effects of Carbaryl in Rats." *Journal of Hum Exp Toxicol,* 1996; vol. 15:736–738.

Pitcairn, Richard, D.V.M., Ph.D., and Susan Hubble Pitcairn. *Dr. Pitcairn's Complete Guide to Natural Health for Dogs and Cats.* Emmaus, PA: Rodale Press, Inc., 1995.

Sherman, J. D. "Chlorpyrifos (Dursban)-Associated Birth Defects: A Report of Four Cases." *Arch Environ Health,* 1996; vol. 51:5–8.

Stein, Diane. *The Natural Remedy Book for Dogs and Cats.* Freedom, CA: The Crossing Press, 1994.

Takahashi, R. N., et al., "Behavioral and Biochemical Changes Following Repeated Administration of Carbaryl to Aging Rats." *Journal of Braz J Med Biol Res,* 1990; vol. 23:879–882.

Takahashi, R. N., et al., "Effects of Age on Behavioral and Physiological Responses to Carbaryl in Rats." *Journal of Neurotoxicol Teratol,* 1991; vol. 13:21–26.

PART 4: HOMEOPATHY FOR DOGS

Chapter 8: Understanding Homeopathy

Day, Christopher. *The Homeopathic Treatment of Small Animals: Principles and Practice.* Essex, England: C. W. Daniel Company Limited, 1990.

MacLeod, G., M.R.C.V.S., D.V.S.M. *Dogs: Homeopathic Remedies.* Essex, England: C. W. Daniel Company Limited, 1995.

Pitcairn, Richard, D.V.M., Ph.D., and Susan Hubble Pitcairn. *Dr. Pitcairn's Complete Guide to Natural Health for Dogs and Cats.* Emmaus, PA: Rodale Press, Inc., 1995.

Schoen, Allen M., and Susan G. Wynn, editors. *Complimentary and Alternative Veterinary Medicine, Principles and Practice,* St. Louis, MO: Mosby, Inc., 1998.

"Veterinary Alternatives Can Help Your Pet." *Alternative Medicine Digest,* 1997; issue 19:94–99.

Volhard, Wendy, and Kerry Brown, D.V.M. *The Holistic Guide for a Healthy Dog.* New York: Howell Book House, 1995.

PART 5: THE FIVE MOST COMMON DOG DISEASES

Chapter 9: Natural Prevention and Treatment of Common Dog Diseases

Belfield, Wendell, D.V.M., and Martin Zucker. *How to Have a Healthier Dog.* San Jose, CA: Orthomolecular Specialties, 1981.

Brennan, Mary, D.V.M., and Norma Eckroate. *The Natural Dog.* New York: Penguin Group, 1994.

Carlson, Delbert, and James Giffin. *Dog Owners Home Veterinary Handbook.* New York: Howell Book House, 1992.

Faculty and Staff, School of Veterinary Medicine University of California, Davis. *UCDAVIS School of Veterinary Medicine Book of Dogs.* New York: HarperCollins, 1995.

Pelton, Ross, R.Ph., Ph.D., and Lee Overholser, Ph.D. *Alternatives in Cancer Therapy.* New York: Simon and Schuster, 1994.

Stein, Diane. *The Natural Remedy Book for Dogs and Cats.* Freedom, CA: The Crossing Press, 1994.

Veterinary Product News Staff Report. "Antioxidants May Improve Pet Health." *Veterinary Product News,* 1994; vol. 6, no. 3.

PART 6: NATURAL REMEDIES FOR COMMON AILMENTS

Chapter 10: Natural Healing

Belfield, Wendell, D.V.M., and Martin Zucker. *How to Have a Healthier Dog.* San Jose, CA: Orthomolecular Specialties, 1981.

Brennan, Mary, D.V.M., and Norma Eckroate. *The Natural Dog.* New York: Penguin Group, 1994.

Carlson, Delbert, and James Giffin. *Dog Owners Home Veterinary Handbook.* New York: Howell Book House, 1992.

Faculty and Staff, School of Veterinary Medicine University of California, Davis. *UCDAVIS School of Veterinary Medicine Book of Dogs.* New York: HarperCollins, 1995.

Schoen, Allen M., and Susan G. Wynn, editors. *Complimentary and Alternative Veterinary Medicine: Principles and Practice.* St. Louis, MO: Mosby, Inc., 1998.

Stein, Diane. *The Natural Remedy Book for Dogs and Cats.* Freedom, CA: The Crossing Press, 1994.

Veterinary Product News Staff Report. "Antioxidants May Improve Pet Health." *Veterinary Product News,* 1994; vol. 6, no. 3.

PART 7: THE DOG HIT PARADE

Chapter 11: Breed-Specific Health Problems

The Association of Veterinarians for Animal Rights. *Canine Consumer Report: A Guide to Hereditary and Congenital Diseases in Dogs.* Davis, CA: The Association of Veterinarians for Animal Rights, 1994.

Fogle, Bruce, D.V.M. *The Encyclopedia of the Dog.* New York: Dorling Kindersley Publishing, Inc., 1995.

Lowell, Michelle. *Your Purebred Puppy: A Buyer's Guide.* New York: Henry Holt and Company, Inc., 1990.

The Merck Veterinary Manual, 7th edition. Rahway, NJ: Merck and Co., Inc., 1991.

Pugnetti, Gino. *Simon and Schuster's Guide to Dogs.* New York: Simon and Schuster, Inc., 1980.

Streitferdt, Uwe. *Healthy Dog, Happy Dog.* New York: Barron's Educational Series, Inc., 1994.

Index

The Compassion of Animals

*True Stories of
Animal Courage and Kindness*

Kristin von Kreisler

U.S. $22.95
Can. $29.95
ISBN 0-7615-0990-9
Hardcover

"Nobody writes about animals better than Kristin von Kreisler."
—Chris Willcox,
editor-in-chief, *Reader's Digest*

"These wonderful stories… show once again how
close we are to our evolutionary cousins."
—From the foreword by Jeffrey
Mousaieff Masson, coauthor of *When Elephants Weep*

A dog swallows a lit firecracker to protect a child in strife-torn Belfast. A pet pig steers his human family to safety before a propane gas explosion. A horse keeps vigil over an old woman until help arrives.

With dozens of touching, true-life stories like these, this heartwarming book gathers compelling proof of the intense love that animals feel for humans.

"Nobody writes about animals better than Kristin von Kreisler."
—Christopher Willcox, editor-in-chief, *Reader's Digest*

KRISTIN VON KREISLER

THE COMPASSION OF ANIMALS

TRUE STORIES OF ANIMAL COURAGE AND KINDNESS

Foreword by Jeffrey Moussaieff Masson,
Author of *Dogs Never Lie About Love*

**To order, call (800) 632-8676 or
visit us online at www.primapublishing.com**

To Order Books

Please send me the following items:

Quantity	Title	Unit Price	Total
_____	**The Compassion of Animals** _____	$ 22.95	$ _____
_____	_____	$ _____	$ _____
_____	_____	$ _____	$ _____
_____	_____	$ _____	$ _____
_____	_____	$ _____	$ _____

Subtotal	$ _____
Deduct 10% when ordering 3–5 books	$ _____
7.25% Sales Tax (CA only)	$ _____
8.25% Sales Tax (TN only)	$ _____
5% Sales Tax (MD and IN only)	$ _____
7% G.S.T. Tax (Canada only)	$ _____
Shipping and Handling*	$ _____
Total Order	$ _____

*Shipping and Handling depend on Subtotal.

Subtotal	Shipping/Handling
$0.00–$14.99	$3.00
$15.00–$29.99	$4.00
$30.00–$49.99	$6.00
$50.00–$99.99	$10.00
$100.00–$199.99	$13.50
$200.00+	Call for Quote

Foreign and all Priority Request orders:
Call Order Entry department
for price quote at 916-632-4400
This chart represents the total retail price of books only
(before applicable discounts are taken).

By Telephone: With MC or Visa, call 800-632-8676 or 916-632-4400. Mon–Fri, 8:30-4:30.

WWW: http://www.primapublishing.com

By Internet E-mail: sales@primapub.com

By Mail: Just fill out the information below and send with your remittance to:

**Prima Publishing
P.O. Box 1260BK
Rocklin, CA 95677**

Name _____

Address _____

City _____ State _____ ZIP _____

MC/Visa# _____ Exp. _____

Check/money order enclosed for $ _____ Payable to Prima Publishing

Daytime telephone _____

Signature _____